Graham Truscott
The Power Of His Presence

The Restoration of The Tabernacle of David

THE POWER OF HIS PRESENCE
The Restoration of the Tabernacle of David

PPM

Copyright ©1969, 1972 by Graham Truscott.
This edition copyright ©2025 by Stephen Graham Truscott.
All rights reserved.

No part of this book may be used or reproduced in any manner whatsoever without written permission, except in the case of brief quotations in critical articles and reviews. No part of this book may be used or reproduced in any manner for the purpose of training artificial intelligence technologies or systems.

Published by Presence Pioneers Media, Farmville, NC.
Cover design by Kinsey Schick.
   (https://kinseykateschick.myportfolio.com/work)
Printed in the United States of America.

ISBN 978-1-951611-64-4 (Hardbound)
      978-1-951611-65-1 (Paperback)

All Scripture quotations in this book are taken from the King James Version of the Bible unless otherwise stated.

Contents

Introduction to the New Edition (Matthew Lilley) / v
Author's Preface / ix
What Saith the Scriptures? / xiv
Introduction: The Tabernacle of Who? / 1

PART I: GOD'S NEW THING
1. The Complete Restoration / 7
2. Spiritual Sign-Posts / 15

PART II: WHEN?
3. I Will Build My Church / 25
4. The Ark of the Covenant / 31
5. Of His Fullness / 43
6. Alone With God / 55
7. The Lost Glory / 67

PART III: WHERE?
8. Give Him Your Tabernacle / 79
9. The Church Within the Church / 85
10. Let's Leave Pentecost / 97

PART IV: HOW?
11. The Ark is Coming / 111
12. Let Us Weep / 121
13. A New Unity / 129
14. The Oxen Are Stumbling / 139

15. Preparing a Place / 149
16. Sanctify Yourselves / 157
17. Praise That Pleases / 171
18. Praise Ye the Lord / 181
19. How Shall We Praise? / 187
20. Why Should We Praise? / 203
21. All That is Within Me / 207
22. The Sacrifice of Praise / 217
23. Skeptics Beware! / 223
24. The Praise of Sacrifice / 239
25. Where Do You Worship? / 245

PART V: WHY?

26. The Church Restored / 257
27. The Church Revived / 269
28. The Church Reaping / 281

About the Author / 289

LIST OF ILLUSTRATIONS

Figure 1:   The Ark of the Covenant / 33
Figure 2:   The Tabernacle of Moses / 35
Pigure 3:   The Tabernacle of David / 59
Figure 4:   Journeys of the Ark / 113

INTRODUCTION TO THE NEW EDITION

Have you ever experienced the power of God's presence?

As a young boy, I heard the gospel preached at a Sunday morning church service. Later that day I put my faith in Jesus Christ as my Savior. This was the power of God's presence drawing me to the Lord through His word.

A few years later, an evangelist laid hands on me in a prayer line, and I was baptized in the Holy Spirit. The power of God's presence knocked me to the floor, and I was never the same again.

As I began to cultivate a personal relationship with God — reading my Bible, praying, and worshiping in the secret place — I learned that God's presence was always with me. God was speaking to me, leading me, maturing me, and empowering me in His presence.

After graduating high school, I attended a summer youth camp. One evening, during a time of extended worship, I spent hours on the floor in a life-changing encounter with God's presence. That moment launched me into a ministry of gathering, mobilizing, and teaching God's people to worship, pray, and fast for the last twenty-plus years.

Experiencing and hosting the presence of God has been central to my life and ministry. The name of our ministry is Presence Pioneers, and the subtitle of my first book was *How God's Presence Changes Everything*. I could tell countless stories of the way God manifests His presence among His worshiping people. No one can experience God's presence and remain the same. As we behold Christ, we are inevitably transformed from "glory to glory."

That is why I am thrilled about this re-release of the classic book *The Power of His Presence*.

From the early years of my ministry journey, the story, worship, and tabernacle of King David have fascinated me. David seemed hungry for God's presence like few other people in Scripture. Trying to understand the significance and meaning of David's revolutionary worship tabernacle has been a bit of an obsession for me. While pursuing revelation and teaching on this topic, I was shocked to discover how few books, sermons, or articles have delved into this vitally important biblical subject. My years of study and ministry experience eventually led to the publishing of my book David's Tabernacle.

In my quest for understanding, I became aware of *The Power of His Presence* by Graham Truscott, originally published in 1969. As far as I could tell, this was the very first full-length book treatment on the Tabernacle of David. I thought the book title was perfect, given my passion for God's presence. Unfortunately, it was years before I was able to locate and obtain a copy of the out-of-print book. As I read, I was thrilled to see that it was full of deeply researched and Spirit-filled revelation and insights.

Presence Pioneers Media is honored to make this classic book available again, and we are profoundly grateful to the Truscott family for offering us a license to publish it.

We are releasing this work with the original text fully intact. With that said, the book reflects the moment of time in which it was written. From the 1940s to the 1960s, much of the body of Christ was being impacted by various moves of the Spirit such as the Latter Rain revival and the Charismatic renewal. The influence of these movements on Truscott's writing is clear. Having some context for these movements may help the reader appreciate and understand *The Power of His Presence*. Truscott is from New Zealand, and we have chosen to retain his use of standard English spelling. This book will read just as it did when it was first published in 1969.

Our desire is to honor the life and ministry of the Truscott family. Graham and Pamela Truscott dedicated their lives to Christ as missionaries to

Introduction (by Matthew Lilley)

India, and they saw God move in amazing ways.[1] The seeds planted there are still bearing fruit today.

It is fitting that a missionary published the first book on the Tabernacle of David. A prophecy from Amos 9:11 is quoted in Acts 15:16-17:

"After this I will return And will rebuild the tabernacle of David, which has fallen down; I will rebuild its ruins, And I will set it up; So that the rest of mankind may seek the LORD..."

In this passage, the apostle James declares that God is restoring the Tabernacle of David in this age for a specific purpose: "so that the rest of mankind may seek the Lord." In other words, the rediscovery of Davidic worship, praise, and prayer is unto a great harvest of souls coming into the kingdom of God. As John Piper says, *worship is the fuel and the goal of missions.*[2] Graham Truscott exemplified this principle in his life and ministry. May *The Power of His Presence* inspire us to do the same.

MATTHEW LILLEY
Presence Pioneers Media

---

1 Read more in *Kiwis Can Fly* by Graham and Pamela Truscott
2 See chapter 1 of *Let The Nations Be Glad* by John Piper

Author's Preface

The amazing response to our first book, *YOU SHALL RECEIVE POWER*, has been, to say the least, overwhelming. Letters, testimonies, and orders have been received from Japan, Africa, Europe, America, Australia; in fact, from all over the world, including quite a number of countries that we have never personally visited. We give grateful thanks to God for all who have been filled with the Spirit, and received the promised Power of the Spirit as a result of reading our first book.

YOU SHALL RECEIVE POWER was for those interested in the New Awakening in the Historic Denominations, and those hungry to receive the Baptism in the Holy Spirit. But this book is for a more limited section of the Church—those who desire to go "all the way" with God in this new move of His Spirit taking place today; those who long to see the complete promised Restoration take place in the Church.

Once again I acknowledge my gratitude to all who have helped in supplying material. I thank World Wide Publications, 1313 Hennepin Avenue, Minneapolis, U.S.A., Droke House Publishers, Inc., 309 S. Main, Anderson, S.C., U.S.A. and other authors and publishers for permission to use copyright material. To other books, sermons, and sources that have helped express my thoughts, but the origin of which has been forgotten, I am thankful.

While we praise God for the thousands who have been blessed by *YOU SHALL RECEIVE POWER*, let us remember that the Baptism in the Holy Spirit is but the beginning of the Spirit-filled life. God commands us to "walk in the Spirit." God exhorts us to "grow in grace, and in the knowledge of our Lord and Saviour, Jesus Christ."

THE POWER OF HIS PRESENCE

Therefore, this book goes forth with the earnest prayer that all who read it will be blessed and encouraged—that they will be challenged to take part in the Restoration of the Tabernacle of David, and experience anew the Power of His Presence.

Graham Truscott
Poona, India.
March, 1969.

This original thesis was submitted in partial fulfillment of the requirement for doctorial work to the Clarksville School of Theology, Tennessee, U.S.A.

Author's Preface to the Second Printing (1972)

Less than two years after the first edition of this book was printed, it was nearly sold out. When we received another two orders for 500 copies each we realized a second printing was necessary. I trust this printing will meet the increasing demand for more copies and wider publication of this important message.

I realize that some Bible Teachers prefer to accept only the historical interpretation of the Scriptures. I honor and respect these brethren and have learned much from them, but I do hope they will not object to our enjoyment now of the spiritual blessings prophesied in the Restoration of David's Tabernacle. For we have received so many testimonies of blessings experienced, spiritual bondages broken, joy released, and churches revived as a result of this message. These transformed lives and churches stand as irrefutable proof that the blessings of this Restoration are surely for today.

One of the greatest blessings received has been the release of spirit experienced on entering into praise. Like David, those who praise and worship God in the Biblical ways find they are given "the unquenchable joy of Your Presence" (Psalm 21.6, Living Psalms). For God still dwells in the praises of His people today (Psalm 22:3).

Since the first printing of this book, I have learned that the Lord gave a number of His servants revelation about the Restoration of David's Tabernacle. This has thrilled my heart, and confirmed this is indeed "present truth" for the Church (see 2 Peter 1:12).

THE POWER OF HIS PRESENCE

I take this opportunity again to thank the Lord for His goodness in bringing blessing to so many through the ministry of this book. This second printing of *THE POWER OF HIS PRESENCE* goes forth with the prayer that its message will continue to be a source of study material, inspiration and blessing.

GRAHAM TRUSCOTT
Poona, India June. 1972.

The author has used bold type, italics, and capital letters for emphasis in various places throughout this book.

What Saith the Scriptures?

"In that day will I raise up the Tabernacle of David that is fallen, and close up the breaches thereof; and I will raise up his ruins, and I will build it as in the days of old" (Amos 9:11).

"After this I will return, and will build again the Tabernacle of David, which is fallen down; and 1 will build again the ruins thereof, and I will set it up" (Acts 15:16).

"And the Lord will create upon every dwelling place of mount Zion, and upon her assemblies, a cloud and smoke by day, and the shining of a flaming fire by night: for upon all the glory shall be a defence. And there shall be a Tabernacle for a shadow in the daytime from the heat, and for a place of refuge, and for a covert from storm and from rain" (Isaiah 4:5, 6).

"And David made him houses in the city of David (Zion), and prepared a place for the Ark of God, and pitched for it a Tent (Tabernacle)" (I Chronicles 15:1).

"Repent ye therefore, and be converted, that your sins may be blotted out, when the times of refreshing (and reviving—Amplified Bible) shall come from the presence of the Lord;

And he shall send Jesus Christ, which before was preached unto you:

Whom the heaven must receive (retain) until the times of restitution (complete Restoration— Amplified Bible) of all things, which God hath -spoken by the mouth of all his holy prophets since the world began" (Acts 3:19-2 1).

Introduction

THE TABERNACLE OF WHO?

"You mean the tabernacle of Moses."
"No, the Tabernacle of David."
"The Tabernacle of who?"
"The Tabernacle of David."
"I did not know that David even had a Tabernacle."
"He did. And what's more, you and I are living in the day when God has promised to restore it."

It was in Melbourne, Australia—February, 1968. The friends to whom I was talking seemed very surprised as I told them my sermon topic for the evening service.

"We'll be most interested to hear what you have to say," they said, as we parted to enter the church.

"Why, we've never heard anything about it before!"

"Will you be speaking on this subject anywhere else in Melbourne?"

"The Restoration of David's Tabernacle opens up so many Scriptures I've never understood before!"

After the service, they were all excitedly discussing the sermon. I had not experienced such an enthusiastic response to my preaching for some time.

True, there had been a time when, apart from a hazy recollection that David had once brought the Ark of the Covenant to Zion, I too knew nothing about the Tabernacle of David. Although I later came to understand a little of the Restoration of the Tabernacle of David, it was not until I was desperately seeking God in our Melbourne Motel that something of the significance of this vital truth blazed in my heart. I was kneeling with my Bible open on the bed, asking the Lord for something fresh for my own soul, and for the people to whom I was to minister. I began to read First Chronicles, chapter 13. I do not know how long I was on my knees, but before I realized it, I was so deeply engrossed in this chapter, and the five chapters which follow, that I had read them through many times.

Soon my concordance and some foolscap sheets of note-paper had joined my Bible, and I was engaged in a glorious flurry of turning to Scripture after Scripture, and writing furiously all the while.

But what was taking place on the inside mattered most of all. I was conscious of a very powerful anointing of the Holy Spirit, new liberty to worship my Lord, a new understanding of God's purposes in these Last Days. I knew assuredly that God was speaking to me in a new and precious way from His own Word.

I began to ask questions: When is God restoring the Tabernacle of David? Where? How? Why? I continued writing, praying, praising, asking, receiving, writing again. I knew I had my message for the coming Sunday—and many more messages, for many more Sundays . . .

"Are there any books available about the restoration of the Tabernacle of David?" one of my friends asked.

I thought. I had seen quite a number of books about the tabernacle of Moses. But the Tabernacle of David?

"No. I don't think there are," I said.

"I'm going to pray that the Lord will help you to write one!" was the reply.

As I sit here at my typewriter, God seems to be answering my friend's prayer, and the requests of many who have asked that these studies be produced in book form. The Bible studies given in Australia and added to here

Introduction

at Poona New Life Centre form the basis of this book. When we begin to read our Bibles in the light of the Restoration of David's Tabernacle, the list of Scripture references to this subject is almost limitless. Therefore this book does not cover every aspect of this thrilling truth. The reader will find that many more doors of further blessing and understanding will be unlocked with the keys given in this book.

The Restoration of the Tabernacle of David is not a new denomination. Neither is it a spiritual experience for a select few. All hearts thirsting after God, regardless of race, creed, or denominational affiliation may experience this last mighty move of God's Power and Glory before the Second Coming of the Lord Jesus Christ.

But it is only fair to give a gentle word of warning. "Buy the truth" the wise man said (Prov. 23:23). Like all truth, the Restoration of David's Tabernacle costs something—especially for those who are willing to act upon it. But the Bible teaches that the 'very courageous . . . keep and do all that is written in the book" (Josh. 23:6). May the Lord make us "very courageous."

Well has Dr. A. W. Tozer advised:

... we should press on to enjoy in personal inward experience the exalted privileges that are ours in Christ Jesus; we should insist upon tasting the sweetness of internal worship in spirit as well as in truth; to reach this ideal we should, if necessary, push beyond our contented brethren, and bring upon ourselves whatever opposition may follow as a result.[1]

Are you longing for a closer walk with God? Do you seek to enjoy a deeper personal inward experience of Jesus Christ and His Power? A new dimension in worship? Do you desire to see more of the resurrection Power and Glory of Christ at work in your mission, your church, yourself? Are

---

1 *Keys to the Deeper Life* (Zondervan) by Dr. A. W. Tozer. The late Dr. Tozer was well known in evangelical circles for his long and fruitful editorship of the Alliance Witness, his pastorate of the large Alliance Church in the Chicago area, and especially for his penetrating books on the deeper spiritual life.

you concerned to see more souls come to know Jesus Christ as Saviour and Lord? And are you willing to let opposition come?

Then this book is for you.

Part I
GOD'S NEW THING

The world is in a dreadful state today—are things going to get worse and worse? Or is there going to be a Restoration and Revival before the Second Coming of Christ?

Chapter One
THE COMPLETE RESTORATION

There has never been an age to compare with the one in which you and I are living. In all history there have never been so many famines, wars, and rumours of wars, earthquakes, strikes and riots. Tension and strife, at all levels, are everywhere. Calamity after calamity seems to be tearing our world apart.

Evangelist Dr. Billy Graham, speaking at the opening session of the World Congress on Evangelism in Berlin, November 1966, describes the plight of our world:

"There is the universal feeling that history is running out, that civilization's days are numbered, that the problems of the world are insoluble, that hope has reached its frazzled end." [1]

Day by day the situation is becoming more alarming. New Zealand's Minister of Defence, speaking recently at a University seminar, said, "The world is dangerous now." Reviewing the events of 1968, one of the world's most widely-read magazines stated, "there is a vague anxiety that the machine of the 20th century is beginning to run out of control." More and more respected politicians and scientists agree that we are living in the last moments of time. Our world is no longer able to fully cope with the alarming proportion of its ever-increasing population explosion and ever-decreasing international and interracial harmony.

---

1   Dr. Billy Graham was Honorary Chairman of the World Congress on Evangelism. This quotation is taken from the World Congress on Evangelism Official Reference Volume No. 1, One Race, One Gospel, One Task, published by Worldwide Publications, Minneapolis, Minnesota, U.S.A.

A look at the spiritual situation is even more disturbing. While there has never been such a need for power in the Church, in comparison with the enormous needs of the world today, the Church appears to be making little vital impact and few great advances. Despite the sincere efforts of many true servants of Christ, and a few encouraging reports of spiritual awakening, the Church today seems so vastly different from the dynamic, miracle-working band of simple men that turned the world upside down with the Gospel of Christ nearly 2,000 years ago.

What is going to happen in these last moments of time? Will the masses of humanity living in hopeless despair have a chance to hear the Good News of salvation through Jesus Christ? Will the Church of Jesus Christ be restored to her former glory before the Second Coming of our Lord?

The answer is most definitely "YES," my friend. God has promised to break in upon this present seemingly hopeless situation. He has promised to step once more into the pages of history to rescue His own from defeat, despair, and discouragement, and give all men, everywhere, a chance to call upon the Name of His Son Jesus Christ and be saved. God has indeed promised— and is now doing—a new thing.

He says in Isaiah 43:19 (AMP):

"Behold, I am doing a new thing; now it wrings forth; do you not perceive and know it, and will you not give heed to it?"

Let us then, be encouraged! The Lord in the following verses tells us what this new thing is. "A way in the wilderness." "Rivers in the desert." "I give waters in the wilderness." "Drink to my people, my chosen." "This people ,.. shall show forth my praise."[2]

Rivers. Restoration. Revival. Praise.

This is the new thing God is doing today. This new last move of the Spirit is of such magnitude and power that the Lord even warns us we may not completely understand it, or even believe it:

---

2 Isaiah 43:19-21.

"Look around you . . . among the nations and see! And be astonished! Astounded! For I am putting into effect a work in your days that you would not believe if it were told you" (Hab. 1:5, Amplified Bible).

Again, here is His promise in Jeremiah 33:3:

"Call unto me, and I will answer thee, and shew thee great and mighty things, which, thou knowest not."

Let US then, be prepared for an altogether new move of God—a quickening, an outpouring of His Spirit, a Restoration such as has never been seen before in history. Although it is God's Own Word, it almost reads like a beautiful heresy. In spite of the fact that it is God's promise to us, at first glance it seems almost too good to be true. But it is true. It is real. It is His Word. And, as our Lord clearly told us, "The Scripture cannot be broken"(John 10:35).

God's Promised Restoration

Here are two of the most important Scriptures about God's promised Restoration in the whole Bible. Read them through prayerfully. Meditate upon them.

AMOS 9:11-13:

"In that day will I raise up the Tabernacle of David that is fallen, and close up the breaches thereof; and I will raise up his ruins, and I will build it in the days of old:

That they may possess the remnant of Edom, and of all the heathen, which are called by my name, saith the Lord that doeth this.

Behold the days come, saith the Lord, that the plowman shall overtake the reaper, and the treader of grapes him that soweth seed; and the mounains shall drop sweet wine, and all the hills shall melt."

ACTS 15:13-18:

"And after they had held their peace. James answered, saying, Men and brethren, hearken unto me:

Simeon hath declared how God at the first did visit the Gentiles, to take out of them a people for his name.

And to this agree the words of the prophets; as it is written,

After this I will return, and will build again the Tabernacle of David, which is fallen down; and I will build again the ruins thereof, and I will set it up

That the residue of men might seek after the Lord, and all the Gentiles, upon whom my name is called, saith the Lord, who doeth all these things.

Known unto God are all his works from the beginning of the world."[3]

The glorious Gospel Age had commenced. The Holy Spirit had fallen upon the waiting disciples. Filled with His Power they had preached the Good News of salvation in Christ to the multitudes. Thousands were swept into the Kingdom of God.

But Peter had done something which had not been done before. Instead of preaching to the Jews only, he had taken the Gospel, under the guidance of the Holy Spirit, to the Gentile household of Cornelius. Defending, from Scripture, what Peter had done, James, speaking under the inspiration of the Spirit, quotes from the book of the prophet Amos. He speaks of the restoration of the Tabernacle of David, the building up of a glorious habitation for the Spirit of God, to bring a harvest of souls to Christ.

While the book of Acts most certainly records the commencement of this Restoration, it is obvious that in the book of Acts the Restoration was neither completed nor perfected. Under the unction of the Holy Spirit James, together with all of the Old Testament prophets, looks down the corridors of time to an age when there will be a complete Restoration of the Tabernacle of David as a dwelling place for God's Presence. By comparing Scripture with Scripture, we shall see that this glorious Restoration is speaking of the great world-wide move of the Spirit of God at the end of the Gospel Age, just before the Second Coming of the Lord Jesus Christ.

---

[3] Or, "says the Lord who has been making these things known from the beginning of the world" (Amplified Bible).

The Complete Restoration

To these Old Testament prophecies many New Testament Scriptures agree. For example, Paul told the Christians at Rome that the revelation of the mystery of his Gospel was now made manifest, "by the scriptures of the prophets, according to the commandment of the everlasting God, made known to all nations for the obedience of faith"(Romans 16:25-26). The thought here is clearly that the power of the Gospel, and the revelation of the mystery, is found in the prophets. Now, says Paul, these Scriptures of the prophets are to be made known to all nations, that they may become obedient to the faith of the Gospel of Christ by the Power of God.

One of the most lucid New Testament Scriptures concerning the promised Restoration is found in Acts 3:19-21:

"Repent ye therefore, and be converted, that your sins may be blotted out, when the times of refreshing (and reviving—Amplified Bible) *shall come from the presence of the Lord;*

And he shall send Jesus Christ, which before was preached unto you:

Whom the heaven must receive (retain) *until the times of restitution* (complete restoration—Amplified Bible) *of all things, which God hath spoken by the mouth of all his holy prophets since the world began."*

Here Peter teaches that all the prophets spoke of this complete restoration of all that God had promised—a restoration that supersedes anything ever known before. How good God is to encourage us in this way! And this is not some vague promise for the "sweet bye and bye"—it has commenced! It is taking place today. I have travelled through thirty nations in the last three years, and have been blessed to see first-hand that where hungry hearts are seeking God and are open to His Word, churches and assemblies are seeing this wonderful restoration in their midst. And the Lord will perfect and complete this restoration, ushering in the return of our Lord Jesus Christ.

Reformation to Restoration

Restoration—what a wonderful and expressive word! What an encouragement! What a challenge! The word "restoration" in our English Bible (and its equivalent, "restitution"), come from varied picturesque Hebrew and Greek words. One means "to make whole, or complete." Another means "to make alive." Others have the meaning "to give," "to cause to turn back, to put down again." Are not these the needs of the Church in this hour?

According to Webster's Dictionary, "restoration" is "the act of returning to an original state, or condition", or "the act of giving anything back to an owner." Both of these definitions are exciting expressions of this glorious Restoration which God is doing today. Firstly, the Bible clearly teaches the Lord desires to restore the Church of Jesus Christ to its original condition—and even more than this—for it is written, "the glory of this latter house shall be greater than the former, saith the Lord of hosts" (Haggai 2:9). Secondly, the Lord desires to give back to His children their rightful inheritance in Christ—every blessing purchased for them on Calvary.

In every century since the birth of the Church on the day of Pentecost there have been those who have experienced something of God's Spirit in their lives. But this last day restoration commenced with the Reformation. When the Holy Spirit anointed Romans 1:17, "the just shall live by faith," to the heart of Martin Luther, God restored to His Church the truth of justification by faith. In the 18th Century God used the Wesleys to restore the message of scriptural holiness. This brought about a move of the Spirit of God which swept the whole of England and beyond. Restoration continued through the 19th Century when men like William Booth, D. L. Moody, F. B. Meyer, and many others were used of God in extraordinary ways. At the turn of this century the Spirit of God was poured out in many places throughout the world—America, Scandinavia, India, China, and other countries. At that time the truths of the Baptism in the Holy Spirit, and the gifts of the Holy Spirit were restored to many churches.[4]

All this was very wonderful but the restoration we are seeing today is even more dynamic and penetrating. Not that the present restoration is taking away from the truths that God previously restored to His Church. On the contrary, in the current Restoration these truths are being emphasized with renewed enthusiasm. But in addition, all that has been lost is being restored. And surely all of us will admit, when we compare our churches today with the Church of the book of Acts, that we have most certainly lost something.

Today's Restoration

When we compare the cold formalism, and even the stereotyped evangelical habits of today's churches with the miraculous Power of God in action through the first century Church, we must ask ourselves, "could anything be more different?"

In his translators preface to his paraphrase of the Acts of the Apostles, "The Young Church in Action," J. B. Philips contrasts the power of God in action in the early Christian Church, with the traditional forms and historic pride of our churches today. Commenting on the Acts of the Apostles he says:

Yet we cannot help feeling disturbed as well as moved, for this surely is the Church as it was meant to be. It is vigorous and flexible, for these are the days before it ever became fat and short of breath through prosperity, or muscle bound by over-organization. These men did not make 'acts of faith', they believed; they did not 'say their prayers', they really prayed. They did not hold conferences on psychosomatic medicine, they simply healed the sick. But if they were uncomplicated and naive by modern standards we have ruefully to admit that they were open on the God-ward side in a way that is almost unknown today . . .We in the modern Church have unquestionably lost something.

---

[4] For a more detailed account see "The Testimony of History," in the author's book, *You Shall Receive Power*.

THE POWER OF HIS PRESENCE

In King David's day, we see the same situation. The Ark of the Covenant"[5] was lost to God's people. Because of this, they had lost also the presence, power, and glory of the Living God. The presence of God—this Ark of the Covenant—had to be restored. David, by bringing back the Ark of the Covenant, restored the power of His presence to Israel. He put the Ark in a Tabernacle, from which the light of God's glory, power, victory, and peace shone out to all who came to Mount Zion. This is the Tabernacle that God has promised to restore! A restoration of the power of God's Presence!

---

5   See Chapter 4, "The Ark of the Covenant."

Chapter Two

SPIRITUAL SIGN-POSTS

There is no clearer picture of the end of time given anywhere in the Bible than in Matthew chapter 24. It is Christ's own description of these days in which you and I live.

> *The disciples came to Jesus and asked, "Tell us, when shall these things be? and what shall be the sign of thy coming, and of the end of the world?" (verse 3).*

The list of signs of the End Time which follows almost reads like the headlines from the daily newspaper. Wars, famines, pestilences, earthquakes, sorrows (Matt. 24:7). Jesus also foretold spiritual deception (Matt. 24:4, 5, 11, 24). A cold formal church (Matt. 24:12). And, thank God, the powerful preaching of the Gospel throughout all nations (Matt. 24:14).

Nobody can deny these sign-posts, pointing to the soon-coming of our Lord Jesus Christ, are being seen before our very eyes. But the verse to particularly notice is verse 34:

> *"Verily I say unto you. This generation shall not pass, till all these things be fulfilled."*

"This generation." The generation in which you and I live. We are seeing these signs fulfilled. You and I are living in the last generation. Today we are perfectly justified in looking for, and seeing, the signs of the Second Coming of our Lord. They are being fulfilled at an alarming rate.

But one rather disturbing trend is that many Bible scholars today are putting too much emphasis on the physical signs of His Coming, and not enough on the spiritual sign-posts pointing to the Coming of the Lord. Indeed, some completely pass by great spiritual signs which God has promised. For example, in their effort to see the physical signs of the Coming of Christ, many sincere Christians are missing a great spiritual work which God is doing.

One spiritual sign that is going on virtually unrecognized is the operation of the nine miraculous gifts of the Spirit[1] in the historic denominations. Throughout the world members of all churches and missions are receiving the Holy Spirit just as the early disciples did.

That this phenomenon is a sign of the Second Coming of Christ there can be no doubt. The Rev. R. C. Firebrace, Anglican Minister in New Zealand, writes in Logos under the heading "The Gifts—Signs of the End":

The Charismatic Renewal can only be viewed in its true perspective as an eschatological event. That is to say, it is only when we realize that we are living in the Time of the End, the days leading up to the Return of Christ, that we begin to understand the significance and purpose of this movement, as yet, only in its preliminary stage... it is a special outpouring of the Spirit, a new Pentecost in fact, of which the object is to 'accomplish the number of God's elect' (Burial Service, Book of Common Prayer) and fit them to play their part in the work of the Kingdom. The 'early rain' of the first Pentecost caused the seed sown by the Apostolic preaching to spring up; the 'latter rain' brings the Harvest to full maturity, prior to being gathered in. Each is accompanied by the charismatic gifts of the Spirit 'confirming the word with signs following' (Mark 16:20).

"*There have of course been other mighty movements of the Spirit at critical points in Church History. But the 'gifts' of I Cor. 12 have played a very minor part in these revivals. And why? One hesitates to dogmatise, but one possible answer appeals to me more. Is it not possible that these manifestations in their fullness are reserved for those vital turning points of history, when the Harvest of one age is gathered and the seed sown for the next? In other words, the gifts are eschatological signs. When they are seen operating on a big scale we know that*

---

1   1 Cor. 12:1-11.

we stand on the edge of tremendous happenings. An End is at hand, also a Beginning.[2]

Let us be sure not to miss out on what God is doing in these days.

The Temple in Jerusalem

One of the most prominent physical signs many are looking for in these days is the rebuilding of the Jewish temple on Mount Moriah in Jerusalem. I want to be careful here. I do not say the temple will not be rebuilt. I do not say it cannot be rebuilt. I have been there, and seen the site. The Mosque of Omar will not be easily moved but I do not say it could not happen.

What I do say is this—let us be careful not to place too much emphasis on the rebuilding of a physical temple.

Jesus Himself placed very little emphasis on it. At the beginning of His ministry, the Lord Jesus spoke of the temple (which was neither Solomon's temple nor Ezra's—it was the temple built by Herod), as "My Father's house" (John 2:16).

But later Jesus completely disowned it, saying unto the people of Jerusalem, "Behold, your house is left unto you desolate" (Matthew 23:38).

Since the death of Christ on the cross, and His triumphant resurrection, any temple erected after the old order is not only left desolate—those sacrifices offered in it are an abomination to God.

Furthermore, I do not find a direct statement, in the Old Testament or the New, where God said that He would specifically rebuild the temple in Jerusalem.

Recently I read a book on the Second Coming of Christ. In this book, the author has a whole section about the Jews rebuilding their temple in Jerusalem, and various things that will happen in the temple. However, even in this book not a single verse is quoted proving the temple will be rebuilt. Once again I say I am not denying it could happen. But should we not

---

[2] From Logos Magazine, March 1968. The Rev. R. C. Firebrace, M.A., A.K.C. is Minister of St. Peter's Anglican Church, Raglan, New Zealand. He was for some time, a teacher in India.

give more heed unto that which God has categorically stated that He will rebuild?

What God is Definitely Building

Many Scriptures teach that God is far more interested in doing a spiritual work in hearts that seek Him, than He is in any physical temple that man can build. For example, in Isaiah 66:1 and 2:

Thus saith the Lord, The heaven is my throne, and the earth is my footstool: where is the house that ye build unto me? and where is the place of my rest?

For all those things hath mine hand made, and all those things have been, saith the Lord; but to this man will I look, even to him that is poor and of a contrite spirit, and trembleth at my word.

Here is a spiritual work God says He will do. Here is something God says He will definitely rebuild:

"I will raise up the Tabernacle of David that is fallen ... I will build it" (Amos 9:11).

"I will build again the Tabernacle of David which is fallen down; and I will build again the ruins thereof" (Acts 15:16).

God is doing a spiritual work. The Bible is full of spiritual sign-posts. God is rebuilding. He is restoring and refreshing His Church with the greatest deluge of Holy Ghost power ever received from heaven. See the physical signs by all means. But above all, look for, seek, and experience the spiritual.

I do not advocate spiritualizing everything in the Bible. Far from it. But here is another verse that will help us. Speaking of Old Testament Scriptures and events, Paul says:

Now all these things happened unto them for ensamples (margin, 'types'): *and they are written for our admonition, upon whom the ends of the world are come (I Cor. 10:11).*

In the Amplified Bible, this verse is even more illuminating:

Now these things befell them by way of a figure—as an example and warning (to us) ; they were written to admonish and fit us for right action by good instruction, we in whose days the ages have reached their climax —their consummation and concluding period.

People in the Old Testament did many things which are spiritual sign-posts for us today. The things they did are to teach us, bless us, challenge us, and warn us—we who are living at the end of this age. And one of the greatest sign-posts, one of the great events of the Old Testament which God clearly says is for our instruction today, is the building of the Tabernacle of David. After the Tabernacle of David had fallen down, God specifically said twice—once in the Old Testament and once in the New—that He would rebuild it. "At the mouth of two ... or three witnesses, shall the matter be established."[3] The Holy Spirit Himself, through James, uses David's Tabernacle to teach New Testament truth to the young Church (Acts 15:16). How much more would God teach us from it today, we who are, as Paul says, those "upon whom the ends of the world are come."

The Old Testament in the New

It is important to understand the Apostles used Old Testament Scriptures and events to prove New Testament doctrines.

In his epistle to the Romans, the Apostle Paul takes a verse from the Old Testament Prophet Habakkuk (Hab. 2:4) and develops the doctrine of Justification by Faith. In First Corinthians chapter 10 Paul tells us the events in the history of the Nation of Israel "were our examples" (verse 6). In Galatians Paul teaches that Abraham, his wife, handmaid and sons, together with Sinai and Jerusalem "are an allegory" (Gal. 4:24) which he uses to illustrate our freedom in Christ.

On the day of Pentecost, the Apostle Peter justifies the one hundred and twenty speaking in unknown tongues by quoting from the Old Testament prophet Joel, saying:

---

3   Deut. 19:15: See also Matt. 18:16.

"This is that which was spoken by the prophet Joel; And it shall come to pass in the last days, saith God, I will pour out of my Spirit upon all flesh" (Acts 2:16, 17).

It is interesting to note there are far more evidences of Joel's prophecy being fulfilled today than there were on the day Peter used these verses from Joel. Today we see the Spirit of God being poured out not just on one hundred and twenty disciples in a room in Jerusalem, but on many thousands of disciples around the world—indeed, "on all flesh."

In the same way, in Acts 15:15-18 when James is proving the ingathering of Gentile souls which had taken place under Peter's ministry was Scriptural, he too turns to the Old Testament—to Amos chapter 9. Notice here James did not quote the whole portion from Amos which speaks of the Restoration of David's Tabernacle. For, as Joel's prophecy quoted by Peter had the commencement of its fulfilment in the book of Acts, and the completion of its fulfilment in our day and generation, so Amos' prophecy quoted by James, has the commencement of its fulfilment with the outpouring of the Spirit on the Gentiles, and the climax of its fulfilment in our generation.

Old Testament Scriptures were "spiritual signposts", pointing to New Testament truths and experiences. Concerning the Old and New Testaments as one harmonious whole, it has been said:

"The New is in the Old contained,
The Old is in the New explained."

Or, in the language of the Bible, the "vail . . . in the reading of the Old Testament... is done away in Christ" (2 Cor. 3:14). The symbols, types, shadows, and examples given to us in the Old Testament are being fulfilled by Christ in His Church.

Spiritual Interpretation

While we shall see that each detail of the actual event of the building of the Tabernacle of David, and the resultant return of the Power of God's Presence is an example for us today, and has a spiritual interpretation, it is even more clear that the prophecies of the restoration of David's Tabernacle must have a spiritual interpretation. Just a quick glance at Amos chapter 9 reveals this:

> *In that day will I raise up the Tabernacle of David that is fallen . . .*
> *Behold, the days come, saith the Lord,, that the plowman shall overtake the reaper, and the treader of grapes him that soweth seed; and the mountains shall drop sweet wine, and all the hills shall melt (Amos 9:11. 13).*

As a physical phenomenon, the plowman overtaking the reaper is an impossibility. No natural seed grows that quickly, but there is a seed, which when watered sufficiently by the rain from Heaven, will. That seed is "the word of the kingdom," the Word of the Living God (Matt. 13:19). Thus the prophet is speaking of the sowing of the Word of God, and an ingathering of souls. And this is exactly how James uses this prophecy in Acts 15:16. Not only is a quick harvest foretold, but many harvests, one upon another.

In the same way, no one has seen a mountain dropping sweet wine. This also must have a spiritual interpretation. In the Bible, mountains often speak of obstacles, problems, and difficulties. In the Restoration of David's Tabernacle, God will turn these into "sweet wine"—into glorious victory. Likewise, the melting hills speak of obstacles before us being flattened out by the power of the Lord. The Amplified Bible interprets these promises as spiritual blessings, adding to verse thirteen, "that is, everything heretofore barren and unfruitful shall overflow with spiritual blessing."

Today's spiritual sign-posts point to the fact that God is doing, as He promised, "a new thing." There is coming, in this generation, an outpouring of the Holy Spirit upon His Church, a return of the Power of God's Presence, and a harvest of souls turning to God such as has never been experienced before in all history. This is the promise of the Restoration of the Tabernacle of David. This vital truth unlocks the keys to the house of David.[4]

---

4   See Isaiah 22:22; Rev. 3:7.

THE POWER OF HIS PRESENCE

We see many Scriptures clearly teach the Tabernacle of David will be restored. But when? Where? How? Why?

Part II
WHEN?

WHEN is God restoring the Tabernacle of David?

Chapter Three

I WILL BUILD MY CHURCH

When is God rebuilding the Tabernacle of David? Did He completely rebuild it in the early Church? Will He rebuild it after the Second Coming of Christ? Or is the Restoration of David's Tabernacle part of this Last Day Restoration?

The answer to this most important question can be found from:

(1) The literal wording of the actual prophecies ;

(2) The spiritual message prophesied by the actual events which took place during the building of the first Tabernacle of David.

The first we will deal with in this chapter, and in subsequent chapters the spiritual message which comes to us from the building of the first Tabernacle of David.[1]

God's Building

The literal wording of the prophecy is, "1 will . . . build again the Tabernacle of David which is fallen down" (Acts 15:16).

Jesus said, "I will build my church" (Matthew 16:18).

Paul said, "You are God's building" (1 Cor. 3:9).

Peter said, "You also, as lively stones, are built up a spiritual house" (1 Peter 2:5).

God is not building one, two, or three things. God is vitally concerned with the building of one thing, and one alone—His Church. Oh, that we

---

1   See 1 Cor. 10:11

might receive a fresh insight of how precious the building of God's Church is to Him. When we look to Calvary, and contemplate the price God paid to purchase this Building, surely we can see God's concern, God's great heart of love for His Building, His Church.

"... built up a spiritual house." But when we compare the Church in the book of Acts and the Epistles as it was, with the Church as we see it today, we must confess that God's Building is, like David's Tabernacle, in ruins.

When we read the exploits of the early Church in the midst of fiery persecutions, do we not long, every one of us, for a return to New Testament faith and power?

In the third chapter of Ezra we read of the rebuilding of the foundation of the temple. Solomon's magnificent temple had been destroyed. Cyrus, King of Persia, proclaimed that it be built again. Many returned from Babylon to Jerusalem to help in the work. When the builders laid the foundation of the temple of the Lord, "all the people shouted with a great shout, when they praised the Lord, because the foundation of the house of the Lord was laid" (verse 11).

But in comparison with the New Testament Church, is the Christian Church of today really worth shouting about? There were some in Ezra's company who did not shout and praise the Lord. They remembered with broken, longing hearts, the majesty and power of the foundation of the first temple. The record says they "wept with a loud' voice" (verse 12).

In which group do we find ourselves today? Contented? Satisfied? Making a great noise about these few broken stones we call Christianity? Or do we long to return to the Biblical foundation which gave us our heritage in Christ?

There must be a rebuilding, a Restoration, of the habitation of God. It must be built again.

Do you think the Lord Jesus Christ will come for a half-built Church? Or a Church which is falling down and in ruins? Will God present to His Son a sick, weak, sin-stained, defeated Bride? Never! The Bible teaches

Christ will come for a perfect Church, which is built up "unto the measure of the stature of the fullness of Christ" (Ephesians 4:13). Therefore we see this glorious rebuilding must take place before the Second Coming of the Lord Jesus Christ.

The Restoration of God's Glory

"In that day will I raise up the Tabernacle of David that has fallen ... I will build it as in the days of old" (Amos 9:11). David's Tabernacle will be rebuilt at a time when similar conditions are prevailing as at the time of the first building of David's Tabernacle. The time will be "as in the days of old."

David built his Tabernacle at a time when the Glory of God and the Power of His Presence had been lost. The Ark of the Covenant, which was the focal point of God's Presence, Glory and Power in Israel, had been captured by the Philistines. The Glory of God had departed from the people. But the Philistines returned the Ark to Israel, and the time had come to bring God's Presence back. In preparation for the return of the Ark of the Covenant of God, David built a Tabernacle for it. When the joyful procession arrived at Mount Zion, David set up the Ark in the Tabernacle he had built.

The Presence of God as seen in the Shekinah Glory above the Ark of the Covenant was restored. His Presence and Glory transformed all who worshipped at David's Tabernacle.

This was altogether different from the tabernacle which Moses had built. This was a new thing. A new order. There was rejoicing, praise, and worship. The Psalms we love so well were born at David's Tabernacle. David himself entered in to a new ministry. God's glory had been restored in the midst of His people.

The Need Today

What a striking parallel we see today! The time we live in is indeed "as in the days of old," when David's Tabernacle was built to receive the Ark of God's Presence. We must confess to our shame that we too, compared with the early Church, have lost much of the glorious Power and intimate Presence which God wills for His people. As one describes it:

> *"If the Holy Spirit were taken away from the Church, as the shekinah glory departed from the temple in Ezekiel's vision (Ezek. 11 : 22 ff.), one wonders if a great deal of our meetings and activities would not continue unaltered. In other words, as somebody else put it, a great deal of church activity can be attributed to natural rather than to supernatural causes. They are just carried on as a matter of convention and established custom without reliance on the Holy Spirit at all."*[2]

But "as in the days of old," God has promised to rebuild a dwelling place like David's Tabernacle. Once again He wants to dwell in His fullness with His people, refining them, bringing them into a closer fellowship with Himself, and giving them new Power to be witnesses of the Resurrection Life of His Son Jesus Christ. Truly God is preparing His Church for the dynamic impact it will have on this End Time generation. This is taking place today, before the Second Coming of Jesus Christ. What a blessed privilege it is to be living in such a day as this. How the heart thrills to know that God is at work in our day in a new way!

Restoration—Revolution by the Spirit

One well-informed observer of this rebuilding and Restoration taking place today is the Rev. John Myers, Editor of the Magazine Voice in the Wilderness, which has a world-wide circulation. A few years ago Rev. Myers was interviewed by David Davies, Church Editor of the newspaper Post-Advocate. Under the headline. "Editor Says Church Being Revolutionized by Spirit," Rev. Myers shows clearly the Restoration has most definitely begun:[3]

> *"A Spiritual Revolution of far-reaching consequences is taking place within the Church of the Lord Jesus Christ.*

---

2   *Take My Life* by M. Griffiths (I.V.F.)
3   Many thousands of reprints of this interview have been circulated worldwide.

> *"The restored New Testament church is emerging from its chrysalis and will yet burst forth in all its destined power and fullness of spiritual life upon the church world.*
>
> *"We see growing evidence on every side of this glorious revolution, which will break down sectarian isolation and prejudice and sweep away the mass of tradition and dead formality which has so long divided 'God's people and bogged them down in the emptiness of merely 'playing church' instead of actually meeting the living God.*
>
> *"Many do not realize that the spiritual awakening they are enjoying is part of God's over-all plan to restore His Church back to the New Testament pattern and fullness . . . this is the work of God and not of man. He is able to take care of it. As the restoration moves on towards maturity there will come more and more a glorious blending of the different aspects until in the triumph of a balanced whole the Church will truly become the 'fullness of Christ' in the earth.*
>
> *"The restoration of the Church is not a new movement. It began with Luther and the early reformers and was continued by Wesley, Darby, Booth, Andrew Murray and other great spiritual leaders. But the full restoration has yet to be completed before the Church can come fully into its Divine purpose in this age."*

Rev. Myers believes that the Divine purpose for the Church is that every aspect of New Testament Christianity be blended together into a balanced entity. When asked what effect the restored Church would have on the world, he answered:

> *"Once again the Church will turn the world upside down and shake the foundations of Hell. It will be a unified, Spirit-filled and fully functioning organism, even a many-membered Body in which shall be displayed before both men and angels the very fullness of the risen Christ!"*

This world-wide spiritual Revolution is continuing to gain momentum all the time as more and more Christians open their hearts to what God is doing in these days.

Rebuilding. Restoration. Revolution. And the outcome of these is Revival, and a great Reaping of souls by the Rebuilt, Revived Church.

Do not our hearts respond to these things? Do we not long for this spiritual revolution to take place in our hearts? And in our congregations?

> O Breath of Life, come sweeping through us.
> Revive Thy Church with life and power;
> O Breath of Life, come, cleanse, renew us
> And fit Thy Church to meet this hour.
> O Breath of Love, come breathe within us.
> Renewing thought and will and heart:
> Come, Love of Christ, afresh to win us.
> Revive Thy Church in ev'ry part.

When is God rebuilding the Tabernacle of David? When is Christ building His Church?

Now!

Chapter Four

THE ARK OF THE COVENANT

Before we can continue our study on the Restoration of David's Tabernacle, it is absolutely essential for us to have a clear understanding of the Ark of the Covenant. Because, until the time that Jesus Himself was born, the Ark of the Covenant was the most important thing on the face of the earth.

"And they shall make an Ark" (Exod. 25:10). Thus commenced God's instructions for the building of the tabernacle of Moses. This lone piece of furniture within the Most Holy Place, where God manifested His Glory and spoke, comes first. Of course, all six pieces of furniture in the tabernacle of Moses are important. But we see clearly, in the Word of God, that the Ark of the Covenant is by far the most important of all.

Three Arks

It is significant to note that there are three arks described for us in the Bible—the Ark of Noah, the Ark of Moses, and the Ark of the Covenant. Each one of these three speaks of deliverance from judgment, refuge from the storms of life, the blessing of obedience, trust in God, and the Presence of God.

In the first ark, the Ark of Noah, a God-fearing family of eight was kept safe and secure from the flood, which was God's judgment upon the sin of the world. All others outside the Ark of Noah perished in the waters. Noah's Ark was a large boat sealed both inside and out with pitch. The storm and floods could not harm those within the ark, because they were shut in by God, and shut in with God. Today Christ is our refuge from the storms of life. The words of the Lord to Noah are our invitation today: "Come thou and all thy house into the ark" (Genesis 7:1).

The mother of Moses, Jochebed, made the second ark. Once again, we see this ark also was a refuge from judgment. Pharaoh, King of Egypt, had pronounced the sentence of death upon all sons born to the Israelites. Again judgment was by water. "Every son that is born ye shall cast into the river, and every daughter ye shall save alive" (Exod. 1:22). The mother of Moses made a small ark or boat of bulrushes, and placed the baby Moses in it, laying the little vessel in the weeds by the river bank. Here Moses was safe and secure in the ark. God honoured his mother's faith, and God's Presence was with him.

Both of these arks were made secure, waterproofed by being lined with pitch. The Hebrew word for pitch is **kaphar**. This is the same word used in the Old Testament for "atonement." This Hebrew word is also translated in our Bible "to be merciful," "to forgive," "to be cleansed," and "to pardon." So we see the pitch is a picture, or type, of the Blood of the Lord Jesus Christ which cleanses us from all sin and keeps us cleansed and safe in Him.

The Ark of the Covenant (see Figure 1)

The first two arks were but a preparation for the third ark, the Ark of the Covenant. The Ark of the Covenant was also a place of refuge and shelter from the judgment of God. But it was much more than this. For the Ark of the Covenant is essentially a picture of the Lord Jesus Christ Himself. The Ark of the Covenant was the place of deep, spiritual, intimate communion and fellowship with God; a place of victory. The place where God manifested His Power, Presence, and Glory.

The Ark itself was an oblong-shaped box, 3 3/4 feet long, and 2 1/4 feet wide and 2 1/4 feet high. The box was made of wood, and was overlaid, both inside and out, with gold. Time and space forbid us from looking more closely into all the details, but this gold-covered box speaks of the

Figure 1: The Ark of the Covenant

Lord Jesus Christ. The wood reminds us that the Lord Jesus took upon Himself human flesh, and on the wooden Cross bore our sins in His own body (1 Pet. 2:24). Gold, of course, speaks of His deity. Thus the two-fold nature of our Lord—God and Man, "Emmanuel," God with us—are revealed in this Ark. The three layers —gold, wood, gold—remind us there is one God eternally existent in three Persons, the Father, the Son, and the Holy Spirit (1 John 5:7).

A Crown of Gold

The Ark of the Covenant wore a crown. In the pattern given for its construction we read:

"And thou . . . shalt make upon it a crown of gold round about" (Exod. 25:11 b).

The subject of crowns in the Bible is a very intriguing and blessed study, but we must leave it for another time and place. Suffice to say here, crowns are for kings to wear. A crown speaks of lordship, sovereignty and power. The Ark of the Covenant, as we have already seen, speaks of the Lord Jesus Christ. Thus the golden crown upon the Ark reminds us of our beloved Lord Jesus in His exalted office as King of kings:

"And I looked, and behold a white cloud, and upon the cloud one sat like unto the Son of man, having on his head a golden crown" (Rev. 14:14).

"We see Jesus . . . crowned with glory and honour" (Heb. 2:9).

"And he hath on his vesture and on his thigh a name written, KING OF KINGS, AND LORD OF LORDS" (Rev. 19:16).

The Bible teaches that our Lord Jesus Christ has three offices—those of Prophet, Priest, and King, in the tabernacle of Moses, there were three main divisions—the Outer Court, the Holy Place, and the Holy of Holies (see Figure 2). Each one of these places speaks to us of Christ in one of His ministries or offices.

In the Outer Court of the tabernacle of Moses was the brazen altar. Upon this altar were placed the offerings for sin. Innocent victims shed their blood to cover the sins of the guilty. The brazen altar and the offerings on it point to Jesus and His first coming, when He came as the Lamb of God to die on the Cross of Calvary for our sins. A prophet is one who comes from the presence of God with God's message for man. Jesus became our Prophet to wash away our sins, and to bring us God's message of salvation.

Going inside the tabernacle of Moses proper, the "tent of meeting,"[1] we come first into the Holy Place. In the Holy Place, the priest offered incense upon the golden altar of incense. In the Bible incense speaks to us of prayer. A priest intercedes for the people.

Today the ministry of the Priest in the Holy Place is fulfilled by the Lord Jesus Himself, Who is in the Holy Place in Heaven, where "He ever liveth to make intercession for (us)" (Heb. 7:25).

---

1   See Rev. 5:8

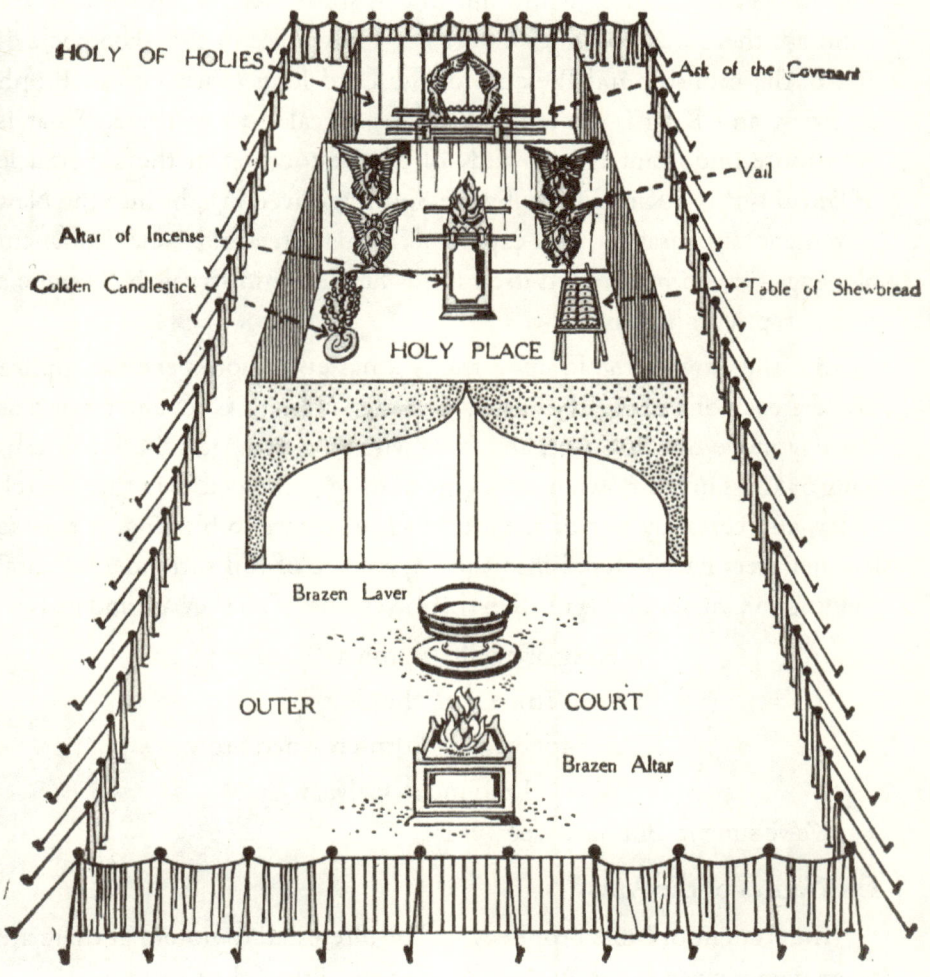

Figure 2: The Tabernacle of Moses (not drawn to scale)

However, when we enter in behind the veil, right into the Holy of Holies, we meet Christ in His ministry and office of King of kings, as typified to us by the golden crown upon the Ark of the Covenant there.

These facts are most significant in this study, because, as we shall see, although there was no Outer Court nor Holy Place in the Tabernacle of David, the ministry and Presence of the Lord Jesus Christ as our Prophet, Priest and King is nevertheless clearly revealed to us there. What is even more important in our study of the Restoration of the Tabernacle of David is this—King David, by the Spirit, received insight into the New Testament dispensation, and experienced this three-fold New Testament blessing—which manifested itself in his life and ministry as he became a prophet, priest and king.[2]

But the crown of gold upon the Ark has even more personal application for each one of us. Those who would go on with God, and enjoy this last day move of His Spirit, are those who have crowned the Lord Jesus King of kings in their own hearts. One of the great tragedies in the Church today, and certainly one of the greatest hindrances to blessing, is that so few believers have entered into this experience of full surrender, of total yielding to Christ as King of all in their lives, and of all they are and possess.

> King of my life I crown Thee now.
> Thine shall the glory be;
> Lest I forget Thy thorn-crowned brow,
> Lead me to Calvary.

We've sung it. But have we *done* it?

The Names of the Ark

The student of Bible prophecy will be interested to note that there are seven names given in the Word of God to the Ark of the Covenant.[3]

---

2   See Chapter 22, "Skeptics—Beware!"
3   The number seven in the Bible speaks of Dispensational Completeness, and Perfection in that which is Temporary. Just a few examples: In seven days God completed the earth's creation and rested; the seven years of plenty and the seven years of famine in the time of Joseph; in the conquest of Jericho we see seven priests, seven trumpets, and the people marched around the city seven times on the seventh day; Naaman went down into the waters seven times; the seven letters to the seven churches in the book of Revelation; etc. Someone has said, "As a water-

These names also speak to us today:

(1) The Ark of the Testimony (Exod. 25:22),
(2) The Ark of the Covenant (Num. 10:33),
(3) The Ark of the Lord God (1 Kings 2:26),
(4) The Ark of the Lord, the Lord of all the earth (Josh. 3:13),
(5) The Ark of God (1 Sam. 3:3),
(6) The Holy Ark (2 Chron. 35:3),
(7) The Ark of Thy Strength (Psalm 132:8).

The Contents of the Ark

Before we examine what was in the Ark of the Covenant, let us be reminded again that **it was to house this Ark—the only piece of furniture in David's Tabernacle—together with its contents, that David pitched his Tabernacle.**

Not only is the Tabernacle of David being restored today. The Ark of the Covenant, together with its contents, is also being restored in *spiritual application* to God's people who are willing to move on with Him. Both Old and New Testaments clearly teach that there were *three* things in the Ark of the Covenant. For instance, we see from Hebrews 9:4 the Ark of the Covenant contained:

(1) The Tables of the Covenant, or the Law;
(2) The Golden Pot of Manna;
(3) Aaron's Rod that budded.

We also read in Deuteronomy 31:26:

"Take this Book of the Law, and put it by the side of the Ark of the Covenant of Jehovah your God, that it may be there for a witness against thee." (American Standard Version)

So we see in addition there was:

(4) The Book of the Law by the side of the Ark.

---

mark on paper shows the mill from which the paper comes, so the number seven bears witness that the Bible is the work of the Holy Spirit."

"Important Lessons for Us Today"

In Hebrews 9:9 we read that the facts concerning Moses' tabernacle, and the Ark of the Covenant, were "a parable—a visible symbol or type or picture of the present age,"(Amplified Bible) or as the same verse is rendered in the *Living Letters* Paraphrase:

"This has an important lesson for us today."

(1) **The Two Tables of the Covenant** were of course, the two slabs of stone given to Moses on Mount Sinai. On these were written the Ten Commandments. In Exodus 25:16 God commanded Moses:

"And thou shalt put into the Ark the testimony which I shall give thee."

And again in Exodus 40:20:

"He (Moses) took the testimony (the Ten Commandments) and put it into the Ark" (Amplified Bible).

One of the fundamental teachings underlying the Law was Holiness. "Ye shall be holy; for I am holy"(Lev. 11:44). The Apostle Peter takes this up in his Epistle:

"But as he which hath called you is holy, so be ye holy in all manner of conversation; Because it is written, 'Be ye holy; for I am holy'" (1 Pet. 1:15-16).

So we see the lesson for us today contained in the two Tables of the Law in the Ark of the Covenant is Holiness.

(2) **The Golden Pot of Manna** contained a portion of that manna, that heavenly food, which God gave the children of Israel in the wilderness (Exod. 16:4-26). The commandment for a pot full of manna to be preserved in the Ark of the Covenant is recorded in Exodus 16:32-34.

This bread from heaven speaks to us today of the **Word of God, the Bible**. God has given His Word to be bread—food—for our souls.[4]

(3) **Aaron's Rod that Budded** was commanded to be kept in the Ark of the Covenant in Numbers 17:10:

---

[4] For example, sec 2 Cor. 9:10

"And the Lord told Moses, Put Aaron's rod back before the testimony (in the Ark), to be kept as a (warning) sign for the rebels; and you shall make an end of their murmurings against Me, lest they die" (Amplified Bible).

The lesson we learn today from Aaron's rod which budded is that it speaks of *the anointing*. This fruitfulness, the budding of Aaron's rod, proved that Aaron was the true anointed servant of God.[5] Aaron and his sons were anointed with the holy anointing oil.[6] God said that Aaron was given charge of the offerings of all the hallowed things of the children of Israel "by reason of the anointing" (Num. 18:8).

(4) **The Book of the Law by the side of the Ark** was not actually inside the Ark of the Covenant but was placed beside it. However, one thing is sure—the Book of the Law was an integral part of the Ark of the Covenant. The details of how this book was commended to be put by the Ark of the Covenant may be read in Deuteronomy 31:24-30.

This Book of the Law also speaks to us of the Word of God. Such is the extreme importance of God's Word that it was, as it were, "doubly" or twice preserved—in the Tables of the Law and in the Book of the Law. It is interesting to note in passing that in the complete armour which the Christian is commanded to put on, we see the Word of God is also mentioned twice. We are to stand having our "loins girt about with truth" (Eph. 6:14). Jesus said, "Thy Word is truth" (John 17:17). We are also told to "take . . . the sword of the Spirit which is the Word of God" (Eph. 6:17). We can never over emphasize the utmost importance of the Word of God.

But the Book of the Law by the side of the Ark speaks to us, in these days of Restoration, with even more impact. In the book of Second Kings, we read of King Josiah. The Bible says that "he did that which was right in the sight of the Lord, and walked in all the way of David his father, and turned not aside to the right hand or to the left" (2 Kings 22: 2). There was

---

5   See Numbers chapter 17
6   Exod. 40:15, 16

a wonderful restoration during Josiah's reign, and in the midst of this an astounding discovery was made. The high priest announced excitedly to the scribe:

*"I have found the **Book of the Law** in the house of the Lord" (2 Kings 22:8).*

Shaphan the scribe anxiously read it to the king. When the king heard the words of the Book of the Law he rent his clothes, realising that neither he nor his people had kept the Word of God. Therefore the judgments of God would come upon him. But then King Josiah renewed the Covenant, kept the feast of the Lord, and was assured they would escape the coming judgments if they kept the Word of the Law. How this speaks to us today of *The Book of Revelation*. God's judgments are coming upon the earth. But, thank God, those who keep His Word and live according to it shall be delivered from the judgments to come.

The Ark Fulfills the Holy Place

As we have seen, there was both a Holy Place, and a Holy of Holies in the tabernacle of Moses. However, there was no Holy Place in the Tabernacle of David. What David did, in effect, was to *transfer only the Holy of Holies to Mount Zion* when he built his Tabernacle there.

The reason for this is that the three pieces of furniture in the Holy Place have their fulfilment in the contents of the Ark of the Covenant. Thus we see with added emphasis and urgency, the extreme importance of this one thing—the Ark of the Covenant.

Concerning the furniture in the Holy Place, we see briefly:

(1) *The Altar of Incense* points forward to the **Tables of Stone** in the Ark of the Covenant. The Altar of Incense speaks not only of prayer, but holiness; because the blood of sin offerings which had been shed on the brazen altar was sprinkled upon the Altar of Incense once a year for the holiness of the people.

(2) *The Table of Shewbread* has its fulfilment in the **Golden Pot of Manna**. The loaves of bread for the Table were placed there fresh and hot

once a week. But that bread from heaven in the Ark of the Covenant did not need to be renewed. It was there always as a testimony of God's provision of food for His people.

(3) The *Golden Candlestick* in the Holy Place points forward to, and has its fulfilment in, **Aaron's Rod that budded** which was in the Ark of the Covenant. The Golden Candlestick had seven branches. Each branch was made up of three groups of a knop, a flower, and a fruit.[7] The oil, speaking to us of anointing, had to be renewed from time to time. Aaron's Rod was in the Ark of the Covenant as a constant reminder of the fruitful power of the anointing of God's Spirit.

The Contents of the Ark seen in Christ

We have already seen the Ark of the Covenant and its contents speak in every detail of Jesus Christ our Lord. He is its fulfilment. He is God with us, "Emmanuel." "In Him dwelleth all the fullness of the Godhead bodily" (Col. 2:9).

(1) The Tables of the Law speak of **Holiness**. The Bible teaches that God has made Christ holiness unto us:

"But of Him are ye in Christ Jesus, who of God is made unto us wisdom, and righteousness (or holiness)" (1 Cor. 1:30).

We have no holiness of our own. But how wonderful to know God says in His Word "that we might be partakers of His holiness" (Heb. 12:10).

(2) The Manna in the Ark, speaking to us of the **Word of God** is also fulfilled in the Lord Jesus Christ. From eternities past He has always been the Word (John 1:1). When He was on earth He was "the Word made flesh" (John 1:14). And when He comes again, in Power and great Glory, the Bible says, "His Name is called The Word of God" (Rev. 19:13).

---

7   That is, *nine* portions to each branch. Nine in the Bible is the number of the Holy Spirit. For example, there are *nine* fruit of the Spirit mentioned in Galatians 5:22, 23; *nine* gifts of the Spirit listed in 1 Corinthians 12:1-11; *nine* references to the Latter Rain Outpouring of the Spirit of God upon the earth in the Last Days, etc.

(3) Aaron's Rod, a picture of the **Anointing**, is fulfilled in our Lord Jesus Christ. He was anointed with the Holy Spirit in the River Jordan (Matt. 3:16). The Bible says:

"God, thy God, hath anointed thee with the oil of gladness above thy fellows" (Psalm 45:7).

Jesus testified:

"The Spirit of the Lord is upon me, because He hath anointed me to preach the gospel to the poor..." (Luke 4:18).

Peter said:

"God anointed Jesus of Nazareth with the Holy Ghost and with power: who went about doing good, and healing all that were oppressed of the devil; for God was with Him" (Acts 10:38).

Jesus is the "Rod of all rods," the "rod out of the stem of Jesse... and the Spirit of the Lord shall rest upon Him" (Isaiah 11:1-2).

It is absolutely imperative that these truths burn deep into our hearts. The Presence of the Ark of the Covenant has its fulfilment in the Presence with us of the Lord Jesus Christ in all His fullness by the Power of the Spirit. It was for the entrance of the fullness of God's Presence that David erected his Tabernacle. This is the Tabernacle God is restoring in these days.

To sum up, let us remember Jesus said in the well-known verse, John 14:6:

"I AM

(1) "the Way," (Tables of Stone—Holiness),

(2) "the Truth," (Pot of Manna—the Word),

(3) "and the Life" (Aaron's Rod—the Anointing).

Blessed be His wonderful Name!

Chapter Five

OF HIS FULLNESS

"And David . . . prepared a place for the Ark of God, and pitched for it a tent (a tabernacle)" (I Chron. 15:1).

Because our subject, the Restoration of the Tabernacle of David, is so intimately connected with the Ark of the Covenant, let us continue to search the Scriptures for more concerning this amazing piece of tabernacle furniture. Not that we have room in this book to plumb all the depths of this teaching and blessing. We can only bring out some of the "important lessons for us today"[1] in its relationship to the Restoration of the Tabernacle of David.

The Contents of the Ark in Us

"And of His fullness have all we received, and grace for grace" (John 1:16).

It almost reads like a translator's error in the Gospels. His fullness? In us?

But it is confirmed in the Epistles:

"That you might be filled with all the fullness of God" (Eph. 3:19).

We saw in our last chapter that all the fullness of the contents of the Ark of the Covenant is fulfilled in Christ. Holiness (the Tables of the Law), the Word (the Pot of Manna), the Anointing of the Holy Spirit (Aaron's Rod which budded).

---

1   Heb. 9:9—*Living Letters*

Dear friend, here is the most important lesson for you and me—God wills that this same fullness dwell in us! Dare we even contemplate it? It shatters our intellect. It challenges our faith.

The fullness of Christ in us!

This is really what the Restoration of the Tabernacle of David is all about. Not the pitching of a tent on a hill in a far-away land. But the Restoration of the fullness of the Presence of Christ in His people now!

Not after He comes again.

Now!

Not in the next world. In this world. Even as it is written, "As He is, so are we in this world" (1 John 4:17).

Am I? Are you? If not, then a Restoration is urgently needed. Praise be to God, He has promised one:

"I will build again the Tabernacle of David which is fallen down" (Acts 15:16).

(1) The Tables of the Law Restored—*Holiness*

The Bible is insistent on this one thing—if God wants us to be anything. He wants us to be holy. Because of its extreme importance we shall deal with this subject a little later in more detail. But let us remind ourselves here that "God hath . . . called us . . . unto holiness" (1 Thess. 4:7). "Perfecting holiness in the fear of God" (2 Cor. 7:1). God wills that our hearts be "unblameable in holiness before God, even our Father, at the coming of our Lord Jesus Christ with all his saints" (1 Thess. 3:13).

Bible holiness is no "1-am-holier-than-thou" air. Neither is it a legalistic bondage to man-made rules or regulations. It is a spiritual experience of the Cross of Christ in the believer's life.

The Lord Jesus did not die on the Cross only that we might be forgiven. He died to make us holy. God's commandment "Be ye holy; for I am holy" (1 Pet. 1:16) is not in the Bible to frustrate us. The exhortation to "be holy in all your conduct and manner of living" (1 Pet. 1:15—*Amplified*

Bible) is given to be obeyed! Indeed, God warns that without holiness, no man shall see the Lord (Heb. 12:14). Around the world today, thousands of Christians are entering into the glorious liberty of Bible holiness. God is restoring to His Church the truth that Christ is our Holiness, and that we can experience the Power of His Cross in our lives today.

(2) **The Pot of Manna Restored**—*the Word*

Even as the Pot of Manna was in the Ark of the Covenant, so God wills that His Word dwell in our hearts:

"Let the Word of Christ dwell in you richly in all wisdom" (Col. 3:16).

"Thy Word have I hid in mine heart, that I might not sin against Thee" (Psalm 119:11).

While some sections of the Church seem to desire allegiance with manmade systems and doctrines, there are also many turning to God with hungry hearts for Him to feed them from His Word. Despite attacks upon it by modern critics, the Word of God stands sure. God is restoring confidence and faith in His Word in these days.

Again, in these days of the outpouring of the Spirit, we hear God saying:

"Give ear, O ye heavens, and I will speak; and hear, O earth, the words of my mouth. My doctrine shall drop as the rain, my speech shall distil as the dew, as the small rain upon the tender herb, and as the showers upon the grass" (Deut. 32:1, 2).

Manna from heaven. Blessed food indeed. The Bible teaches that at the end of the week, on the sixth day, God gave His people a double portion of bread from heaven (Exod. 16:5, 23-25). Today we are living at the end of the sixth day of God's week. The Bible says in both Old and New Testaments, that we should "be not ignorant of this one thing, that one day is with the Lord as a thousand years, and a thousand years as one day" (2 Pt. 3:8; Psalm 90:4). It is an historical fact that we are fast approaching the end of the sixth thousand-year period since the fall of Adam, or the-end—of the sixth day. Therefore, we must gather a double portion of Manna. And is it not written, "To him that overcometh will I give to eat of the hidden Manna" (Rev. 2:17)?

(3) **The Rod of Aaron Restored**—*the Anointing*

No one can deny that today we are seeing throughout the whole earth the commencement of a mighty outpouring of the Spirit of God upon all flesh. Magazines with world-wide circulation have reported it. Leaders of all denominations are discussing it.

Many Christians throughout the world are receiving an experience of the anointing in the same way as Christ's followers in the book of Acts were anointed.

Time magazine, with the largest weekly circulation in the world, reports under their heading "Charisma on the Rise":

"The so-called 'charismatic gifts'—prophecy, spiritual healing and glossolalia, or speaking in tongues—have long been characteristic of the zealous, fundamentalist Pentecostal sects. Increasingly, though, these unusual outpourings of spiritual feeling can be found in mainstream Protestant and even Roman Catholic congregations...[2]

God is restoring the anointing of His Spirit to hungry hearts everywhere—together with the Biblical manifestations of this anointing.

Thousands of Christians in all branches of the Church are discovering a new anointing of Power, a new dynamic for Christian living, and a new dimension of communion with God.

God wills such an anointing for every believer in Christ. The Bible teaches this anointing of the Holy Spirit, this Baptism with the Holy Ghost and fire, this infilling of the Holy Spirit is not the same as conversion, or receiving the Lord Jesus as Saviour.

It comes as a shock. It challenges our experience. It upsets our theology. But the disturbing fact is this: the believers at Samaria had received the Word of God, they were believers in the Lord Jesus Christ, they had been baptized in water, they had seen mighty miracles performed in the Name of

---

2   *Time Magazine*, June 14, 1968

the Lord, and the joy of salvation filled their whole city. But the Bible says, "As yet He (the Holy Spirit) was fallen upon none of them" (Acts 8:16).

The Jews wanted to know what to do when they heard the Spirit had been poured out upon the disciples of Christ. They were told to repent of their sins, to be baptized in water, and after this they would receive the Gift of the Holy Ghost (Acts 2:37-38).

The Apostle Paul was converted to Christ, receiving Him as Lord and Saviour on the Damascus road. But three days later, when Ananias laid hands upon Paul, he received the anointing of the Holy Spirit (Acts 9:1-19).

Cornelius and his company first became believers, and the Lord purified their hearts by faith. Then possibly just a few minutes, or even a few seconds later, as a subsequent step to their conversion the Holy Spirit fell upon them (Acts 10:34-48; 15:7, 9).

The Apostle Paul found disciples at Ephesus who had believed in Jesus for conversion long before Paul visited them. But when Paul challenged them, asking, "Have you received the Holy Ghost since you believed?" their lack was seen. Paul laid his hands upon them and they received the Holy Spirit (Acts 19:1-7).

Thus, the Bible proves to us beyond a shadow of doubt, that in every case there were two distinct operations of God's power—being born of the Spirit, or converted, or saved; and later, sometimes seconds, sometimes days, sometimes possibly years, receiving the blessed anointing of the Holy Spirit. None received the filling of the Spirit at the moment of their conversion.

In the words of Andrew Murray:

"All these facts teach us that there are two ways in which the Holy Spirit works in us. The first is the preparatory operation in which He simply acts on us, but does not yet take up His abode (fully) within us, though leading us to conversion and faith, and ever urging us to all that is good and holy.

"The second is the higher and more advanced phase of His working,

when we receive Him as an abiding gift, as an indwelling Person, concerning whom we know that He assumes responsibility for our whole inner being, working in it both to will and to do. This is the ideal of the full Christian life."[3]

The founder of Gordon College of Theology and Missions, Dr. A. J. Gordon, contemporary of Spurgeon, Moody and Myer, affirms; "It is clearly an experience belonging to one who has already been converted."[4]

Are You Anointed?

The Apostle Paul asks the disciples at Ephesus this searching question. It challenges everyone of us today:

"Have you received the Holy Ghost since you believed?"

They had to answer the question:

"We have not so much as heard whether there be any Holy Ghost"(Acts 19:1-7).

What a tragic reply! They could have been enjoying the fullness of the blessing of the Holy Spirit. Paul laid his hands upon them, and they received the Holy Spirit, spoke in tongues, and prophesied.

Friend, what is your reply? "Have you received the Holy Ghost since you believed?"(Acts 19:2—*Amplified Bible*).

In their futile endeavour to excuse themselves from an experience such as the early Ephesians had, many remind us that modern translators render this question a little differently. In the Greek, the word "when" is used, instead of "since." Thus the question reads, "Did you receive the Holy Spirit when you believed on Jesus as the Christ?" This is a good translation, for it speaks of receiving the Spirit as part of the first foundation of Christian experience, agreeing with Peter's words in Acts 2:38. But the question put this way, clearly underlines this alarming truth:—*It is possible to believe in*

---

3   *The Full Blessing of Pentecost—The One Thing Needful* (Oliphants), by Andrew Murray. Andrew Murray (author of *The Holiest of All*), is one of today's most widely- read Christian authors.

4   *The Ministry of the Spirit* (Judson Press), by A. J. Gordon.

Christ as Saviour and yet NOT receive the Spirit's fullness! It is possible to know Christ as Saviour, and yet not be anointed by His Spirit. As Dr. Torrey, first Principal of Moody Bible Institute, writes:

> "*It is evident that the baptism with the Holy Spirit is an operation of the Holy Spirit distinct from and additional to His regenerating work ... A man may be regenerated by the Holy Spirit and still not be baptized with the Holy Spirit. In regeneration, there is the impartation of life, by the Spirit's power, and the one who receives is saved: in the baptism with Holy Spirit, there is the impartation of power, and the one who receives it is fitted for service...*[5]

Have you received this New Testament Anointing of Power? Has this fruitful budding Rod-of-Aaron experience been restored in your life?

But let us be careful to emphasize here that this is not a "once-for-all" experience. The Bible clearly teaches the Christian who is enjoying the fullness of the Holy Spirit is living a continuously Spirit-filled life by being constantly filled with the Holy Spirit. Paul testified: "Though our outward man perish, yet the inward man is renewed day by day" (2 Cor. 4:16). How is the inward man to be daily renewed? The answer is found in Ephesians 3:16:

> "*That He would grant you, according to the riches of His glory, to be strengthened with might by His Spirit in the inner man.*"

Oh for a new anointing.
Oh for the Heavenly Flame!
Oh for a new anointing.
To glorify Thy Name.
Oh from sin and self to cease.
Oh for a sense of inward peace.
Lord, that Thy Glory may increase,
Saviour, anoint me now.

---

[5] *The Person and Work of the Holy Spirit* (Fleming H. Revell) by Dr. R. A. Torrey

Maybe for years you have lived a defeated, frustrated Christian life. Be encouraged. The Ark is coming. God has promised, "I will restore to you the years that the locust hath eaten" (Joel 2:25).

God will restore the fullness of Christ's anointing to all who believe, and act upon His Word. Expect Him to do exactly what He has promised in His Word to do.

The Mercy Seat

"And thou shalt make a Mercy Seat of pure gold . . . and thou shalt put the Mercy Seat upon the Ark; and in the Ark thou shalt put the Testimony that I shall give thee. And there will I meet with thee, and I will commune with thee from above the Mercy Seat" (Exod. 25:17, 21. 22).

Above this gold-plated, oblong box of the Ark of the Covenant, was the Mercy Seat. Like the rest of the Ark, the Mercy Seat speaks to us of the Lord Jesus Christ.

If there had been no blood-sprinkled Mercy Seat, God would have looked down from above the Ark of the Covenant and seen the Law which the people had repeatedly broken. The Bible defines sin as "the transgression of the Law" (1 John 3:4). Thus, had there been no Mercy Seat, God would have looked directly upon the sins of the people, and death would have been the result.

But behold the mercy of God! Upon this Mercy Seat, which covered the Ark, was sprinkled the blood of the innocent animal which had been slain on the altar of burnt offering, the brazen altar. Thus, when God looked down upon the Ark, instead of beholding the broken Law and the sins of the people, He saw the blood of atonement. Therefore God could not slay the people because He Himself had promised:

"When I see the blood, I will pass over you" (Exod. 12:13).

The Mercy Seat was made from beaten gold. The Lord Jesus became our Mercy Seat by the beating He received at Gethsemane, at the whipping post, and the Cross of Calvary, where He shed His Blood to wash away our sins. There He met the demands and the penalty of the Law which we all have broken. Jesus is called our "Mercy Seat" in Romans chapter three:

"Being justified freely by his grace through the redemption that is in Christ Jesus: Whom God hath set forth to be a propitiation (Greek— Mercy Seat) through faith in his blood" (Rom. 3:24, 25).

The Greek word for "propitiation" is *"hilasterion,"* and means literally the "seat of mercy." Therefore, God has set forth Jesus Christ to be our Mercy Seat through faith in His precious Blood.

As we shall see later in our study, the men of Bethshemesh made the tragic mistake of looking into the Ark.[6] Unless blood covers that broken Law, we are dead in our trespasses and sins. God smote them dead and the people lamented. Death results where there is no blood to wash away sin.

The Shekinah Glory of His Presence

Some would have us think that the Ark of the Covenant was a picture or a type of the Presence of God to the people of Israel. That it was a picture or a type which speaks to us today, we most definitely agree. But a symbol of God's Presence to Israel? Never! The Ark of the Covenant was no more a symbol of God's Presence to Israel than Christ was a symbol of God's Presence when He was on earth. Christ was no symbol. Christ was no type. He was "Emmanuel . . . God with us" (Matt. 1:23). Our precious Saviour was "the Word made flesh" ((John 1:14). The Bible says "that God was in Christ, reconciling the world unto Himself" (2 Cor. 5:19). Christ was the Second Person of the Triune Godhead incarnate. When He was on earth He was, as it were, the "focal point" of God's Presence with us.

Similarly, the Ark of the Covenant was the literal, real Presence of God with His people. It was the focal point of God's Presence upon the earth. Let us follow this very closely, for this truth can revolutionize our lives, and give us much understanding concerning the Restoration of the Tabernacle of David.

---

6   See 1 Sam. 6:19

Concerning the construction of the Ark of the Covenant, it is written: *"And thou shalt make two cherubims of gold, of beaten work shalt thou make them, in the two ends of the mercy seat . . . And there I will meet with thee, and I will commune with thee from above the mercy seat"* (Exod. 25:18, 22).

The cherubim were two symbolical figures placed one each end of the mercy seat with outstretched wings. Their wings were to be stretched upwards, and their faces toward each other and toward the mercy seat. They were symbols of the holiness of God.

The essential thing to note here is, that God said, "*There* **I will meet with thee, and I will commune with thee** from above the mercy seat." God would meet, God would speak from a place above the mercy seat, between the cherubim. **We cannot over-emphasize this important fact.** Here lies one of the most essential keys for us to understand the Ark of the Covenant, and its return to the Restored Tabernacle of David. Time and again God repeats this truth in His Word. Let us just give a few examples here:

"I will appear in the cloud upon the mercy seat" (Lev. 16:2).

Not a type. Not a symbol. Not a picture. But God Himself!

"In the tent of meeting before (the Ark of) the Testimony, where I will meet with you" (Num. 17:4, Amplified Bible).

This was no apparition. This was no vision. This was a literal meeting with the Living God.

"The Ark of the Covenant of the Lord of hosts, which dwelleth between the cherubims" (1 Sam. 4:4).

Once again, not a picture. God dwelling, God Himself living between the cherubim. We are aware, of course, that God is omnipresent. He is everywhere at once. He was also omnipresent when our Lord Jesus walked this earth. But just as our Lord was the revelation of God upon the earth at that time, so the Ark of the Covenant was the revelation of God to His people in those days when the Ark was with them.

Now we can understand why Joshua "fell to the earth upon his face before the Ark of the Lord until eventide" (Josh. 7:6). He interceded before the Ark and God spoke to him from the Ark. At the Ark of the Covenant of the Lord, Joshua ministered the Word of God to the people (Joshua 8:32-35). And so we could go on right through our Bibles.

But what about the Tabernacle of David? David most certainly knew where to meet His God:

"The Lord reigneth; let the people tremble: He sitteth between the cherubim; let the earth be moved.

"The Lord is great in Zion . . (Psalm 99:1-2).

"Give ear, O Shepherd of Israel, thou that leadest Joseph like a flock; thou that dwellest between the cherubims, shine forth" (Psalm 80:1).

In another place, David said:

"I will not give sleep to mine eyes, or slumber to mine eyelids.

Until I find out a place for the Lord, an habitation for the mighty God of Jacob" (Psalm 132:4, 5).

And where was this habitation?

"Let us go into His Tabernacle; let us worship at His foot-stool" (verse 7, Amplified Bible).

And what was in this Tabernacle?

"Arise, O Lord, into Thy rest; Thou, and the Ark of Thy strength" (verse 8).

Little wonder then, that David desired never to leave his Tabernacle. There he could at all times see the Glory and Presence of God between the wings of the cherubim, and there receive assurance and confidence toward God in his heart:

"I will dwell in Your Tabernacle for ever; let me find refuge and trust in the shelter of Your wings. Selah (pause, and calmly think of that)!" (Psalm 61:4, Amplified Bible).

Do we realize that in David's most famous Psalm, which most of us know by heart, he is speaking of his Tabernacle?

"Surely or only goodness, mercy and unfailing love shall follow me all the days of my life; and through the length of days the house of the Lord (and His presence) shall be my dwelling place" (Psalm 23:6, Amplified Bible*).*

David met with God; David worshipped God; David heard from God, as he waited upon Him before the Ark of the Covenant. The Shekinah of God's Glory, God's Power, God's Presence, dwelt between the cherubim of the Ark. God Himself was there. And this is the Ark which God is restoring back into the Tabernacle of David today. Does not this make our hearts worship this Mighty God of ours?

The Fullness of His Presence in Us

Now we are commencing to see why God has so clearly and specifically promised to restore the Tabernacle of David in these last days. God gives back this fullness of His Divine Power and Glory, as manifested in the Ark of the Covenant, and revealed and fulfilled in Christ our Lord, to dwell in us. This is the very reason we were created—that God's Loving, Father-heart might express His love towards His creation, and make us His children, and dwell in us. This He has done for us in Christ. "Christ in you, the hope of glory" (Col. 1:27).

And so, now we can say with John:

"Of His fullness have all we received, and grace for grace" (John 1:16).

Now we can see why He wants us "to know the love of Christ, which passeth knowledge, that ye might be filled with all the fullness of God (Eph. 3:19).

"And they shall make an Ark" (Exod. 25:10). This Ark, all the fullness of God's Glory and Presence as revealed in Christ, shall again dwell in the Tabernacle of David which God is restoring today.

Chapter Six
ALONE WITH GOD

The God of the Bible is the God of action. He moves on. The very first verse in the Bible says "God created" (Gen. 1:1). The very next verse says "the Spirit of God moved" (Gen. 1:2).

Some, by relegating the miracles of God to a bygone era, have tried to make God appear a patient Observer of the affairs of men. Never! God is neither dead nor asleep. He is working. He is moving. Today.

God does not change. "I am the Lord, I change not" (Mal. 3:6). Our Saviour is "Jesus Christ, the same yesterday, and today, and forever" (Heb. 13:8).

Change: no. But move; most certainly yes! The Bible says of Samson "the Spirit of the Lord began to move him at times" (Judges 13:25). And from time to time it pleases God to move by His Spirit, and He is most certainly doing so today.

The Ark of the Covenant did not change. But it did move. In a later chapter we shall examine more closely some of the journeys of the Ark. But let us here keep in mind that God wants us to experience today the "moving of the Ark" in our lives in the fullness of the blessing of the Gospel.

Alone with God

We are now beginning to see what a place of intimate communion with God the Ark of the Covenant was. A place where God met with His people, where He revealed the Glory of His Presence, where He spoke "face to face" with His people.

But let us also see the progressive revelation of His blessing. With the exception of a few, like Joshua who had power with God, in the tabernacle of Moses, only the high priest, once a year, and that not without blood, could enter into the Holy of Holies and stand before the Ark of the Covenant to enjoy this intimate fellowship with Almighty God. This was the climax of spiritual experience. One man, alone with God.

In the Holy Place, all the priests were permitted to assemble and worship together at the Table of Shewbread by the light of the Golden Candlestick. But in the Holy of Holies, that innermost sanctuary behind the veil, only personal, individual fellowship was permitted with God at the Ark of the Covenant. Let us also remember that the time which the high priest spent alone with God on the day of atonement, when he entered in beyond the veil and presented the blood of atonement, was far more important than all the hundreds of days of service in the Outer Court and worship in the Holy Place.

How this challenges us today to spend more time alone with God! For today, because of all that our blessed Saviour has done for us, we may at any time enter beyond the veil, right into the brightness of His Glory before the Ark of the Covenant in the Holy of Holies, to have personal, individual fellowship with our Lord.

> Alone with God,
> The world forbidden;
> Alone with God,
> O bless'd retreat,
> Alone with God,
> And in Him hidden
> To hold with Him communion sweet.

Christ Has Entered

It becomes obvious from a study of the tabernacle of Moses, that the work of the high priest was but a type of the work of Him who was still to come. Every year the sprinkling of blood on the Mercy Seat had to be repeated on the day of atonement. However, the blood of bulls and goats could only cover sin; it could never wash sin away. The blood of innocent animals shed on behalf of the people; could only atone for a little while. Even though the blood was sprinkled annually, it could never pay the price of sin. This is what we are taught in the book of Hebrews;

> *"For the law having a shadow of good things to come, and not the very image of the things, can never with those sacrifices 'which they offered year by year continually make the comers thereunto perfect. For then would they not have ceased to be offered? because that the worshippers once purged should have had no more conscience of sins. But in those sacrifices there is a remembrance again made of sins every year. For it is not possible that the blood of bulls and of goats should take away sins. But this man, (Jesus) after he had offered one sacrifice for sins for ever, sat down on the right hand of God" (Heb. 10:1-4, 12).*

> *"Neither by the blood of goats and calves, but by His own blood He entered in once into the holy place, having obtained eternal redemption for us" (Heb. 9:12).*

Our invitation to fellowship with God at the Ark of the Covenant in the Holy of Holies is even more dramatically revealed to us when we see—

The Rent Veil

For one thousand five hundred years the way into the Holy of Holies was completely blocked by a heavy veil or curtain, which forbade anyone to go in except the high priest once a year with the blood of atonement.

But when our precious Saviour shed His Blood upon the Cross, and completed the perfect atoning sacrifice for sin, crying "It is finished!" what happened to this veil which stopped us entering into the glorious Presence of God? It is written:

> *"Jesus, when he had cried again with a loud voice, yielded up the ghost. And, behold, the veil of the temple was; rent in twain from the top to the bottom; and the earth did quake, and the rocks rent'" (Matt. 27:50, 51).*

The barrier was broken down. The veil was torn in two. Hallelujah! The veil into the Most Holy Sanctuary, the pathway into intimate fellowship with our Lord, was made open.

Again, we read in the book of Hebrews, we can now come:

"by a new and living way, which he (Jesus) hath consecrated for us, through the veil, that is to say, his flesh" (Heb. 10:20).

How beautifully we see this truth in Hebrews 6:18-20 (*Amplified Bible*):

"This was so that by two unchangeable things (His promise and His oath), in which it is impossible for God ever to prove false or deceive us, we who have fled (to Him) for refuge might have mighty indwelling strength and strong encouragement to grasp and hold fast the hope appointed for us and set before (us). (Now) we have this (hope) as a sure and steadfast anchor of the soul—it cannot slip and it cannot break down under whoever steps out upon it—(a hope) that reaches farther and enters into (the very certainty of the Presence) **within the veil, where Jesus has entered in for us (in advance), a Forerunner having become a High Priest forever after the order (with the rank) of Melchizedek."**

> Once our blessed Christ of beauty
> Was veiled off from human view;
> But thro' suff'ring death and sorrow
> He has rent the veil in two.
>
> O behold the man of sorrows,
> O behold Him in plain view,
> Lo! He is the mighty conq'ror.
> Since He rent the veil in two.

Praise His most wonderful and worthy Name!

These truths are vital for understanding the Tabernacle of David, and our study of its Restoration. For while there was in the tabernacle of Moses a veil separating man from the Light and Glory of God's Presence in the

Holy of Holies, the thrill of David's Tabernacle is that before the Ark of the Covenant there was—

No Veil!

No veil! No hindrance. No "Keep Out" sign as there was in the tabernacle of Moses. This truth can transform our prayer lives. It revolutionizes our fellowship with the Lord. Not just a high priest coming on behalf of all the people. For it is written:

> "He appointed certain of the Levites to minister before the ark of the Lord, and to record, and to thank and praise the Lord God of Israel" (1 Chron. 16:4).

And not just once a year, but:

> "...priests with trumpets **continually** before the Ark of the Covenant of God" (I Chron. 16:6).

Continuous praise and worship right before the Ark of the Covenant. There was nothing between the priests and their God. If we experience the cleansing blood of Christ in our lives, we are priests unto God now:

> "Unto him that loved us, and washed us from our sins in his own blood. And hath made us kings and priests unto God and His Father; to Him be glory and dominion for ever and ever. Amen" (Rev. 1:5,6).

Figure 3: The Tabernacle of David

Peter says we who are born again of the Word of God are an "holy priesthood"(1 Pet. 2:5). And again, "a royal priesthood" (1 Pet. 2:9). One of the main teachings of that great reformer, Martin Luther, is "The priesthood of all believers."

Oh, don't you see the significance of all this? God is restoring a Tabernacle without a veil. God has washed us in the blood of His Son, and made us priests. Now we can boldly come "within the veil" to stand right in front of the Ark of the Covenant, and experience His Presence, His Fellowship, His Power, His Voice, His Shekinah Glory in the Holy of Holies. For to put it very simply, what David actually did was to set up on Mount Zion the Most Holy Place—the Holy of Holies with the Ark of the Covenant in it. For as we have seen, all that was in the Holy Place had its fulfillment in the Ark of the Covenant in the Holy of Holies.

In David's day the Holy Place was still in Moses' tabernacle on the hill of Gibeon. You could continue with that old formal worship if you wanted to. But the fullness of the Presence of God was not there on the hill at Gibeon. God's Presence was in the Tabernacle of David on another hill, Mount Zion! This is why David said of Mount Zion:

"Why leap ye, ye high hills? **this** *is the hill which God desireth to dwell in; yea, the Lord will dwell in it for ever" (Psalm 68:16).*

Again David said:

"Sing praises to the Lord, which dwelleth in Zion" (Psalm 9:11).

My friend, God's Presence is returning to this Tabernacle of David which God has promised to restore. There is no veil in this Tabernacle. We may commune directly with the Holy One of Israel. We may behold His Presence and Glory in His sanctuary. No wonder then, we are invited to:

"Come boldly unto the throne of grace, that we may obtain mercy, and find grace to help in time of need" (Heb. 4:16).

As we continue our studies of this glorious truth, there will be no doubt as to the answer to our question, "WHEN is God restoring the Tabernacle of David?"

The Ark Moves On

The Bible teaches that this magnificent Ark of the Covenant was placed in three main sanctuaries. These were:—

> (1) The Tabernacle of Moses;
> (2) The Tabernacle of David;
> (3) The Temple of Solomon.

(1) **The Tabernacle of Moses** pictures for us today the kind of worship and ministry we see in the Christian Church even until these last of the Last Days. It was essentially silent worship in the Tabernacle of Moses. It was formal. It followed a very distinct order of service. The regulations and rules of liturgy were rigidly adhered to. The only noise you could hear in the Tabernacle of Moses was the quiet tinkling of the bells on the garments of the priests. You will recall that around the border of his garments the priest had bells and pomegranates. Small bells, and small fruit. These represent for us the gifts, and the fruit of the Spirit. These are, of course, most essential parts of our Christian living and worship. But apart from operating the gifts of the Spirit, and endeavouring to cultivate the fruit of the Spirit in our lives, by and large most of our worship today is rather silent.

But God moved on. The Ark of God did not stay in the Tabernacle of Moses. As long as the Ark of God was there, it was correct, and right, and proper to worship God there in that way. But when the Ark of His Presence is no longer in that Tabernacle, how is it possible for us to worship Him in that way?

(2) **The Tabernacle of David** is, as we have seen, a new move of the Spirit of God. No longer is the Ark of His Presence in the old, silent tabernacle. This is a new Tabernacle. This is a deeper, more intimate fellowship with the Lord.

The tabernacle of Moses was wonderful as long as His Presence was there. But you cannot, you dare not, stay when God's fullness is no longer there, when God is doing something new.

In the Tabernacle of David pitched on Mount Zion, the Glory of God was visible to all the people. This is why we read in the Bible that the Glory of God's Presence shone out from Mount Zion. We see in the tabernacle of Moses, the Glory of God and the Light of His Presence had been confined to a tiny room, the Holy of Holies, fifteen feet square. But, as we have seen, there was no veil to contain or hide the Glory of God and the Light of His Presence in the Tabernacle of David. This was why Asaph, who was appointed to record the Songs (i.e. Psalms) that came forth in the Spirit (how many of us have fully appreciated that so many of the Psalms were written in conjunction with the Tabernacle of David?), was able to testify:

"Out of Zion, the perfection of beauty,
God hath shined" (Psalm 50:2).

And did not our Lord Himself link "light" with "a city"? "Ye are the light of the world. A city that is set on an hill cannot be hid"(Matt. 5:14). I wonder what city He was referring to? We read in Hebrews, "Ye are come unto Mount Zion"(Heb. 12:22).

One fact is abundantly clear. David's Tabernacle was an altogether new experience of God's Power and Presence, which caused the people to worship God, not silently, but rather "making a noise" (1 Chron. 15:28).

(3) **The Temple of Solomon** speaks to us of the thousand years when Christ will reign upon the earth, the Millennium. The Temple was solid. It was more permanent.

The Bible teaches that the staves, or poles, which were used to carry the Ark of the Covenant, were taken out of the Ark when it was placed in Solomon's Temple (2 Chron. 5:9; 1 Kings 8:8). Travelling was over. There were no more journeys. This, of course, reminds us that our earthly pilgrimage will be over when Jesus comes again (see 1 Pet. 2:11; Heb. 11:13).

Furthermore, when the Ark of the Covenant was placed in Solomon's Temple, it no longer contained the Pot of Manna See 1 Kings 8:9. We have already observed that the Bible teaches no manna fell on the seventh day of the week (Exodus 16:26). We have also seen a day with the Lord is as a thousand years (see Psalm 90:4; 2 Pet. 3:8). We may liken the thousand-year millennial reign of Christ to the seventh day, or sabbath, of God's week. We had better gather our double portion during this evening time of the sixth day! (See Exod. 16:5.)

When the Ark of the Covenant came to rest in the Temple of Solomon, it was also without Aaron's Rod which budded (see 1 Kings 8:9). The redemptive work of the Word of God and the Holy Spirit will finish at the Second Coming of the Lord Jesus Christ, heralding the end of this Gospel Dispensation.[1]

Furthermore, whereas the priests were to minister before the Ark of the Lord continually in the Tabernacle of David, we read in the Temple of Solomon that the priests "could not stand to minister (2 Chron. 5:14).

Thus we see that in between the tabernacle of Moses and the Temple of Solomon, the Tabernacle of David is chronologically placed. But note also that David's Tabernacle was pitched only a generation before the staves of the Ark were taken out, and it moved no more. In exactly the same way in this generation, just before that millennial rest of which the Temple of Solomon is a type—this generation which "shall not pass till all these things be fulfilled (Matt. 24:34)—this generation will see the Tabernacle of David restored according to the promise of the Lord. God is leading us out from the worship of which the tabernacle of Moses speaks, into a new experience of the Glory and Power of His Presence in this generation, just before the Second Coming of the Lord Jesus Christ. Before we see His Temple in that "new Jerusalem," we shall see the Tabernacle of David restored in this Jerusalem, which is the Church of Jesus Christ (see Revelation chapter 21; Heb. 12:22).

In The Last Days

Many other Scriptures confirm that God is restoring the Tabernacle

---

1 Of course, both the Word and the Spirit are eternal. We refer here only to the completion of the ministry of the Word and the Spirit at the end of the Gospel Dispensation.

of David in the Last Days, just before the Second Coming of Christ. The prophet Isaiah prophesied:

"And it shall come to pass in the last days, that the mountain {Mount Zion) of the Lord's house (the Tabernacle of David) shall be established in the top of the mountains, and shall be exalted above the hills; and all nations shall flow unto it.

And many people shall go and say. Come ye, and let us go up to the mountain of the Lord {Mount Zion), to the house of the God of Jacob; {the Tabernacle of David) and he will teach us of his ways, and we will walk in his paths: for out of Zion shall go forth the law, and the word of the Lord from Jerusalem" (Isaiah 2:2, 3).

Here we read of the establishment and exaltation of David's Tabernacle in Zion "in the Last Days." We read also of the great harvest of souls that shall take place as a result of this establishment, of which we shall speak in more detail in a later chapter. Notice how this Restoration of the Tabernacle of David is wedged in just before the Second Coming of the Lord, some of the results of which are mentioned in the following verse four.

Move with God

King David was not satisfied. Nor were his people. Yes, they had known something of the blessing of God. But oh I how they longed for the return of the Ark of the Covenant. How they wished to experience the fullness of the Power of His Glorious Presence. They wept. They lamented. And then they made their momentous decision—a decision which changed the course of history, and will do so again:

"Let us bring again the Ark of our God" to us" (1 Chron. 13:3).

And what was the people's response?

"And all the congregation said that they would do so: for the thing was right in the eyes of all the people" (verse 4).

May all respond the same way today!

Let us arise. Let us move with God. Let us not rob ourselves of so much blessing by not taking part in this new move of His Spirit. But rather let us, in the words of the chorus well-known to so many:

Move, move, move, move on with God!
>   Glory, Hallelujah!
Where true sons of God have trod.
>   Glory, Hallelujah!
God is moving by His Spirit,
>   These are Revival Days,
So let us then determine in our hearts
>   The way God's moving.
>   And move with God!

Follow the Ark

It was a new experience. They had heard how God had parted the Red Sea. They had heard of all the miracles that had taken place by the hand of God's servant Moses. But now Moses was dead. But the God of Moses was not dead I He was very much alive. And He was about to lead His people into the Promised Land. He was about to lead His people over the Jordan River (or rather, through it), so that they could possess all He had promised them. And as they moved forward, notice the essential part the Ark of the Covenant played in their crossing over Jordan:

*"And they commanded the people, saying, When ye see the Ark of the Covenant of the Lord your God, and the priests the Levites bearing it, then ye shall remove from your place, and **go after it**" (Josh. 3:3).*

Keep your eyes upon the Ark. And when you see it moving, get up from where you are, and "go after it." Because the people obeyed this commandment of the Lord, the waters of the River Jordan divided, and they passed over as if on dry land. As long as they followed the Ark they were victorious. Following the Ark of the Covenant around the city of Jericho, shouting and blowing trumpets, they saw the walls of Jericho fall down flat before their eyes, and conquered the city.

Friend, once again the Ark is moving! It has been removed from the old tabernacle of Moses, and God is rebuilding a new Tabernacle, wherein the Ark of His Presence and Glory may dwell.

Will you "follow the Ark"?

The True Tabernacle

We are now in a position to consider Hebrews 8:1 and 2 :

*"We have such an high priest, who is set on the right hand of the throne of the Majesty in the heavens; A minister of the sanctuary, and of the **true tabernacle**, which the Lord pitched, and not man."*

What is this "true tabernacle" the Bible speaks to us of? The answer is found in the words "which the Lord pitched, and not man."

Moses pitched the tabernacle of Moses.

David pitched the Tabernacle of David.

But what tabernacle has "the Lord pitched"? In all of Scripture, there is only one Tabernacle God has ever promised to build, the restored Tabernacle of David: "I . . . will build again the Tabernacle of David" (Acts 15:16).

In the Tabernacle of David which God is restoring the Lord Jesus Christ is the Ark of the Covenant. He is the Manna. He is the Rod. He is the Word. He is the Glory of God. He is the High Priest. He is the cover. He is the cords. He is all in all! Oh, may we allow Him to do this great Restoration in our hearts, in our churches and missions, in these desperate days in which we live!

Are you willing?

When is God restoring the Tabernacle of David?

Now.

Without doubt the Tabernacle of David is to be completely restored in this generation—just before the Second Coming of the Lord Jesus Christ.

God is moving. Will you pray in the words of the song:

> God is moving by His Spirit,
>   Moving through all the earth.
> Signs and wonders, when God moves.
>   Move, O Lord, in me.

God is moving. He commands us to "Follow the Ark." Are we willing to move with God? Are you willing to follow the Ark?

Chapter Seven

THE LOST GLORY

"His heart trembled for the Ark of God." "The Glory is departed from Israel; because the Ark of God is taken."

About four thousand of their soldiers lay dead in the field. They were badly beaten. The army of Israel was defeated by the enemy, the Philistines (see 1 Samuel chapter 4).

> "Let us bring the Ark of the Covenant of the Lord here from Shiloh, that He may come among us and save us from the power of our enemies," the people said (1 Samuel 4:3—Amplified Bible).

So they went to Shiloh, and brought the Ark of the Covenant to the front lines of the battle.

When the Ark arrived, together with Hophni and Phinehas, the two wicked sons of Eli, "all Israel shouted with a great shout, so that the earth resounded" (1 Sam. 4:5—*Amplified Bible*). But all their shouting was to no avail. They had gone too far. Sin had been tolerated in the camp. The Ark was to no advantage, because the priesthood was profaned. The ministry had forsaken the ways of the Lord. Consequently, Israel suffered an even worse defeat, and "there was a very great slaughter, for 30,000 foot soldiers of Israel fell" (1 Sam. 4:10—*Amplified Bible*). In the slaughter, Hophni and Phinehas were slain. But worst of all:

"The Ark of God was taken" (1 Sam. 4:1 1).

Trembling for the Ark

Back in the city of Shiloh, Eli the priest sits anxiously by the side of the road. Although blind, he is "watching." Although old, he cannot stay at home. Eli had one concern—one great apprehension. Not his own welfare. Not even the welfare of his own two sons. But what about the Ark of God? Would they lose the Presence of God?

"His heart trembled for the Ark" (1 Sam. 4:13).

What profound importance there is in this Ark! Can we fully plumb the depths of its terrifying significance? Brother, sister—does your "heart tremble for the Ark"? Is the Presence of the Living God with you and your people the consuming passion of your life? Is your chief desire to see Christ, of Whom the Ark speaks today, manifest His Resurrection Power and Glory in your midst?

A soldier rushes back to Shiloh with the tragic news. So stricken with grief is this messenger that he has torn his clothes, and covered his head with earth. The Lord had already told Samuel that He was "about to do a thing in Israel, at which both ears of all who hear it shall tingle" (1 Samuel 3:11—*Amplified Bible*). It does even more than this. It causes all the city to cry out. When Eli hears the people crying out, he hurriedly asks, "What is this uproar?"

The eye-witness of the battle rushes to Eli giving him the sad account of the defeat of the army of the Lord. The slaughter of so many soldiers is extremely grievous to Eli as a judge.

Next he hears how his two sons have been killed. The death of his sons, especially when he has cause to fear they died in their sins, tears at his heart as a father. But he does not interrupt the story (as David did for his son Absalom) with passionate lamentations for his dead sons. His most important interest is the Ark of the Covenant. Surely this Benjamite soldier must have news of the Ark of God. If only he could hear the glad tidings, "But the Ark of God is safe, and still with us, and we are bringing it home to Shiloh," then his joy for the Ark would overcome his grief for all these other disasters.

Then the fate of the Ark is told him:

"The Ark of God is taken" (verse 17).

The impact of these words hits him like a thunderbolt. He is completely overcome, and swept off his seat. He crashes to the ground, breaks his neck and dies.

"Our Warning"

"Now these things befell them by way of a figure—as an example and warning to us" (I Cor. 10:11—Amplified Bible).

What a lesson. What a warning there is for us in this account of the loss of the Ark of the Covenant! God would have all Christians be priests unto Himself (Rev. 1:5-6; 1 Pet. 2:5,9). Priests who enjoy the blessed fellowship of ministering unto the Lord, and enter into the burden of the needs of those around them.

But Satan has blinded us. Like Eli, our eyes are dim. Let us open our eyes wide and behold all that God has promised us in the fullness of the blessing of His Presence. Do we really see our need? Or do we, like the Laodiceans, say "I have need of nothing" (Rev. 3:17)? May we anoint our eyes with the eye-salve of the Spirit that we may see (Rev. 3:18).

Eli was old. And some of us are stuck with rituals and spiritual habits ninety-eight years old, instead of opening our hearts for this new move of the Spirit in these Last Days. Eli was heavy. How many of our churches today are burdened down with man-invented offices, conferences, and committees, the names of which do not appear in the Sacred Record!

But worst of all, because we no longer believe certain portions of the Word of God are for today, Satan has taken away the Ark. The miraculous manifestations of the Spirit? The supernatural Power of God? The Baptism with the Holy Ghost and Fire? Biblical methods of praise and worship? "Oh, that's not for today," the Deceiver has taught us to say. And the shameful result is, compared to the Spirit-filled New Testament Church, we lack the Powerful Presence of our Risen Lord.

Where are these anointed, unlearned men, who preach the 'Gospel with signs following, turning thousands to Christ? Where are these firebrands, who so know the Presence of the Ark of God's Power with them, they turn the world upside down (Acts 17:6). Might we not well ask with Elisha, "Where is the Lord God of Elijah?" (2 Kings 2:14). Shall we not search our hearts, and confess with Gideon, "If the Lord be with us . . . where be all His miracles which our fathers told us of?" (Judges 6:13).

How tragic it is that we have been taught so long and so persistently about our weaknesses, our lack of ability, and our unworthiness, we hardly dare say Jesus is **really** "the same yesterday, and today, and forever" (Heb. 13:8). We are afraid that people will misunderstand us, close their doors to us, and think we have become fanatical. Friends, have we taken the Bible seriously? Have we acted as though it were true?

The result of the enemy capturing the Ark from us is also the same. Like Eli, we have fallen backward. We have fallen from what God wants us to be.

When Eli fell his neck broke. The neck connects the body to the head. Messages are sent from the head to the whole body by means of the great trunk nerves in the spinal column through the neck.

Many Scriptures teach that we, the Church, are the Body of Christ, and Christ is our Head. For example, we read in Ephesians 1:22 and 23 that God has given Christ "to be the Head over all things to the *Church, which is His body*" (see also Eph. 4:15, 5:23; Col. 1:18).

But Eli's neck was broken. The connection between the head and the body was severed. When we compare our churches and missions with the New Testament Church, we may rightly ask if the same thing has not happened to us. Where is that vital, intimate link with Christ our Head?

The result of the broken neck was that Eli died. We do not need to elaborate here. Suffice to say it is the will of God that His Body, the Church, be pulsating and motivated by the Resurrection Life of Jesus Christ.

Ichabod

The prophesied desolation of Eli's house, and the mournful loss of the

The Lost Glory

Ark of the Covenant is climaxed with the death of Eli's daughter-in-law.

Despite the fact she is the wife of Phinehas, one of those sinful sons of Eli who had such a part in bringing these calamities on Israel, the foremost affections of her heart are for the Ark of God. Although concerned for the death of her father-in-law, the death of her husband, and the birth of her newborn son, the Bible says she "set not her heart" on these things (1 Sam. 4:20, marginal rendering). Her all-important interest is the Ark of the Lord. Though she has strength to give birth to her baby, she dies soon afterwards.

With her last breath she names

"the child Ichabod saying, the glory is departed from Israel! Because the Ark of God had been captured and because of her father-in-law and her husband. She said, The glory is gone from Israel, for the Ark of God has been taken" (1 Samuel 4:21-22—Amplified Bible).

What joy is there in having a son to one who is lamenting the loss of the Ark of God? What comfort is there in a child born in Israel when the Glory of the God of Israel has departed, and the Ark of the Lord is in the land of the Philistines?

Thus she gives the babe a name to preserve for all future generations the magnitude of the tragic loss of God's Presence. "Ichabod". The name means, "Where is the Glory?", "Alas for the Glory!", "There is no Glory", "The Glory is departed."

"The Glory is departed."

Revival for Survival

Many chapters could be written about this sorrowful incident. For it serves, in every detail, to rebuke and challenge us for our departure from Biblical faith and practice, and the resultant loss of the fullness of the Glory and Majesty of God's Power from our midst. When we compare our puny efforts with the world-shaking Dynamic and Glory that motivated the New Testament Church, can we not weep with shame the word, *"Ichabod!"*

THE POWER OF HIS PRESENCE

Wherever the New Testament disciples went the Glory of God, by the Power of the Spirit, was working with them and through them, to the end that men and women might believe in Christ and experience His transforming salvation. Indeed, "they went forth, and preached everywhere, the Lord working with them, and confirming the word with signs following" (Mark 16:20).

On the Day of Pentecost, the one hundred and twenty were filled with the Spirit and spoke with other tongues. Peter preached under the unction of the Spirit. The result was three thousand souls came to the Lord (Acts 2:41). Next a crippled beggar was healed. Five thousand souls came to Christ (Acts chapters 3 and 4). In the eighth chapter of the Acts of the Apostles, the wicked city of Samaria was filled with the joy of the Lord, and turned to Christ, hearing and seeing the miracles which Philip did by the Power and Glory with him.

Aeneas, who was sick of the palsy, is healed. The result? "All that dwelt at Lydda and Saron saw him, and turned to the Lord" (Acts 9:35). In the same chapter, Dorcas is raised from the dead. The result? "And it was known throughout all Joppa; and many believed in the Lord" (Acts 9:42). And so the record goes on.

Has the Glory of God changed? Is our Lord no longer able to do these things with the same alarming regularity that He did in Bible days? Or is it, rather than having changed, His Glory is lost to us. Our enemy has blinded our eyes and robbed us of so much of the blessing of the Gospel of Christ. Ichabod! The Glory is departed! Death!

And what of the few souls we do bring to the Lord? When they read, in simple faith and trust, the New Testament blessings which are promised to all believers, we immediately tell them, "Oh, that's not for today, you see." God will hold us responsible for the way we are not only robbing ourselves but robbing our "spiritual children" from the blessing of experiencing the Glory and Power of God in their lives. J. B. Philips has described the plight of many of us:

The Lost Glory

"When we compare the strength and vigour of the Spirit-filled early Church with the confused and sometimes feeble performance of the Church today, we might perhaps conclude that when man's rigidity attempts to canalise the free and flexible flow of the Spirit, he is left to his own devices." [1]

The Glory departed! In 1967 something happened in New Zealand which, in the words of Anglican priest the Rev. R. C. Firebrace (see page 13) "to serious students of Scripture Prophecy should be a warning signal of the first magnitude." One of the country's largest denominations, acting through its official machinery deliberately placed on record that a minister who does not believe in the literal Resurrection of Christ (as it is taught in the Bible), in life after death, in the divinity of Christ, and in a prayer-answering God, not only commits no doctrinal error but has the church's full confidence even as the principal of its ministers' training college! Well has the Rev. Firebrace called this "the deliberate, fully conscious rejection of the basic fundamentals of the Christian faith, or, what amounts to the same thing, the turning of them into options which the church member can accept or deny without in any way affecting his status."

We appreciate the "faithful remnant" who believe God would have them stay in this church to witness to the old truths as long as they can. We also appreciate that the historic announcement of November 6, 1967 caused many to think seriously about their faith. But, when this kind of wholesale departure from the Scriptures takes place, is not the Church losing the Glory and Presence of the Ark of the Lord?

Concerning the Spirit's Power and Presence, Andrew Murray has this true criticism to make— **"How little it is enjoyed!"**

"It is one of the saddest tokens of the unspiritual condition of the Church that so many are content with things just as they are, and have no desire to know more of this seeking for the reality of the Spirit's power." [2]

---

1   *The Young Church in Action*, Translator's Preface.
2   *The Full Blessing of Pentecost—the One Thing Needful* (Oliphants), by Andrew Murray

Yes, it seems a very gloomy picture. But God in His grace is far more merciful to us than we ever deserve. King David was not content to be without the fullness of the Presence of God—the Ark of the Covenant. So he determined to bring it back into the midst of his people.

Today, many of all denominations in the Christian Church, not content with the status quo, are experiencing the return of the Ark anew. Let us not take the dangerous stand of unbelief, and resist the Spirit of God. Let us rather, like David, admit that the Ark is not with us. Let us own up to the fact that we of the Christian Church are simply not examples of New Testament witness Faith and Power. Well has Dr. Howard Ervin, graduate of Princeton Theological Seminary and Baptist Minister, pointed to the heart of the matter:

"If the book of Acts bears witness to normative Christian experience—and it indubitably does—then by every standard of measurement, contemporary Church-life is subnormal. Consequently, it does not speak meaningfully, much less authoritatively to our fragmented modern world...

"In the face of need so staggering, and opportunity so unparalleled, the Church must live 'the Life, the Truth, the Way,' or get out of the way. It must have Charismatic Revival for survival." [3]

Despite our limiting God in so many ways. He has Power to restore to His Church the Glory that rocked Imperial Rome itself. He has Power to restore His Church to her former state upon the earth—Power to make her a firebrand, a victorious, living witness. Indeed, He is doing just this. What sorrow will be ours if we fail to put ourselves into the life-stream of "living waters"! Behold, the Ark is coming. Look, the Tabernacle of David is being restored. The exalted Christ is pouring out again "this which you now see and hear" (Acts 2:33). Will we continue to stand afar off and raise objections while multitudes perish without Christ and without hope? Can we afford to deny ourselves the very Power of the Holy Spirit promised to

---

[3] From the Editorial of *View* (No. 2, 1965), adapted from *These Are Not Drunken, As Ye Suppose* By Howard M. Ervin

us, and thereby deny those for whom Christ died the chance of accepting eternal life? Dare we disobey God's will for us and take no part in this Restoration of the Tabernacle of David?

God has promised:

"After this I will return, and will build again the Tabernacle of David, which is fallen down; and I will build again the ruins thereof, and I will set it up: That the residue of men might seek after the Lord, and all the Gentiles, upon whom my Name is called, saith the Lord, who doeth all these things" (Acts 15:16, 17).

"WHEN is God Restoring the Tabernacle of David?"

Now! And who can deny that we desperately need it?

But, "WHERE is God Restoring the Tabernacle of David?"

Part III
WHERE?

WHERE is God restoring the Tabernacle of David?

Chapter Eight
GIVE HIM YOUR TABERNACLE

The Restoration of the Tabernacle of David cannot be understood by studying the political situation in the Middle East. The Restoration of the Tabernacle of David has nothing to do with the recent capture of Jerusalem. Neither does it have anything to do with the nation of Israel, a physical hill, or a tabernacle or tent we see with the natural eye. Rather, the Restoration of David's Tabernacle is the spiritual Restoration of the Power of His Presence promised by God to all Christians who look for it in these last days.

David Pitched a Tent

The people of Israel lamented after God's Presence. They decided to do all they could to bring the Ark of God, the Power of God's Presence, to them.

The Bible tells us that in the midst of this preparation David pitched a tent to receive the Ark of the Covenant:

"David made him houses in the city of David, and prepared a place for the Ark of God, and pitched for it a tent" (1 Chronicles 15:1).

The Bible goes on to teach it was in this very tent, or Tabernacle as it is called in 2 Samuel 6:17, that the Ark of His Presence was placed:

"So they brought the Ark of God, and set it in the midst of the tent that David had pitched for it" (1 Chron. 16:1).

The various Hebrew and Greek words, from which the word "tabernacle" and "tent" appear in our Bible, have three main meanings. Firstly, "a tent;" secondly, "a tabernacle, dwelling place;" thirdly, "a covering, a hiding place, or booth." From these various shades of meaning, we have many wonderful insights into the Tabernacle of David.

In New Zealand and Australia, during the summer vacation many people leave their homes for a "camping" holiday. In the back of the car is placed a small, folded, fabric, temporary dwelling place—a tent. When an inviting place is found the tent is pitched, serving as a temporary dwelling place for the holiday motorist.

Tents are also a familiar sight in India. Outside our front gate is a large animal bazaar, where bulls and goats are bought and sold. Around the edge of the market place are small tents, or tabernacles, which are used by tea vendors and others wanting to shelter their wares from the intense heat of the sun. From time immemorial tents have been used by man.

His Body

In the New Testament we see the word "tabernacle" used to speak of the physical Body of Christ. We are all familiar with the well-known words of John 1:14:

> *"And the Word was made flesh, and dwelt among us, and we beheld his glory, the glory as of the only begotten of the Father, full of grace and truth."*

The word "dwelt" in this verse is the Greek word *skenoo* which means "to pitch a tent (*skene*)," or "to tabernacle." The marginal rendering in the Revised Version is "tabernacled." The Amplified Bible is also very clear here:

> *"And the Word (Christ) became flesh (human, incarnate) and **tabernacled—fixed His tent of flesh**, lived awhile—among us" (John 1:14).*

The word "tabernacle" also appears in Hebrews 9:11 in conjunction with the Body or Flesh of Christ:

> *"But Christ being come an High Priest of good things to come, by a greater and more perfect tabernacle, not made with hands, that is to say, not of this building."*[1]

---

[1] Of what "more perfect tabernacle not made with hands" is Christ the "High Priest of good things" today?

Thus we see the word "tabernacle" truly speaks of the Body of Christ. The Lord Jesus pitched His Tent, was present with us here on earth. Blessed, be His Name!

We have already seen that the Body of Christ, in the New Testament, also speaks of His Church.[2] Praise God that He is again "pitching His Tent" in His Church, manifesting His Presence in a new and wonderful way. God indeed is restoring the Tabernacle of David IN HIS CHURCH.

1 do not say the Jews do not have an important place in history. Neither do 1 say it is insignificant that Israel is again restored as a nation. But is not His **Church** even dearer to the Heart of God? Does He not have even more love for those who have accepted Christ, the Messiah, the One final Sacrifice for sin? While there are many ramifications and aspects of the teaching of "Israel" in the Bible, is not "Israel, even to such as are of a clean heart" (Psalm 73:1) "the Israel of God" (Gal. 6:16)—those who are cleansed in the Blood of the Lamb, the Church, His Body, most important of all to God? Surely those who have received great David's Greater Son as King and Shepherd (Ezek. 37:24) will know His promise, "My Tabernacle also shall be with them: yea, I will be their God, and they shall be My people" (Ezekiel 37:27).

Present Your Bodies

However, the Power of His Presence, the Restoration of the Tabernacle of David is even more personal in its application to our individual lives. For in the New Testament, the word "tabernacle" does not only refer to the Body of Christ.

It also speaks of us as individuals. The Apostle Peter speaks of his body as his tabernacle:

> *"Yea, I think it right, as long as I am in this tabernacle (tent, body—* Amplified Bible), *to stir you up by putting you in remembrance; Knowing that shortly I must put off this my tabernacle* (the folding up of my tent— Moffatt), *even as our Lord Jesus Christ hath shewed me" (2 Peter 1:13, 14).*

---

2   See Eph. 1:22, 23; 4:15, 16: etc.

The Apostle Paul also speaks about our bodies as tabernacles: *"For we know that if our earthly house of this tabernacle were dissolved, we have a building of God, an house not made with hands, eternal in the heavens"* (2 Cor. 5:1).

Thus we see the Christian's body is called in the Bible, a tabernacle, a tent, a dwelling place. And more than this, a dwelling place for the Spirit and Glory of God:

"Do you not know that your body is the temple—the very sanctuary—of the Holy Spirit who lives within you?" (1 Cor. 6:19, Amplified Bible*).*

Clearly God wants to dwell in this sanctuary, the tabernacle of our body. Not only this. He wants to restore His Tabernacle there, the Tabernacle of David. Shall we not then, obey the Word of the Lord to present our tabernacles unto Him:

"I beseech you therefore, brethren, by the mercies of God, that ye present your bodies a living sacrifice, holy, acceptable unto God, which is your reasonable service.

And be not conformed to this world: but be ye transformed by the renewing of your mind, that ye may prove what is that good, and acceptable, and perfect, will of God" (Rom. 12:1, 2).

The Tabernacle Prepared

David prepared the Tabernacle. He made it ready for the coming of the Ark. God then enabled David to restore the Power of His Presence to the people. The Ark of the Covenant, with much praise, joy, and blessing, was placed in the Tabernacle of David.

Is your tabernacle prepared? Or is the lamentation of Jeremiah concerning the place in which God would dwell true:

"My tabernacle is spoiled, and all my cords are broken: my children are gone forth of me, and they are not: there is none to stretch forth my tent any more, and to set up my curtains" (Jer. 10:20).[3]

---

3   Notice the next verse tells us the pastors are to blame for this calamity.

Give Him Your Tabernacle

Let us then prepare our tabernacles for the return of the Power of His Presence. Let us cease from committing the sin of disobeying and disbelieving His Word:

"Receive, I pray thee, the law from His mouth, and lay up His words in thine heart.

If thou return to the Almighty, thou shalt be built up, thou shalt put away iniquity far from thy tabernacles" (Job 22:22, 23).

Let us be ready. Let us present unto the Lord clean, prepared tabernacles for the Restoration of David's Tabernacle in our hearts.

What a tremendous responsibility is theirs who pastor the flock of God!

Chapter Nine

THE CHURCH WITHIN THE CHURCH

The Bible teaches that God is building the Tabernacle of David in His Church. The Bible further teaches that God is building the Tabernacle of David in two particular places within the Church:

(1) **In Individual Christians** who are longing after the Presence of God in a new way;

(2) **In Individual Congregations or Assemblies** where the ministry and people have open hearts for this Restoration, this new move of God taking place today.

The City of David

The Tabernacle of David was pitched "in the city of David" (1 Chron. 15:1), and the Ark of God was set up in this Tabernacle (I Chron. 16:1). The name of David's city was Zion:

"David took the strong hold of Zion: the same is the city of David" (2 Sam. 5:7).

Actually, Zion was a City within a city. Today we think of Jerusalem as the city of God. And rightly so, for it is. But it was not always "The Holy City." Indeed, the Bible teaches it was once inhabited by Canaanites, Perizzites, and Jebusites; people who did not love God, neither served Him, nor cared to worship Him. God delivered Jerusalem into the hands of the tribe of Judah, who smote the city with the edge of the sword, and set the city on fire (Judges 1:8).

However, the Jebusites were not driven out until God raised up King David. He captured the southwest stronghold of the city, and dwelt in the fort, building up Zion and its walls.[1]

The visitor to Jerusalem readily sees what a fortress this city is. As Dr. F. N. Peloubet says in his Bible Dictionary,

"Jerusalem was an almost impregnable Gibraltar. The steep sides of the ravines on the east, the south and the west provided bulwarks against siege. The north was the only direction from which a foe could attack the city under the conditions of ancient warfare."

Another peculiarity of the defence of Jerusalem is that although there is a good supply of spring water and many cisterns and reservoirs, the area round about is barren and dry, offering the would-be invaders of the city little sustenance. Even if attack was from the north, the chances of success were very small.

If Jerusalem was an almost impregnable city, Zion was even more so. Situated to the southwest of Jerusalem, Zion was higher than the rest of the city. It was this City within a city, Zion within Jerusalem, which David built up, and where he built his Tabernacle to receive the Ark of the Covenant. Little wonder we are invited to:

"Walk about Zion, and go round about her: tell the towers thereof.
Mark ye well her bulwarks, consider her palaces; that ye may tell it to the generation following" (Psalm 48:12, 13).

The very name "Zion" means "fortress." However, the main thing is that God wants us to see the spiritual lessons there are for us concerning Zion. Let us remember our earlier exhortation not to keep our eyes too steadily fastened on the physical things. Well I remember, when my wife and I were in Jerusalem in 1965, standing with Dr. Mattar on the Mount of Olives, and asking him to point out Mount Zion. We looked in vain for some enormous mountain, and were surprised to see that Mount Zion was

---

1   See 2 Sam. 5:6-10.

only a relatively small hill! Yet another lesson not to look too intently for that which attracts the natural eye.[2]

Zion, Joy of the Whole Earth

Some years ago when reading through the book of Psalms, I was so impressed by the constant repetition of the extraordinary descriptions of Zion, commandments given to Zion, and blessings promised to Zion, that I took some sheets of paper and wrote them all out. While I was blessed in that little study, I totally failed to see the significance of it all. Why Zion? Why, out of all the blessed mountains spoken of in the Bible, was Zion singled out for particular emphasis? I pondered the words of the well-known hymn—what was the hymn-writer really trying to convey when he wrote:

> Glorious things of thee are spoken,
> Zion, city of our God:
> He, whose word cannot be broken.
> Formed thee for His own abode.
> On the Rock of Ages founded.
> What can shake thy sure repose?
> With salvation's walls surrounded.
> Thou may'st smile at all thy foes.

The hymn-writer had no doubt received his inspiration from Psalm 87: *"The Lord loveth the gates of Zion more than all the dwellings of Jacob. Glorious things are spoken of thee, O city of God"* (Psalm 87:2, 3).

What a wonderful and blessed place Zion was in David's time! There are scores of almost staggering Scriptural promises, blessings, and commandments concerning Zion. Here are just a few:

---

2   The author and his wife were privileged to stay with Dr. Mattar and his family in their home next to the Garden Tomb. At that time Dr. Mattar was the Keeper of the Garden Tomb. On Pentecost Sunday in June 1965 we had the joy of preaching the Gospel right outside the Garden Tomb and seeing souls come to Christ there. During the Arab-Israeli conflict Dr. Mattar was killed in the shooting.

(1) **Zion is the Place Chosen of God:**

"For the Lord hath chosen Zion; He hath desired it for His habitation" (Psalm 132:13).

(2) **God Dwells in Zion:**

"Sing praises to the Lord, which dwelleth in Zion" (Psalm 9:11).

"The Lord of hosts, which dwelleth in mount Zion" (Isaiah 8:18).

"Sing and rejoice, O daughter of Zion: for, lo, I come, and I will dwell in the midst of thee, saith the Lord" (Zech. 2:10).

(3) **Zion Is Beautiful, the Joy of the Whole Earth:**

"Beautiful for situation, the joy of the whole earth, is mount Zion" (Psalm 48:2).

"Out of Zion, the perfection of beauty, God hath shined" (Psalm 50:2).

(4) **Zion is a Place of Rejoicing:**

"Let mount Zion rejoice" (Psalm 48:11).

(5) **The Inhabitants of Zion are Commanded to Praise God:**

"Praise thy God, O Zion" (Psalm 147:12).

(6) **The Inhabitants of Zion are Commanded to Make a Noise:**

"Cry out and shout, thou inhabitant of Zion: for great is the Holy One of Israel in the midst of thee" (Isaiah 12:6).[3]

(7) **Zion is the Place Where God Has Commanded Blessing:**

"As the dew of Hermon, and as the dew that descended upon the mountains of Zion: for there the Lord commanded the blessing, even life forevermore" (Psalm 133:3).

---

3   The Hebrew word for "inhabitant" in this verse actually designates the feminine article. Literally, this reads (as it does in our Marathi Bible), "Cry out and shout, thou inhabitants of Zion." This is also the marginal rendering of this verse. It is interesting to note throughout the Bible, that so very often God has chosen women to lead His people in praise and worship, e.g. "And Miriam the prophetess, the sister of Aaron, took a timbrel in her hand; and all the women went out after her with timbrels and dances" (Exod. 15:20); "The women came out of all the cities of Israel, singing and dancing" (1 Sam. 18:6); etc.

"The Lord shall bless thee out of Zion" (Psalm 128:5).
"The Lord that made heaven and earth bless thee out of Zion" (Psalm 134:3).

(8) Zion is a Place of Health and Strength, Especially in the Day of Trouble:

"The Lord hear thee in the day of trouble; the name of the God of Jacob defend thee;

Send thee help from the sanctuary, and strengthen thee (margin, support thee) out of Zion" (Psalm 20:1, 2).

(9) The Fire of God is in Zion:

"The Lord, whose fire is in Zion" (Isaiah 31:9).

The list goes on and on. Why this special choice of Zion?

Why Zion?

There are many blessed and outstanding mountains described for us in the Bible—Sinai, Hebron, Carmel, Horeb, just to mention a few. But Zion stands out from them all. The reason for this is not only because it was the city of David. The Bible clearly teaches the reason Zion is so special in the sight of God is because the Tabernacle of David was pitched there, and the Ark of God was set up there. God's Presence was at Mount Zion. God's Power was at Mount Zion. God's Glory shone forth from Mount Zion. Because the Tabernacle of David containing the Ark of the Covenant was there.

Without the Tabernacle of David, Zion would have been just another one of the hills in Jerusalem. Yes, the Power of His Presence in the Ark of the Covenant transformed Mount Zion into "the joy of the whole earth."[4] Now we can understand why the Tabernacle of David is also called "the Tabernacle of the daughter of Zion."[5]

Reference has already been made to the fact that there was a time when the tabernacle of Moses was pitched at Shiloh. We have also mentioned

---

4   Psalm 48:2.
5   Lam. 2:4.

that David transferred the Holy of Holies only, with the Ark of the Covenant, to Mount Zion. God replaced Shiloh with Mount Zion. This is shown in Psalm 78:

> *"So that He forsook the tabernacle at Shiloh, the tent in which He had dwelt among men (and never returned to it again)...*
>
> *But He chose the tribe of Judah (as Israel's leader), Mount Zion which He loves (to replace Shiloh as His capital)"* (Psalm 78:60, 68, Amplified Bible).

Where Is Zion Today?

It is prophesied in Scripture that in the Last Days, Zion, together with the Lord's House in it (the Tabernacle of David) shall be established. And as we have already seen, in both Old and New Testaments, the words "Last Days" in the Bible are always referring to the days before the Second Coming of the Lord:

> *"And it shall come to pass in the last days, that the mountain (Zion) of the Lord's house (the Tabernacle of David) shall be established in the top of the mountains, and shall be exalted above the hills; and all nations shall flow unto it.*
>
> *And many people shall go and say, Come ye, and let us go up to the mountain of the Lord, to the house of the God of Jacob; and he will teach us of his ways, and we will walk in his paths: for out of Zion shall go forth the law, and the word of the Lord from Jerusalem"* (Isaiah 2:2, 3).

What blessed verses these are on which to meditate. How wonderful to know that all nations, multitudes from every tribe and kindred shall turn to this spiritual Tabernacle of David established on spiritual Zion, receiving the Lord God as their God, and Jesus as their Saviour. As we shall see in a later chapter, this agrees with what is taught in Acts 15:17, and Amos 9:12, 13.[6] Already, it is becoming clear where God is restoring the Tabernacle of David.

---

6   See Chapter 28, "The Church Reaping."

The Church Within the Church

Let us now turn to the fourth chapter of Isaiah. More facts concerning where and what Mount Zion is are revealed:

"And the Lord will create upon every dwelling place of Mount Zion, and upon her assemblies, a cloud and smoke by day, and the shining of a flaming fire by night: for upon all the glory shall be a defence (Hebrew, covering).

And there shall be a Tabernacle for a shadow In the day time from the heat, and for a place of refuge, and for a covert from storm and from rain" (Isaiah 4:5, 6).

"Mount Zion." "Her assemblies." Here we are expressly told Mount Zion is made up of assemblies, or, if you like, churches. And this is exactly what we are taught In Hebrews chapter 12:

"But ye are come unto Mount Zion, and unto the city of the living God, the heavenly Jerusalem, and to an innumerable company of angels. To the general assembly and church of the firstborn, which are written (margin, enrolled) in heaven" (Heb. 12:22,23).

Remember the writer of Hebrews was writing to a church experiencing the New Testament Power of God in their midst.[7] They were exhorted to continue in praise (Heb. 13:15). Jesus Christ had not changed, and His Presence was mighty in their midst to do all He had done when He was on earth (Heb. 13:8).

Thus we are left in no doubt. God says in His Word that those who belong to an assembly of people knowing the mighty Resurrection Power and Presence of God with them are indeed a church dwelling on spiritual Zion. Here God is again building the Tabernacle of David.

Many well-known authorities agree with this interpretation. For example, in his *Commentary on the Whole Bible*, Matthew Henry writes concerning Amos 9:11:

"It is promised, that in the Messiah the kingdom of David shall be restored (v 11). The church militant, in its present state, dwelling as in

---

7   See Heb. 2:4.

shepherds' tents to feed, as in soldiers' tents to fight, is the Tabernacle of David. The royal family was so impoverished, its power abridged, for many of that race degenerated, and in the captivity it lost the imperial dignity. So it was with the church of the Jews; in the latter days its glory departed: it was like a tabernacle brought to ruin. By Jesus Christ these tabernacles were raised and rebuilt. In Him God's covenant with David had its accomplishment; and the glory of that house revived again. The spiritual glory of the family of Christ far exceeded the temporal glory of the family of David. In Him also God's covenant with Israel had its accomplishment, and in the gospel-church the tabernacle of God was set up among men again. This is quoted in the first council at Jerusalem as referring to the calling in of the Gentiles and God's 'taking out of them a people for his name."

Commenting on God's promise to restore the Tabernacle of David in Acts 15:16, Matthew Henry has this to say:

" 'It is written,' Amos 9:11, 12, where is foretold, the setting up of the Kingdom of the Messiah (verse 16): 'I will raise up the Tabernacle of David that is fallen.' This Tabernacle was ruined and 'fallen down'; there had not been for many ages a king of the House of David. But God, 'will return, and will build it again,' raise it out of its ruins, a phoenix out of its ashes; and this was now lately fulfilled, when our Lord Jesus was raised out of that family. **The Church of Christ may be called the Tabernacle of David**" (emphasis ours).

There are many more Scriptures we could consider in our study of Zion. The place where God is restoring the Power of His Presence. We have room for only one more here:

"Look upon Zion, the city of our solemnities: thine eyes shall see Jerusalem a quiet[8] habitation, a **Tabernacle** *that shall not be taken down; not one of the stakes thereof shall ever be removed, neither shall any of*

---

8 The word "quiet" in this verse has nothing to do with noise, or rather, lack of noise. The Hebrew word shaanan from which it is derived means "to be at ease, or rest." You can be sure it does not mean "silence" because the same Hebrew word shaanan is translated twice in the Old Testament as "tumult."

the cords thereof be broken.

But there the glorious Lord will be unto us a place of broad rivers and streams . . . And the inhabitant shall not say, I am sick; the people that dwell therein shall be forgiven their iniquity" (Isaiah 33:20, 21, 24).

Here we see that the assemblies dwelling in the Tabernacle of David upon Mount Zion know the healing Power of Jesus Christ, and the Power of His Blood to wash away sin. Again, we are left in no doubt. Zion clearly speaks of churches knowing the Power of His Presence, and the life-transforming, miraculous manifestations of His Presence.

The Church Within the Church

The Bible is clear on this one thing. Zion was a city within a city. Individual Christians, and assemblies or churches, making up Zion today are, in like manner, a city within a city, a Church within a Church.

Once again we would emphasise we are not speaking of any particular group or denomination. David's Tabernacle on Zion is a spiritual experience of Bible faith and Power.

That which was true of Zion of old is true of this Last Day restored Zion. Above we listed just nine qualifications, descriptions, or marks which identify Zion. These are spiritually true in the Zion of God today.

All of Zion was in Jerusalem. But not all Jerusalem was in Zion! In the same way we see the distinction between New Testament Zion and Jerusalem. All believers—all who have truly repented from their sins and accepted Jesus Christ as their personal Saviour—are members of that New Jerusalem. But, even as all Jerusalem was not Zion in the times of the first Tabernacle of David, so shall it be at the Restoration of the Tabernacle of David. God is, as we have seen, restoring the Tabernacle of David in Zion, which is a city within a city, a Church within a Church.

Let us consider for a moment—are all believers who are truly saved, really born again, and having eternal life, experiencing the blessings of Zion? Are they interested to see this great Restoration Revival take place in their lives, in their missions, in their churches? The answer is obvious. Not all want revival. Not all are hungry for revival. Not all are willing to pay the price for revival.

I want to be very careful here. I am not suggesting for a moment that these are losing their eternal life. As long as they remain in Christ, they are eternally secure. But surely there is much more to the Christian life than only having assurance of salvation. The whole teaching of the New Testament is that God is calling a people to go on to perfection. And there are those who are so hungry for God, those who are longing for God to do a new thing, that they are seeking to "grow in grace, and in the knowledge of our Lord and Saviour Jesus Christ" (2 Pet. 3:18).

May God deliver us from a cheap, easy, "only believe" Gospel. Surely there are those among us who are not interested only in "pie in the sky when we die." Praise God, there are those who want to be useful here below. Those who desire not to be ashamed at His Coming. Those who long to go on to perfection. Those who know the Bible teaches it is possible to grow unto the measure of the stature of the fullness of Christ—know that God is Restoring the Ark of His Powerful Presence—know that God is Restoring the Tabernacle of David—know that God's Glory again shall be seen in His people as at the beginning. For too long the blessings of Zion have been placed in the millennium, or in eternity. God says He is restoring the Tabernacle of David, before the Second Coming of Jesus Christ. He is restoring it in Zion—in all individuals and churches who will receive this Restoration of the Power of His Presence. Let us then, sing anew:

> Come, ye that love the Lord
> And let your joys be known;
> Join in the song with sweet accord.
> And thus surround the Throne.

> We're marching to Zion
> Beautiful, beautiful Zion,
> We're marching upward to Zion,
> The Beautiful City of God.

The Church Within the Church

The writer of this hymn certainly had some insight into the things the Bible teaches concerning Zion:

> The hill of Zion yields
> A thousand sacred sweets.
> Before we reach the heavenly fields,
> Or walk the golden streets.

Zion—the city within a city. Zion—the Church within the Church. Not a man-made division. Not a carnal splitting of churches. Merely our heart's response to God's claim for a full dedication of our lives to Him, that He might restore His tabernacle in us.

There were ten virgins. They were clean. They were not defiled. There is only one cleansing agent, the Blood of Christ. Moreover, they all had lamps. This means, they were experiencing the Word of God—"Thy Word is a lamp unto my feet" (Psalm 119:103). But five of these virgins were foolish, and five were wise. Because the foolish took no extra oil, when the cry went up to go out to meet the Bridegroom they were not ready. They missed out on some intimate experience with the Bridegroom. The Bible does not say they did not receive eternal life. The Bible says they were foolish. They did not have sufficient oil.

The oil speaks of the Power of the Presence of God by the anointing of the Holy Spirit. Reader, is there enough oil in your vessel? Here is just another of the many examples in both Old and New Testaments which teach us there is a spiritual division in the people of God.[9] Even when our Lord Himself was on earth, there were those who lived in more intimate fellowship with Him than others.

A city within a city. A Church within a Church. Zion or Jerusalem? Foolish or wise? Anointed or not? Living for the Restoration of the Tabernacle of David or not? Longing for the Presence of the Ark or not? Which are we?

---

9   See Matt. 25:1-13.

"*WHERE* is God restoring again the Tabernacle of David?" Wherever He can find hearts who long to be lifted from sub-standard, sub-normal, sub-New Testament Christian living. He is restoring the Power of His Presence in such hearts.

Will you give Him yours?

CHAPTER TEN

LET'S LEAVE PENTECOST

For ye are not come unto the mount that might be touched, and that burned with fire, nor unto blackness, and darkness, and tempest. And the sound of a trumpet, and the Voice of Words; which voice they that heard intreated that the word should not be spoken to them any more: (For they could not endure that which was commanded. And if so much as a beast touch the mountain, it shall be stoned, or thrust through with a dart: And so terrible was the sight, that Moses said, I exceedingly fear and quake:) But ye are come unto mount Zion, and unto the city of the living God, the heavenly Jerusalem, and to an innumerable company of angels. To the general assembly and church of the firstborn, which are written in heaven" (Heb. 12:18-23).

"Upon . . . mount Zion, and upon her assemblies . . . there shall be a Tabernacle (Isaiah 4:5, 6).

For any ministers of Pentecostal churches who may find the title of this chapter a shock, let me say immediately, I am not suggesting they, or their members, leave their churches! While it is not essential to be a member of a Pentecostal church to experience the Restoration of the Tabernacle of David, it is not necessary to leave one either. What I am urging is a new look at this Pentecostal experience, that experience of enduement with Power such as the early disciples received on the Day of Pentecost. This enduement with Power is being experienced by thousands throughout the world today.

Just A Beginning

On the Day of Pentecost the exalted Christ filled His waiting disciples with the Power of the Spirit. As the disciples began to speak in utterances given by the Spirit Himself, the Jews who had gathered in Jerusalem to keep the Old Testament Feast of Pentecost wondered what was happening. Some mocked. Others asked, "What meaneth this?" (Acts 2:12).

Peter preached his dynamic sermon. He told the crowd that God was pouring out His Spirit. He boldly proclaimed the Gospel of the Lord he had once denied, preaching the death, resurrection, and ascension of Christ. He testified that, as disciples of Jesus, the one hundred and twenty were enjoying His Presence and blessing in their lives by the Power of the Spirit.

He who had come to convict of sin (John 16:8) was working in the hearts of those who heard the Word. The Spirit's conviction cut deep into their hearts, and they asked the Spirit-baptized witnesses of Christ this all-important question: "What shall we do?" (Acts 2:37).

"What shall we do?" Remember—unconverted, unregenerate sinners are talking. Souls outside the Kingdom of God. But they see their need of the Saviour. They want to become followers of Jesus of Nazareth and experience His Presence and Power even as the one hundred and twenty are doing. To begin their Christian life, here is the commandment they are given:

*"Then Peter said unto them. **Repent**, and be baptized every one of you in the Name of Jesus Christ for the remission of sins, and ye shall receive the gift of the Holy Ghost" (Acts 2:38).*

"What shall we do?"

(1) "Repent,"

(2) "Be baptized,"

(3) "Receive the Holy Ghost."

Here the Bible clearly teaches the way the Christian life begins. Acts 2:38 teaches the **first foundation** of the initial Christian experience. The experience has three steps.

Many teach that there are one, or two experiences. The Bible teaches there are **three** fundamental, foundation steps, each forming part of the **whole beginning** of the Christian life.

Yet others would teach our Christian experience is complete when we have obeyed these three foundation steps. But the Bible teaches our Christian life has not really started without them! It is clear that Peter, under the unction of God, preached these words to unbelievers for the **commencement** of their Christian life.

On hearing this, some get angry. Others are filled with questions and doubts. Some mock. Others say, "It's not for today." Say what we will, we cannot change God's Word. But sometimes, we have to change our thinking.

You Have Only Started!

Again, let it be emphasized. This experience of a personal Pentecost is not a suggestion to believers in Christ for the deepening of their spiritual lives. It is a **commandment** to unregenerate men and women for a Biblical **commencement** of their Christian lives![1]

The fullness or Baptism of the Holy Spirit, is nothing added or extra. It is not an experience received by a select few after years of godly living to make them "super-Christians." It is the normal initial step through the door into full salvation.

Some churches have over-emphasized the infilling of the Spirit as a second work of grace subsequent to conversion and regeneration, only to be realized after a **second** act of consecration. It is true that in these modern days many of us do not hear about the fullness of the Spirit until years after our conversion. (I heard nothing at all about the fullness of the Holy Spirit until nearly five years after 1 became a Christian). As a result, we often have to re-read the New Testament. A second operation of the Holy Spirit—Yes. But never let us lose sight of the fact that in the New Testament, these three steps are meant for the Christian **from the beginning**.

For example, the Christians at Samaria (Acts chapter 8) had a deficient initial experience, but the situation was soon remedied. The tragedy is this.

---

[1] For a more detailed treatment of this subject, see Chapter 4 of the author's book, *You Shall Receive Power*.

The exceptional situation at Samaria has become the common one today. This needs to be remedied. The Bible foundation is, "Repent," "be baptized," "receive the Holy Ghost."

How beautifully Dr. Tozer expresses it:

"The Spirit-filled life is not a special, deluxe edition of Christianity. It is part and parcel of the total plan of God for His people.

"You must be satisfied that it is not abnormal. I admit that it is unusual, because there are so few people who walk in the light of it or enjoy it. But it is not abnormal. In a world where everybody was sick, health would be unusual, but it wouldn't be abnormal. This (Spirit-filled life) is unusual only because our spiritual lives are so wretchedly sick, and so far down from where they should be."[2]

Renewed Daily

To be baptized with the Spirit or filled with the Spirit is not a "once for all" experience. I cannot emphasize this too strongly. The baptism with the Spirit is a gift received from the hand of God. The fullness of the Spirit is not an experience to be attained. It is a spiritual condition to be maintained. You do not struggle and strive for "your baptism", and step up on to a super-spiritual level when you receive. You do not "have all God has for you, brother" when you receive the baptism with the Spirit. You have not arrived. You have only just started!

We sometimes hear the expression, "One baptism; many fillings." True, but I would say, "One baptism: daily fillings" is the need of every Christian. For it is written: "The inward man is renewed day by day" (2 Cor. 4:16). How? "Strengthened with might by His Spirit in the inner man" (Eph. 3:16). We do not have Power for holy living and a radiant testimony today from last year's baptism, but from this morning's filling. God is not looking for "Spirit-baptized" Christians. He needs "Spirit-filled" Christians.

---

2   Tozer, A. W., *How to be Filled with the Holy Spirit* (Christian Publications, Inc.)

I do not wish in any way to minimize the satisfying, liberating, Christ-revealing Power of the baptism with the Spirit, and all that it has meant to me in my life and ministry. But the baptism with the Spirit does not automatically guarantee a Spirit-filled life from that moment on. It is recorded many times that the New Testament followers of Christ were filled with the Spirit after their initial baptism or filling on the Day of Pentecost. If this need of a daily filling with the Holy Spirit had been taught, some of the tragedies that have happened in the Pentecostal Awakening could possibly have been averted. I wonder how many have been put off the Spirit-filled life through listening to a testimony about "My baptism. Hallelujah," from a person once baptized with the Spirit but now hard, cold, and long since dried up. They remember the vocabulary, the actions are still there, but no "rivers of living water" flow from their innermost being.[3]

The Origin of Pentecost

Once in a Pentecostal Convention (I won't say where!) when I was asked to preach the opening message, I chose as my subject, "The First Pentecostal Meeting with God." As there was a pleasant informal atmosphere, I asked the audience, in which there were at least thirty preachers, a few questions.

"Which portion of Scripture do you think I will be using as my text?" I asked, after I had announced my subject.

"Why, the second chapter of Acts, of course!" came the reply from everyone.

"Where does the word 'Pentecostal' come from?" I asked.

"From the second chapter of Acts," was the unanimous reply.

"Come now, many of you here are Pentecostal preachers. Where does this name 'Pentecostal' come from?"

After quite a bit of enthusiasm and curiosity had been aroused, I went on to read my text:

---

3   See John 7:38

"And Moses brought forth the people out of the camp to meet with God; and they stood at the nether part of the mount" (Exod. 19;17).

Many are under the misapprehension that the day the waiting disciples received the Holy Spirit, is called the Day of Pentecost because the Lord poured out His Spirit on that day. But the wording is, "And when the Day of Pentecost was fully come" (Acts 2:1). The fact is, the Day of Pentecost had been celebrated annually for 1500 years before the outpouring of the Spirit recorded in Acts chapter 2! The Feast Day of Pentecost was a feast kept in remembrance of an historical event in Israel which is recorded for us in Exodus chapters 19 to 23.

Fifty days after the children of Israel had been delivered from the bondage of Egypt by the blood of the Passover lamb, they came to Mount Sinai. It was at this mount that the Presence of God came down in a way that God's people had never known before. It was a new manifestation of God's Power and Presence. The Bible says that Mount Sinai was shaking and on fire. The voice of God was heard out of the midst of the fire in a new way. The words God spoke on Mount Sinai are the Ten Commandments (Exodus 20), and various other commandments given to Moses for the people. It is very important to notice the commandments to build the tabernacle of Moses were given on Mount Sinai.[4] God commanded the people of Israel to keep the Feast of Pentecost to remind them of their experience at Sinai.[5]

The two loaves, the ten sacrificial animals offered with the bread, (called an offering made by fire), the new meat offering, and all the details of the Feast of Pentecost pointed back to the Power and Glory of God when He met with His people at Mount Sinai. But it also pointed forward in time. It was a shadow of something to come—a New Testament manifestation of God's Power.

The Fulfillment of Pentecost

For fifteen hundred years Israel kept the Feast of Pentecost. One Pentecostal season, when Jews from many places were gathered together in

---

4   See Exodus chapters 25 to 31.
5   See Lev. 23:15-21; Deut. 16:10-12.

the city of Jerusalem to keep the Old Testament Feast, they heard strange sounds coming from an upper room. While Jews in the temple continued to keep the old Feast, the one hundred and twenty followers of the despised Nazarene were experiencing the New Testament fulfillment of Pentecost.

While the Jews were keeping the Feast of Pentecost 50 days after the Feast of Passover, the disciples were experiencing its fulfillment 50 days after the Passover Lamb had been slain on Calvary.

While the Jews keeping the Feast of Pentecost in the Temple were remembering they were bondsmen in Egypt (Deut. 16:12), the disciples, by the Spirit, were entering into "the glorious liberty of the children of God" (Rom. 8:21). For, "where the Spirit of the Lord is, there is liberty" (2 Cor. 3:17).

While the Jews, according to the old commandment, were offering in the temple the two wave loaves of bread made of the same flour (Lev. 23:16-17), the disciples receiving their Pentecostal experience were entering into the experience of becoming one bread in Christ, being all "partakers of that one Bread" (1 Cor. 10:17). Jesus the Bread of Life (John 6:48) was being made real in their lives by the Power of the Holy Spirit, according to the promise of the Lord (John 16:13-14).

God spoke with His people in an altogether new way from Mount Sinai. He did so again as the hundred and twenty received the spiritual experience of which Sinai was but a type. For, it is written, the one hundred and twenty "began to speak in other tongues, as the Spirit gave them utterance" (Acts 2:4).

God's Presence came down in fire upon Mount Sinai. In like manner, as the hundred and twenty received the outpouring of the Holy Spirit in their lives, "there appeared unto them cloven tongues like as of fire, and it sat upon each of them."

And so we could go on giving detail after detail, showing how that very first "Day of Pentecost" in Exodus 19, corresponds with, and has its fulfillment in the outpouring of the Holy Spirit on the New Testament Church in Acts chapter 2.

Not to Sinai

If the experience of God's children at Sinai corresponds—as it most certainly does—to the personal Pentecostal experience of the Holy Spirit in the believer's life, why then, does it say in the Bible "Ye are not come unto the Mount (Sinai)" (Heb. 12:18)?

Now let us be clear on this point—there is nothing wrong with Mount Sinai, just as there is nothing wrong with a personal, Pentecostal experience of receiving the anointing of the Holy Spirit.

The children of Israel had to go to Sinai. So must we. The Bible commands us to experience that of which Sinai is a type—a personal enduement of Power as the disciples received on the Day of Pentecost.

But Israel did not stay at Mount Sinai. Go through Sinai—yes. But stay there—no. This truth is of utmost importance. The Bible exhorts us not to stay at Sinai.

Here is one of the great tragedies of the first fifty years of the Pentecostal Awakening in this century. The initial experience of receiving a personal Pentecost has been taught by so many as an end—the ultimate. In some literature, we still find such phrases as, "Let us look back to Pentecost." Here we must disagree. We are not to look back On the contrary the Bible teaches us to look for ward. Yes, thank God for the Word and the blessing and the Power that came at Sinai. But, the experience at Sinai, and its New Testament equivalent, the Baptism into the Holy Spirit, is not God's ultimate for our lives. We will never be perfected to meet our Coming Bridegroom, the Lord Jesus Christ, by constantly looking back to the Pentecostal Mountain of Sinai.

One Old Testament type showing why the Feast of Pentecost is not complete in itself, is that leaven, which is always a type of sin, or imperfection, was present at the Feast of Pentecost.[6] Sinai is essential. We must go through Sinai into the promised land. We emphasize there is no other way.

---

6   Lev. 23:17

Yes, we must enjoy a personal powerful enduement with the Pentecostal Power of the Holy Spirit. Amen!

But God help us if that is the limit and ultimate of our experience of the Power of His Presence. God calls us on to Zion, where no sin offerings were made.

The Word of God exhorts us to leave the first principles of the doctrine of Christ—repentance, faith, the doctrine of baptisms, the laying on of hands, etc.—we are commanded to leave these and "go on unto perfection" (see Heb. 6:1-3). This does not mean that we stop believing and enjoying the first principles. Rather, these become more and more precious to us every day. But "perfection" is what we are called unto. Nothing more, nothing less. God not only wills that we receive a personal enduement with the Power of the Holy Spirit. He also wills "that ye might be filled with all the fullness of God" (Eph. 3:19). God wills that we have such a "knowledge of the Son of God," that we grow "unto a perfect man, unto the measure of the stature of the fullness of Christ" (Eph. 4:13). This kind of fullness will never be experienced at Sinai! Thus the Bible exhorts us to—

Come Unto Mount Zion

What a loving invitation. "Come unto Mount Zion." Blessed Mount. Holy Place. On you alone is perfection found (Ps. 50:2). The Presence of God is in your Holy Place. The Presence of the living God on Zion is far more Powerful and blessed than it ever was on Sinai. No wonder it is written:

"The mountains melted from before the Lord, even that Sinai, from before the Lord God of Israel" (Judges 5:5).

Sinai melts before our eyes, when we see the Glory and Power and beauty of Zion.

And why are we exhorted to leave Sinai and come to Zion? Because, we repeat, God is restoring the Tabernacle of David there! Zion, those members of the Church who want a deeper more intimate fellowship with God, shall be restored and revived by the Power of His Presence. The Ark of God in all its Glory—Jesus Christ the Perfect Son of God— shall dwell with His people in a new way.

The Glory of God, we agree, was manifest on Sinai. But His Glory was manifested in a far greater way on Mount Zion.

The people were moved to awe and fear before God at Sinai. But praise and worship ascended to God at Zion.

There was a noise heard at Sinai. But compare the joyous noise of praises to God heard at Zion.

The Commandments of the Lord were given at Sinai. But compare the glorious Psalms given at Zion.

The pattern for the tabernacle of Moses was given at Sinai. But behold the wonder of the Tabernacle of David on Mount Zion, filled with the Glory and Presence of God.

Three Feasts to Keep

God commanded Israel to keep three sacred Feasts unto the Lord.[7] The first Feast, the Feast of Passover, speaks to us of salvation—our being washed in the blood of God's Eternal Passover Lamb, the Lord Jesus. The second Feast, The Feast of Pentecost, speaks of receiving a personal enduement with Power from on high. But there is one Feast more—The Feast of Tabernacles, also called the Feast of "Ingathering" (Exod. 23:16). This third Feast had three phases—the Feast of Trumpets, the Day of Atonement, and the Feast of Tabernacles.[8]

Each of these Feasts point forward to a prophetical fulfillment in the Lord Jesus Christ. But more than this, they also speak to us of a spiritual reality —an experience of God's Power and Presence, which God desires to be fulfilled in the life of every true believer. The Bible teaches:

---

7   See Exod. 23:14-16
8   See Lev. 23:23-44.

Let's Leave Pentecost

"Blessed—happy, fortunate and to be envied—are the people who know the joyful sound (who understand and appreciate the spiritual blessings symbolised by the feasts); they walk, O Lord, in the light and favour of Your countenance!" (Psalm 89:15, Amplified Bible*).*

You have kept the Feast of Passover. We trust that you have also kept the Feast of Pentecost. But will we move on from Mount Sinai to Zion, where we may keep the next Feast, the Feast of Tabernacles? For we see clearly in the Word of God that the Feast of Tabernacles will be experienced by those who offer themselves to God for the Restoration of the Tabernacle of David which is taking place today. The Power of His Presence will be manifested in a way never seen before. There shall be joy, fellowship, praise and worship, an intimate communion with God that you and I never thought possible this side of heaven. This shall be accompanied by the last ingathering of souls, in a Gospel harvest of amazing proportions. So then, friend, let's leave Pentecost!

But remember, the Bible teaches that faith is required to inherit the blessings of God's holy mountain, Zion:

"But he that putteth his trust in Me shall possess the land, and shall inherit my holy mountain (Zion)" (Isaiah 57:13).

We must exercise faith in God's promises of the fullness of the Power of His Presence on Zion, and regardless of what others may think of us, act upon our faith. Pass through the Pentecost of Sinai. But inherit Zion—where we may dwell in the fullness of the Power, liberty, and blessing of His Presence.

Sinai or Zion. Unto which have you come? Toward which mountain is the desire of your heart?

Sinai?

Or Zion?

God is restoring the Power of His Presence on Zion.

Part IV
HOW?

HOW is God restoring the Tabernacle of David?

Chapter Eleven

THE ARK IS COMING

"How shall I bring the Ark of God home to me?" (1 Chron. 13:12). Today, this very question King David asked, is burning in the hearts of many Christians sincerely seeking more of God.

"How can I know the Power of His Presence in a deeper way?" "How can I experience in my life this Restoration which God is doing?" "How can I take part in this great world-wide revival?" "How can I be an effective and fruitful soul-winner for my Lord?"

As In The Days of Old

God has promised to restore the Tabernacle of David. God has promised to restore the Power of His Presence to those of His people who seek Him. God is sending revival.

When? In this generation.

Where? In the hearts of individual Christians who long for more of God, and in assemblies and churches where ministers and congregations long for a new move of God, allowing Him to work in their midst according to His own Word.

But **how**?

The answer is in Amos 9:11:

*"In that day **I will raise up the Tabernacle of David** that is fallen, and close up the breaches thereof; and I will raise up his ruins, and I will build it **as in the days of old.**"*

Here God, specifically and decidedly, answers our question for us. "How is God restoring the Tabernacle of David?" "As in the days of old." And let us remind ourselves again that the vital significance of the Restoration of the Tabernacle of David is **spiritual renewal in our generation**—the return of the Ark of the Covenant—the fullness of the Power of His Presence in us today.

The Restoration Commences (See Figure 4).

Let us now see the journeys of the Ark of the Covenant, remembering Jehovah Himself dwelt between the cherubim of the Ark, and that in every detail the Ark speaks of the Power of the Presence of the Lord.

(1) Shiloh to Ebenezer:

In 1 Samuel chapter 4 we saw that the first journey of the Ark of God, in this study, was from Shiloh to Ebenezer.[1] The Israelites, you will remember, called for the Ark to be brought to them as they did battle with the Philistines, who were at Aphek. But because of their sin, God did not help the Israelites in their battle and the Philistines captured the Ark of the Covenant.

(2) Ebenezer to Ashdod:

"And the Philistines took the Ark of God, and brought it from Ebenezer unto Ashdod" (I Sam. 5:1).

Ashdod was one of the five chief cities of the Philistines. It was a strongly fortified city and was the site of one of the most famous temples to the national god of the Philistines, Dagon. (The other temple, you will remember, was at Gaza, where Samson had slain three thousand Philistines when the Lord restored to him his strength on the day the Philistines were gathered together to offer a great sacrifice unto Dagon, their god).[2] The word Dagon means "fish," and the form of this idol had the face and hands of a man, and the tail of a fish.

The wrath of God on such idolatry is seen here. The Philistines put the Ark of the Covenant of the Lord next to their idol, Dagon. In the morning they found their Dagon thrown to the ground, his head and hands smashed off. This made a lasting impression upon the Philistines, for it is recorded:

---

1   See chapter seven "The Lost Glory."
2   See Judges 16:23

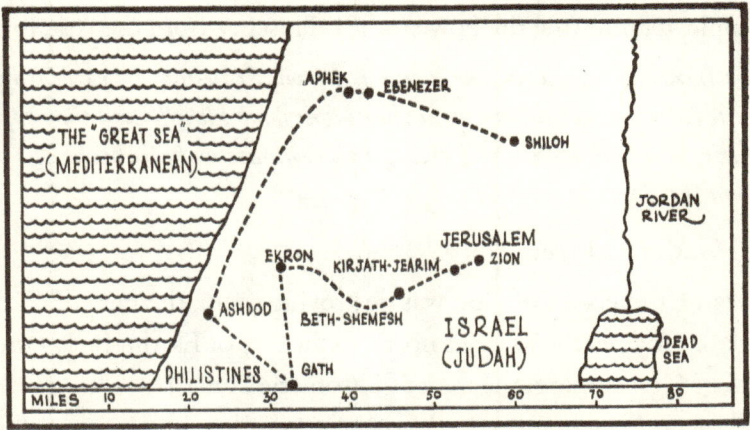

Figure 4: Map showing the journeys of the Ark from Shiloh to Zion.

"Therefore neither the priests of Dagon, nor any that come into Dagon's house, tread on the threshold of Dagon in Ashdod unto this day" (1 Sam. 5:5).

Furthermore, the whole army of Israel, because of sin, had not been able to smite the Philistines. But the Ark of God, without any assistance from men, began to smite the Philistines at Ashdod, causing deadly destruction in their midst:

"But the hand of the Lord was heavy upon the people of Ashdod, and He caused mice to spring up and there was very deadly destruction, and He smote the people with very painful tumours or boils, both Ashdod and its territory" (1 Sam. 5:6, Amplified Bible).

The men of Ashdod decided to get rid of the Ark of God immediately:

"When the men of Ashdod saw that it was so, they said, The Ark of the God of Israel must not remain with us; for His hand is heavy on us and on Dagon our god" (1 Sam. 5:7, Amplified Bible).

(3) Ashdod to Gath;

Seeing that God was against them, the men of Ashdod sent the Ark of God to Gath. But the men of Gath fared little better. God again smote the people, manifesting the Power of His Presence from the Ark, for:

"The hand of the Lord was against the city, causing an exceedingly great panic (at the deaths from the plague), for He afflicted the people of the city, both small and great, and tumours or boils broke out on them" (1 Sam. 5:9, AMP).

(4) Gath to Ekron:

Because the Power of God was destroying them, the men of Gath sent the Ark of God nearly 60 miles north to the city of Ekron. But as they saw the Ark of God coming, the men of Ekron cried out:

"They have brought the Ark of the God of Israel to us, to slay us and our people!" (1 Samuel 5:10, AMP)

Yet again many were slain by the Power of God, and the men who did not die were stricken with very painful tumours or boils and the cry of the city went up to Heaven (1 Sam. 5:12).

Thus we see, for the whole seven months the Ark of the Lord was with the Philistines, God revealed the Power of His Presence among them in no uncertain way. For the Power of His Presence is in the Ark of the Covenant.

(5) Ekron to Bethshemesh:

Realising that the Ark of God was causing them nothing but death and destruction, the Philistines frantically decided to send the Ark of God back to the people of Israel. Since they had been plagued with tumours and mice, they decided to send back a trespass offering with the Ark, of five golden tumours, and five golden mice, one for each of the lords of the Philistines. They remembered with fear and trembling how when Pharaoh, King of Egypt, had hardened his heart against the Lord, God performed His miraculous judgments upon Egypt.

They then made a new cart on which they put the Ark of the Covenant. They took two cows which were still giving milk to their young calves, and tied them in a yoke to pull the cart. Normally, a cow separated from its calf will be deeply distressed and will go nowhere but to look for its suckling calf. But this is no ordinary load they are pulling. The cows went immediately taking the shortest way through the vale of Sorek to Bethshemesh. As the Philistines saw the cows leave their calves and head straight for Bethshemesh, they were assured it was God Himself who had smitten them.[3]

The people of Bethshemesh were reaping their wheat harvest in the valley. Looking up they saw the glorious Ark of God coming towards them, and they rejoiced greatly. "The Ark of God is coming!" they cried. How weak they had been without the Power of the Presence of their God! Little wonder they were so happy to see the Ark of His Presence again.

The cart bearing the Ark of the Covenant finally came into the field of a Bethshemite called Joshua, and stopped by a large stone in the field. The Levites, possibly remembering that the Ark of God was not to be drawn by a cart, but to be carried on their shoulders by the staves according to the commandment of the Law, took the Ark of the Lord down from the cart. The people smashed the wooden cart into pieces, and used the wood to offer the cows as a burnt offering to the Lord. Then the Ark was placed upon the rock.

What a beautiful picture this is. Here the great stone or rock speaks to us of the Lord Jesus Christ. He is the Rock of our salvation (Psalm 89:26). Just as the people of Bethshemesh rejoiced, so also are we exhorted to "make a joyful noise to the Rock of our salvation" (Psalm 95:1). Jesus Himself said, "Upon this Rock (Greek—Petra, meaning a large rock) I will build My Church" (Matt. 16:18).

But the men of Bethshemesh made one tragic mistake. Yes, they were so very happy. They rejoiced because the Presence of God was with them again. But they did not realise the revival had only just started. They did not realise the Ark of God had a long way to go yet. How many people today have been making the same mistake? They have seen wonderful moves of the Spirit, but think God has no more for them. But the move of God in these Last Days has only just begun.

---

3   See 1 Sam. 6:9-12.

Another mistake the Bethshemites made was to forget that God does not only send His Presence among us to bless us. In any genuine move of the Spirit of God, one of the foremost commands of God is to holiness.[4] How tragic it has been that in this wonderful Awakening which has been increasing in Power during this century, some, rejoicing in the blessed liberty which the Presence of God brings have forgotten the awful holiness of God, and His judgment upon sin. The men of Bethshemesh looked into the Ark of the Lord. In doing so they committed a two-fold transgression of the commandments of God.

Firstly, they broke God's commandment which specifically stated they were not to touch the holy things of the Lord. Like Uzzah after them, they paid with their lives.

Secondly, as we have seen, in the Ark of the Lord were the Tables of the Law—commandments which had been broken. God could look down from His Glory between the cherubim and not see the commandments which the people had broken—the sin of the people. This was because in between, placed on the top of the box or chest of the Ark, was the blood-sprinkled Mercy Seat. But if man dared look upon the broken law, without the covering of the blood, he would surely die.

"For the wages of sin is death" (Rom. 6:23).

"Sin . . . bringeth forth death" (Jas. 1:15).

Because they looked into the Ark, God smote them dead. There was no blood, between God and man, covering the broken commandments of God. Thus the joy of revival was abruptly turned into lamenting the consequences of sin. May it not happen again! The dismayed men of Bethshemesh cried:

"Who is able to stand before this Holy Lord God? And to whom shall He go up from us?" (1 Sam. 6:20).

The Bethshemites obviously knew from experience that God Himself was in the Ark of the Covenant. However, because of God's hand of judg-

---

4   See chapter 16 "Sanctify Yourselves."

ment upon them they desired to send the Ark of the Covenant to some other place. They sent messengers to the people of Kirjath-jearim, saying:

> *"The Philistines have brought again the Ark of the Lord; come ye down, and fetch it up to you"* (1 Sam. 6:21).

(6) Bethshemesh to Kirjath-jearim:

Kirjath-jearim was a stronger city than Bethshemesh. It means "the city of forests," and was situated to the northeast of Bethshemesh, on the way to Shiloh, eight miles west of Jerusalem (see Map, Figure 4). Because Kirjath-jearim was on the way from Bethshemesh to Shiloh, it may be that, when the Bethshemites sent to Kirjath-jearim to fetch the Ark of God, they had in mind that the people of Kirjath-jearim should return it to its place in Shiloh, thus completing the full circle. But not only does Shiloh lie desolate (Jer. 7:14). God has other plans for the Ark.

The men of Kirjath-jearim brought the Ark of the Lord from Bethshemesh and took it into the house of Abinadab (Hebrew—*father or source of liberality*) who lived on a hill. They consecrated his son Eleazer (Hebrew—*God is helper*) to keep the Ark of the Lord. Matthew Henry writes of this incident:

> *"God will find out a resting-place for His Ark; if some thrust it from them, yet the hearts of others shall be inclined to receive it. It is no new thing for God's Ark to be thrust into a private house."*

Nevertheless, while the people of Kirjath-jearim housed the Ark (the men of Bethshemesh left it exposed in the field of Joshua), and provided someone to attend the Ark, it is obvious they had no real sense of the potential Power which was available, nor the blessing that this Ark could be to them. Thus, with the exception of an incident concerning the folly of King Saul, to which we shall later refer,[5] there is not one more mention of the Ark of the Covenant until I Chronicles chapter 13. Matthew Henry draws a striking parallel with conditions seen in the Church:

---

5   See 1 Sam. 14:18.

> *"While (the Ark of the Covenant) was absent from the tabernacle, the token of God's special Presence was wanting, nor could they keep the Day of Atonement as it should be kept. They were content with the altars without the Ark; so easily can formal profession rest satisfied in a realm of external performances, without any tokens of God's Presence or acceptance.*

Many things must happen before the Power of His Presence is restored to God's people. Samuel must separate the people from their idols. The absolute futility and folly of trying to serve God without the fullness of His Presence must be realised. Thus the Ark of the Covenant stayed at Kirjath-jearim for nearly one hundred years—through the entire period of Samuel's judgment, through the entire reign of Saul, and well into the reign of King David.[6]

Limiting His Power

Thus we see the Ark of the Covenant sent from city to city with little or no regard, respect, or understanding of its significance being shown. All the mighty Power of Jehovah was available in it, but nobody understood, nobody cared, and nobody paid much attention to it.

This tragic condition is, sad to say, still with us today. All the Might and Majesty of the Power of God is available, through Christ, to His Church today. God wills that His Church be charged with the dynamic Power of the Holy Spirit, mighty, and doing exploits that glorify His Name. But how many believe it? How many understand it? How many see the need? While we sit back and debate, and criticise those who dare believe it is possible to

---

[6] The punctuation and somewhat old-fashioned wording of 1 Sam. 7:2 are slightly misleading here. It would appear, at first glance, that the Ark of God stayed at Kirjath-jearim for only 20 years. But comparing scripture with scripture it becomes clear that it was there during Samuel's judgment (approximately 40 years), Saul's reign (40 years), and was not removed until well into the reign of King David. Thus the 20 years can only refer to the first twenty years of the reign of King David, after which the people began to lament after the Lord. *The Amplified Bible, Adam Clarke's Commentary, Jamieson, Fausset 8t Brown's Commentary,* and other sources, support this.

have the Power of His Presence as in the days of old, multitudes rush into a Christless eternity for lack of the help that we could have, and should have given them. By not understanding the significance of what God wills in these Last Days we thus limit the Holy One of Israel.

But there came a day when God found a man after His own heart, who would not rest until the Ark of God was fully restored to His people in all the Power of His Presence.

Chapter Twelve
LET US WEEP

(1 Chronicles chapter 13, commenced)

"Let us bring again the Ark of our God to us" (1 Chron. 13:3). God has promised to restore the Tabernacle of David "as in the days of old" (Amos 9:11). He is restoring this second Tabernacle of David, in spiritual application, in exactly the same way as the first was built. First and foremost God is doing a spiritual work in His Church today. Therefore, if we really want to know HOW God is restoring David's Tabernacle, we must have a clear understanding of how the first Tabernacle of David was built, and how the Ark of God's Presence was restored to His people.

How was David's Tabernacle built "in the days of old"? For the answer to this question, we must read:

1 CHRONICLES, CHAPTERS THIRTEEN, FOURTEEN, AND SIXTEEN.

May I suggest that you prayerfully read these three chapters two or three times slowly. I am sure you will find it most helpful for our study.

The Important Realisation

In our last chapter we left the Ark of the Covenant at Kirjath-jearim where it stayed for nearly 100 years. However, there came to the people of Israel a time of realisation—an awakening— a time when the people confessed that something was missing.

Nobody would suggest for a moment that God had not been with David. From that first visit of the prophet Samuel to Bethlehem, God had most certainly been with David. For it is written:

"Samuel took the horn of oil, and anointed him (David) in the midst of his brethren: and the Spirit of the Lord came upon David from that day forward" (1 Sam. 16:13).

Neither would anybody deny God was with David's people and his army. Behold the wonderful victories they won! But despite all they had experienced in the past, the hearts of the people ached for more intimate fellowship with God and a more powerful manifestation of His Presence. There was something missing. There was something more.

Dear reader, no one is suggesting for a moment you do not have the Presence of God in your life. Yes, you have most certainly experienced the anointing of the Lord. God has blessed and used you. God has led you, and done many marvellous things for you. But do you not think God has even more in store? Do you not believe He is able to restore the fullness of the Power of His Presence, even before we go to heaven? Do not our hearts long for a closer walk with God?

Let us Weep

"Let us bring again the Ark of our God to us" (1 Chron. 13:3).

This is the cry of hearts which are longing after God. The Bible says while the Ark of God was away at Kirjath-jearim:

"All the house of Israel lamented after the Lord" (I Sam. 7:2).

The Hebrew word for "lamented" means "to show one self a mourner," or "to mourn, be moist (with tears)." Despite all the Lord had done for them, and all He meant to them, they shed tears of mourning, they lamented, they longed for Him to return in all His Power and Glory unto them. And notice the Bible says that all were longing after the Lord. Not just a few, but all the people.

Let Us Weep

While (as we shall see in later chapters), the message of praise, and rejoicing is coming to the fore in these days, the message is not all "rejoice"—especially at the beginning of the Restoration of the Tabernacle of David. The Bible says, there is "a time to weep, and a time to laugh; a time to mourn, and a time to dance" (Eccl. 3:4).

This same Scriptural truth is brought to us in that great Restoration chapter, Joel chapter 2. Here, the responsibility is placed upon the ministry:

"Let the priests, the ministers of the Lord, weep between the porch and the altar" (Joel 2:17).

And what will be the result?

"Then will the Lord be jealous for His land... the Lord will answer... be glad and rejoice; for the Lord will do great things...

Be glad then, ye children of Zion, and rejoice in the Lord your God... I will restore...

And it shall come to pass afterward, that I will pour out My Spirit upon all flesh" (vss. 18, 19. 21, 23. 25, 28).

Weeping—then rejoicing.

Yet again we see this same truth in another wonderful Restoration chapter, Jeremiah chapter 31:

"At the same time (the last days—see chapter 30:24) *saith the Lord...*

Again I will build thee, and thou shalt be built...

Then shall the virgin rejoice in the dance, both young men and old together; for I will turn their mourning into joy, and will comfort them, and make them rejoice from their sorrow" (Jer. 31:1, 4, 13).

On this one thing the Scripture is clear—**until we experience the weeping and mourning of shame, confession, and longing after God, we shall never experience the rejoicing of Zion.**

David had one desire—to seek God, to know God, to love God.

"As the hart pants and longs for the waterbrooks, so I pant and long for You, O God. My inner self thirsts for God, for the Living God...

My tears have been my food day and night" (Psalm 42:1-3, Amplified Bible*).*

So often King David draws his metaphors from his own experiences. No doubt David had seen the deer (the hart) many times while watching his father's flock. If the hart was attacked or injured receiving an open wound, it would immediately cry out rushing to the nearest water. For if the hart could but bathe its wound in the water, there was a possibility the blood would stop flowing, and the wound commence to heal. Oh, that we would long for the Rivers of Living Water of the Power of the Holy Spirit in the same way (John 7:37)!

When we compare all the manifold blessings and Glory promised to Zion, with what we are today, are we not moved to tears? Let us not be ashamed to seek Him with weeping.

Jesus Himself, standing at the grave of His friend, wept unashamedly. If more of His followers wept today, we would see more life in the sick Body of His Church. He said, "Blessed are ye that weep now: for ye shall laugh" (Luke 6:21).

Many Scriptures teach there is a divine connection between the tears of concern and the joy of blessing. Just one more example must suffice;

"They that sow in tears shall reap in joy. He that goeth forth and weepeth, bearing precious seed, shall doubtless come again with rejoicing, bringing his sheaves with him" (Psalm 126:5, 6).

Saul's Tragic Mistake

*"Let us bring again the Ark of our God to us: for we **inquired not at it in the days of Saul**" (1 Chron. 13:3).*

The second part of this verse is one of the saddest statements in the Bible. King Saul had the opportunity to seek the face of God at the Ark of the Covenant. But despite all the miracles and manifestations of God's Power as the result of the Ark, King Saul, like so many before him, did not fully appreciate the Power of His Presence. In all his 40 years as king, only once did he make any move towards the Ark. And even then he committed a tragic mistake.

Let Us Weep

While Saul was waiting around having his conference at Gibeah under a pomegranate tree, his son Jonathan and his armour-bearer were fighting a whole garrison of the Philistines. When the conference began to count up their members, they discovered that Jonathan and his armour-bearer were missing. Suddenly Saul decided to seek God at the Ark of the Covenant. The Ark of God was with the children of Israel for the whole 40 years of his reign. But Saul did not regard or appreciate the significance of the Power of its Presence. So Saul said to Ahiah, "Bring the Ark of God here."

Even while Saul was talking the tumult in the Philistine camp was getting louder and louder.

Panic-stricken, Saul cried to Ahiah, "Quickly, take away your hand!"[1] What a dreadful disregard for the Power of God's Presence!

Saul made many terrible mistakes here:

(1) He chose the wrong priest. Ahiah was the son of Ichabod's brother. And we have clearly seen earlier the full implication of Ichabod—"the Glory is departed!"[2]

(2) Saul would not wait in God's Presence. The Bible teaches we must wait in the Presence of God until we hear Him speak to us.

(3) Saul was not willing to let God speak to him.

(4) Saul feared the enemy. Without waiting to hear from God he said, "Withdraw thine hand. Let's get moving. The Philistines are coming." And yet he was standing before the Ark of the Covenant —that self-same Ark from which God had manifested the Power of His Presence in death and destruction on so many occasions amongst the Philistines. That self-same Ark, which without the help of King Saul or his armies, had caused great discomfort and calamity amongst the Philistines. But Saul is so far from God.

Even though he is the anointed king of Israel, even though he once knew the Power of God in his life, he no longer appreciates it is "not by might (Hebrew—army) nor by power, but by My Spirit, saith the Lord of Hosts" (Zech. 4:6).

---

1 See 1 Sam. 14:1-19.
2 See Chapter 7, "The Lost Glory."

(5) Saul had no need to fear. For the tumult heard was not the Philistine army coming after him, but his son Jonathan, with the miraculous help of God, smiting the Philistine garrison!

(6) As a result of not hearing the voice of God at the Ark of the Covenant, Saul gives his armour-bearer a very unwise commandment hindering the victory. In the next chapter (I Samuel 15), Saul is completely rejected from being king.

How tragic this is. Saul had every opportunity to consult God at the Ark of the Covenant. The Power of God, and His Presence, was there, but he just did not avail himself of his opportunity. Saul was so busy trying to do the work of God, that he had no time to seek God! And the tragedy is, that many are making this same disastrous mistake to-day. They are so caught up and busy in the bustle and rush of God's service, they have no time to wait upon God. God's Power has left them, and they don't know it. "As thy servant was busy here and there, he was gone" (1 Kings 20:40).

Samson is another Biblical example of this condition. When his hair was cut he did not know his strength had gone from him. When Delilah cried, "The Philistines are upon you, Samson!" he woke up "and said, I will go out as I have time after time, and shake myself free. For Samson did not know that the Lord had departed from him" (Judges 16:20). A time of suffering and despair followed. But one day as Samson bowed his head and prayed, the Lord restored unto him his strength (Judges 16:30).

Let us be very careful in these days not to be so busy with activities, all of which may be legitimate, and ministering unto people, that we do not have time to minister unto the Lord.

Saul and David

What a striking comparison there is between Saul and David. Saul had the Presence of God, but he did not want it; David did not have the Presence of God, but he longed for it. Saul left the Presence of God; David sought the Presence of God more than anything else. Saul turned away from the Presence of God; David looked towards the Presence of God. And today, there are people sitting around under their pomegranate trees, holding conferences of little spiritual value and no great import, who are missing the real Presence of God. But, thank God, there are others like David of old who know that the Ark of God is only 8 miles away, and will not rest until they "bring again the Ark of God to us" (1 Chron. 13:3, marginal rendering).

Friends, let us not make the same mistake as Saul. Let us cry and weep and seek God, until we see the promised Restoration of the Power of His Presence.

Chapter Thirteen

A NEW UNITY

(1 Chronicles chapter 13, continued)

One word very prominent in much Christian conversation and dialogue today is, "UNITY."

Christ prayed that His disciples would be united. Churchmen throughout the world, some extremely sincere, are making every effort these days to bring about some semblance of unity. At the time of writing, the latest of these has been an invitation from the Protestant (?) World Council of Churches to the Roman Catholic Church to join together in one large World Super-church. Reporting on the Fourth Assembly of the World Council of Churches held in July 1968 at Uppsala, Sweden, TIME magazine, under the heading "The World Council—From the Sacred to the Secular," says:

> "*Ecumenically, the council took a major step forward by showing, for the first time, an open invitation to the Roman Catholic Church to join the World Council ... Churchmen active in Christian unity proposals have long considered the prospect inevitable.*"[1]

That all the divisions in Christ's Church grieve Him today, there can be no doubt. And let us be honest—these divisions permeate every branch of

---

1   TIME, July 26, 1968. Readers who are members of churches which have now, through the World Council of Churches, invited the Church of Rome to join them, may be interested to know the Roman Catholic Church teaches that Mary is the Ark of the Covenant—"Holy Mary, Holy Mother of God ... Mother of our Creator ... Help of Christians ... Ark of the Covenant ..." From Will You Take

the Church, from the different orders of the Roman Catholic Church to the splits and divisions amongst Protestant groups.

However, it appears that many of the divisions seen today, and many of the attempts at "unity," are largely political. That is, the accounts of the negotiations seem to read more like the reports of mergers between political parties, than the vibrant unity, deep fellowship, and fervent love prayed for by Christ.

Unity In Charismatic Renewal

In spite of all the divisions, there is a new unity being experienced in many parts of Christendom today which is deeply spiritual and in-tensely practical. Too few know very much about it. Some even mock it. Despite this it bears close scrutiny, and one cannot help but feel it resembles something of what New Testament unity really is. For as God restores New Testament faith and experience to people of all denominations who are having a personal encounter with the Holy Spirit— "a personal Pentecost" if you like—many Christians are discovering a warm fellowship with other believers in Christ they were never able to experience before.

As believers of all denominations receive the Holy Spirit, they are beginning to understand "the unity of the Spirit" (Eph. 4:3). Or, in the words of the benediction, "the communion, (or fellowship), of the Holy Ghost" (2 Cor. 13:14). The anointing of the Holy Spirit and the resultant miraculous manifestations, or charisma,[2] are causing Christians who have received this New Testament experience to think less of their particular denomination or group, and more of Christ, and their brother in Christ.

This Sword, a publication printed with Ecclesiastical approval, which concludes with the words, "Recitation daily of Litany and concluding prayer for one month—Plenary Indulgence, usual conditions."

2   The terms Charismatic movement, and Charismatic Renewal, are Anglicized adjectival forms of the Greek word, charisma which means "gift". Personally I do not like the term "charismatic", as it seems to place the emphasis on the gift instead of the Giver. However, it is a term that we should know, for it is widely used today.

A New Unity

Speaking of this Pentecostal Renewal in the Historic churches. Social Historian, Dr. William G. Morgan, writes;

"The current Charismatic Renewal will doubtless have profound implications for the social historian. While there has been no dearth of spiritual awakenings throughout the centuries, the present movement possesses several unique aspects which tend to make it particularly interesting to the student of religious developments."

According to Dr. Morgan, "An obvious characteristic of the Charismatic Renewal is its interdenominational quality." Throughout the world, all denominations have ministers and members who are receiving the baptism with the Holy Spirit. Episcopalians, Anglicans, Lutherans, Presbyterians, Methodists, Mennonites, Baptists, Brethren, and members of nearly all Missionary Societies have been filled with the Spirit, just as believers in Christ were filled in New Testament Days. It is this unity of the Spirit, as compared with the rather superficial harmony resulting from man's efforts, which is bringing about true and deep ecumenism. This is not political and ecclesiastical merger, but the unity of the Spirit—the unity in Christ for which He prayed. According to Dr. Morgan:

"In this day when we see an increasing emphasis on Christian harmony by such groups as the World Council of Churches and the tendency toward mergers between denominations, it is noteworthy that a remarkable degree of unity exists among those who are participating in the Charismatic Renewal. The kindred spirit between such individuals readily transcends denominational barriers."[3]

We have had the privilege of personally seeing first hand in nearly thirty countries of the world something of this precious "unity of the Spirit" in churches and prayer groups of almost all denominations and missions. It is a wonderful and exciting thing to behold. But if there is a commencement of a true Scriptural unity of the Spirit in the experience of Pentecost,

---

3   From *Some Social History Aspects of the Charismatic Renewal* by William G. Morgan, as published in VIEW, No. 2, 1965 (Full Gospel Business Men's Fellowship International).

how much greater will be the unity in the experience of the Tabernacle of David! If there is unity taking place as a result of Sinai, how much more blessed must be the unity at Mount Zion.

Unity In David's Tabernacle

As we have already emphasized, God is restoring the Tabernacle of David in exactly the same way as the first Tabernacle of David was built. The Bible teaches that in the building of David's Tabernacle, and the resultant return of the Power and Presence of God, there was a unity. But what kind of unity was it? This is most important, for this is the very same unity that God is restoring today.

As we have seen, the pitching of David's Tabernacle started with a realization that something was drastically missing from the people of God. Despite all the blessings and victories God had given them, the Ark of the Covenant—the fullness of the Power of His Presence—was still at Kirjath-jearim. As the captains and leaders of the people came together with David (1 Chron. 13:1), this longing after God was in the heart of every one of them. Every leader was dissatisfied. There had to be spiritual renewal.

Today many leaders in the Church of Christ are dissatisfied. This dissatisfaction is a good thing. At the World Congress on Evangelism held in Berlin in 1967, reports were given by leaders from almost every nation on the conditions in their various countries and areas. Despite the fact the main theme of the Congress was Evangelism—the preaching of the Gospel to every race in the world—it is most significant to note that almost without exception, these great church leaders spoke of desperate needs for Spiritual Renewal in the churches of their various countries. Here are what some of these delegates to the World Congress on Evangelism said:

INDIA :

"There is general recognition, therefore, that what the Church in India today needs is revival . . . 'The Church . . . has failed to discharge its spiritual responsibility to the nation mainly because of its spiritual

feebleness . . . Unless the Indian Church is revitalized, there is no future for Christianity in India."[4] *(Mr. I. Ben Wati, Executive Secretary of the Evangelical Fellowship of India).*

THE ARAB WORLD :

"The real problem apparently is with the Church itself." (The Rev. Mr. S. SaJiiouny, executive Secretary of The National Evangelical Synod of Syria and Lebanon).

WEST AFRICA :

". . . unfortunately the general attitude of the average Church has been one of unconcern about reaching unbelievers for Christ." (The Rev. Mr. David I. Olatavo, general secretary of the Evangelical Churches of West Africa).

THE PHILIPPINES :

"Backslidden Christians and anaemic Churches constitute the main obstacle anywhere to the progress of evangelism." (The Rev. Mr. Max. D. Atienza, Vice-President for Asian Evangelism for the Far East Broadcasting Company in Manila, Philippines).

AUSTRALASIA :

" 'Perhaps our greatest need,' one leader said, 'is the motivation of the Spirit, not on an organisational level, but to meet the lack of an explosive power issuing in real concern.' " (The Rev. Mr. Reginald E. Jarrott, Director of Evangelism for the Baptist Union of Queensland in Brisbane, Australia).

SCANDINAVIA :

"The main obstacles (to evangelism), I fear, however, are not outside but inside the Church. Religious divisions weaken the body of Christ. Moreover, many Christians have lost their zeal and love and are spiritually paralyzed. There is an absence of that power which can make the Church dynamic enough to realize a bold programme of evange-

---

4   Quoting another leading Indian Christian, Afr. Rajaiah D. Paul.

lism." (The Rev. Mr. Paulson, National Evangelist with the Mission Covenant Church of Sweden).

THE UNITED STATES OF AMERICA ;

"There are three or four outstanding keys for meeting the great spiritual needs of the United States. In the first place, a spiritual quickening and awakening in the Church is absolutely necessary . . . As things now stand, only a work of the Holy Spirit in great power will make this renewal possible." (Dr. Clyde W. Taylor, Chairman of the World Congress on Evangelism Executive Committee, and executive secretary of the National Association of Evangelicals in Washington, D.C., USA).[5]

This list of quotations could be multiplied many times. And I am sure there are some leaders reading these lines, who, in their heart of hearts are not satisfied. Leaders who would desperately love to see God break forth in mighty Power and do something new—to return in the Power and Glory of His Presence, to awaken His people, and to bring the lost unto Himself by the Power of the Gospel of Christ. Spiritual dissatisfaction, as long as it is satisfied in the Biblical way, is a good thing. For this is when we begin to seek God anew, and He can bless and do something new in our hearts and lives, in our missions and churches.

All the Congregation (1 Chronicles 13:2)

The Bible teaches the unity, which was brought about by this common realization of the lack of the fullness of the Power of God, was not only a unity amongst the leaders. It was a unity of "all the congregation of Israel... our brethren everywhere." The nation had been rent asunder in times past by dissension, strife, jealousies, rivalries and splits—in fact (shame on us for having to say it), more than a little similar to the Church as we see it today. But here was a new commandment. A new unity. As far as we know from

---

[5] Quoted from the Official Reference Volumes-World Congress on Evangelism, One Race, One Gospel, One Ta»k (World-wide Publications, Minneapolis, Minnesota).

A New Unity

the Bible, only one person did not take part in this new unity, and paid very heavily for disobeying the king's commandment.

The Centre and Purpose of Spiritual Unity (verse 3)

"Let us bring again the Ark of our God to us" (1 Chron. 13:3).

"And David gathered all Israel together to Jerusalem, to bring up the Ark of the Lord unto his place, which he had prepared for it" (1 Chron. 15:3).

These two verses show the two vital essentials of the unity God desires:

(1) It is a unity which has the Person of Jesus Christ as its meeting point;

(2) It is a unity which has Spiritual Renewal, by a return to the pattern of the Word of God, as its aim.

(I) The focal point of the coming together of the people of Israel was the Ark of the Covenant. As we have already noted (see Chapter 4, "The Ark of the Covenant") the Ark of the Covenant speaks of the Lord Jesus Christ in all the fullness of His Power, Presence, and blessing. God had revealed to David the tremendous importance of having the Ark in the midst of his people. For it was around this Ark that true fellowship and unity could be experienced in Israel. This unique spiritual unity was attained at the Tabernacle of David as described in Psalm 133, which is clearly referring to the Tabernacle of David:

"Behold, how good and how pleasant it is for brethren to dwell together in unity!

It is like the precious ointment upon the head, that ran down upon the beard, even Aaron's beard; that went down to the skirts of his garments:

As the dew of Hermon, and as the dew that descended upon the mountains of Zion: for there the Lord commanded the blessing, even life for evermore" (Psalm 133:1-3).

The "precious ointment" is, of course, the anointing oil, speaking of the anointing of the Holy Spirit. For without the Holy Spirit there can be no fellowship, in the New Testament sense of the word, between believers. There can be no love or unity. For the Holy Spirit Himself exalts the focal point of our fellowship, the Person of Jesus Christ, and enables us to fix our eyes upon Him (John 16:14).

One more New Testament verse, before we leave this topic, showing that our fellowship and unity is in the Person of God's Son Jesus Christ:

"God is faithful, by whom we were called unto the fellowship of His Son Jesus Christ our Lord" (I Cor. 1:9).

Our unity is not in a doctrine. Our fellowship is not in a denomination. It transcends all man-made tarriers, and brings us together in the unity of Him who is the fulfilment of the Ark of the Covenant, Jesus Christ, our Lord.

The unity seen in the Tabernacle of David had only one aim. Not political. Not denominational gain. But spiritual renewal by a return to the pattern of the Word of God. It was a spiritual unity for a spiritual purpose. David sang about this unity his Tabernacle brought about:

"A Father of the fatherless, and a judge of the widows, is God in His Holy Habitation (David's Tabernacle).

God setteth the solitary in families (margin—in a house): He bringeth out those which are bound with chains; but the rebellious dwell in a dry land" (Psalm 68:5, 6).

God is calling those who are lonely, or by themselves (for this is the meaning of the Hebrew word) to come to His House, His Tabernacle and be loosed from their bondage and brought into deep spiritual union with Himself and with others of like precious faith. But as He says, those who rebel— those who resist the moving of His Spirit—remain in a dry, barren and thirsty land.

The unity God desires includes the nine miraculous gifts of the Spirit in the Body of Christ.[6] It also includes the five "Ascension Gift Ministries" given to the Body of Christ—Apostles, Prophets, Evangelists, Pastors, and

---

6 See 1 Corinthians chapter 12.

Teachers—*"till we all come into the unity of the faith..." (Eph. 4:11-16).*

And it is a unity, once attained, we must endeavour to keep:

"Endeavouring to keep the unity of the Spirit in the bond of peace" (Eph. 4:3).[7]

The People's Response (verse 4)

"And let us bring again the Ark of our God to us: for we enquired not at it in the days of Saul.

*And all the congregation said that they would do so: **for the thing was right in the eyes of all the people**" (1 Chron. 13:3, 4).*

Today God calls us to do all we can—to pray, to seek His face, to praise and worship Him, to be cleansed from sin, to line up our lives and churches according to the Word of God, to prepare ourselves in every way we can—to "bring again the Ark of our God to us" (verse 3, margin).

Oh, may our response be as it was in the day of preparation for the Restoration of the Ark of God to the midst of David's Tabernacle!

A new gathering together. New life. New fellowship. Spiritual unity for a spiritual purpose. Nothing less will satisfy the demand of our God or the need of His Church.

---

[7] That some who claim to have received the fullness of the Holy Spirit do not seem to be able to have fellowship with others, without reason, does not show there is no such thing as "unity of the Spirit." It shows rather, that these may have, like their Galatian brethren of old, "begun in the Spirit and now continue in the flesh" (Gal. 3:3).

Chapter Fourteen

THE OXEN ARE STUMBLING

(1 Chronicles chapter 13, continued)

How is God rebuilding the Tabernacle of David in these days? In exactly the same way as He did the first time, three thousand years ago. Firstly, by causing His people to realise that despite all the many blessings He has given them, they have not yet come "unto a perfect man, unto the measure of the stature of the fullness of Christ" (Eph. 4:13).

Secondly, by a coming together of God's people who are earnestly seeking His face and opening their hearts for this new move of His Spirit. A new. Spirit-empowered unity in the Body of Christ.

All Gathered Together (verse 5)

> "So David gathered all Israel together, from Shihor of Egypt even unto the entering of Hamath, to bring the Ark of God from Kirjath-jearim" (I Chron. 13:5).

We have already stressed that the invitation to bring back the Ark of the Covenant, the Power of God's Presence in all its fullness, to the people of God, is given to all. In this verse we see "David gathered all Israel together, from Shihor of Egypt even unto the entering of Hamath."

The word "**Shihor**" means "slimy", or muddy, or dirty. Note that Shihor was on the borders of Egypt. Shihor speaks to us of sin because sin is unclean. The Bible says, "But we are all as an unclean thing, and all our righteousnesses are as filthy rags" (Isaiah 64:6). And yet, the people of Shihor were called to take part in a spiritual revival. Before entering in they had to sanctify themselves, as we see in 1 Chronicles 15:12. But the point to note here is that God's gracious invitation to take part in the Restoration of the Tabernacle of David is to **all**.

You may feel you are sinful. You may feel you are unworthy. But by the grace of God, the Lord is calling each one of us to take part in this Last Day Restoration Revival. If we will but place our lives in His hands and come to Him, He will cleanse, pardon and transform us into those who will indeed bring back the Ark in these days.

Another important fact encourages our hearts here, giving us the assurance that God can transform all who are willing to heed His invitation into those who can bring back the Ark of His Presence. We have seen from 1 Chronicles 13:1 that King David first consulted with his captains and leaders concerning the bringing back of the Ark into the midst of the people. But who were these leaders? They were men whose lives had been transformed in the presence of the king.

We first read of them:

"And every one that was in distress, and every one that was in debt, and every one that was discontented, gathered themselves unto him; and he (David) became a captain over them" (1 Sam. 22:2).

But in 2 Samuel chapter 23 and 1 Chronicles 1 2 we find these men have been changed into mighty men of valour. In like manner today, our lives can be transformed in the presence of our King—cleansed and strengthened to experience the Power of His Presence. It does not matter how weak or unworthy we feel. The Lord calls all to the Restoration of the Tabernacle of David.

"Hamath" means "defensed, or walled," and was the principal city of upper Syria, a city which was a formidable fortress. The fortress had extremely large and strong walls around it. Hamath is a picture of many of us today, who have "built a wall" around ourselves, and refuse to allow new truth and new blessing to penetrate the defenses we have put up.

The Bible teaches that God speaks judgment against those who build such walls around themselves:

"For the day of the Lord of hosts shall be upon . . . every fenced wall" (Isaiah 2:12, 15).

"The great day of the Lord is near ... A day of the trumpet and alarm against the fenced cities" (Zeph. 1:14-16).

It is also recorded in Leviticus 25:30 that the house in the walled city was not set free in the year of jubilee.[1] Therefore, let us be careful never to get into bondage in "Hamaths," but rather "pull down the barriers" allowing the light and truth of God's Word to shine in. Answer the invitation of our heavenly David to gather together to bring the Ark of His Presence back to His people. In David's day, it did not matter how different the people were. They put aside their differences. For as we have seen, this was a spiritual unity amongst the people of God, with a spiritual purpose. This unity was for the sake of the Ark of the Lord.

It was a unity to bring back the Power of His Presence.

Eight Miles To Go (verse 6)

"And David went up, and all Israel, to Baalah, that is, to Kirjath-jearim, which belonged to Judah, to bring up thence the Ark of God the Lord, that dwelleth between the cherubims, whose name is called on it" (1 Chron. 13:6).

David and his people went from Zion to Kirjath-jearim to bring up the Ark of the Lord. Kirjath-jearim was a land-mark town on the northern boundary of Judah (Josh. 15:9). Kirjath-jearim was only eight miles from the city of Jerusalem . . . eight miles from Zion.

In the Bible, the number eight speaks to us of "Resurrection Life" and "New beginning." Circumcision was performed on the eighth day (Gen. 17:12). The cleansed leper was presented by the priest on the eighth day (Lev. 14:10-11). Noah built an Ark which saved eight people from judg-

---

1   See Lev. 25:8-34.

ment (Genesis chapters 6-8). Jesus rose on the first day of the new week, or on the eighth day. Thus we see something of the significance of the eight miles the people had to go. For it was to be for them, when they brought the Ark of God up to Zion, an altogether new beginning.

Notice that Kirjath-jearim is close to Zion. Friend, this blessed revival is closer to you than you possibly realise. Don't let the Ark stay at Kirjath-jearim. Have a new beginning. Allow God to do this new thing in your life. You will never regret it.

Notice the Ark was in Judah. Judah means "praise." While we may not have seen the complete Restoration of the Tabernacle of David and the return of the Ark, I am sure of this one thing— the Ark is most definitely in Judah! The message of praise and worship is being restored in the Church of God in a wonderful, new and precious way, as we shall see in later chapters.

Again we see emphasized in this sixth verse, that Jehovah Himself "dwelt between the cherubims." David realised that the fullness of the Power of His Presence was with the Ark of the Covenant. Therefore, he was determined to bring the Ark right into the midst of his people.

Man's New Carts (verse 7)

"And they carried the Ark of God in a new cart out of the house of Abinadab: and Uzza and Ahio drave the cart" (1 Chron. 13:7).

With all his success, victories, and blessings, David had not yet brought the Ark of the Covenant back to Zion. There is a real desire in his heart to do so, but in the beginning he goes about it in the wrong way. He has the right desire, is doing the right thing—but is going about it in the wrong way—not according to the Word of God.

You will remember that the Philistines sent the Ark of God back to Israel on a new cart. God had permitted this because of their ignorance. They did not have the Word of God or His commandments. But what God allowed the Philistines to do in ignorance, He judged severely when the

Israelites tried to copy them. Israel had the anointing of God, the priests of God available to carry the Ark of the Covenant in the proper manner, and the Word of God telling them how it should be done. But despite all this the Bible says they "made the Ark to ride in a new cart." What a tragedy that the people of God, despite all their blessings, and all their opportunities, copied the Philistines in this man-made, man-organised, man-oriented way. We read in 1 Samuel 6:14 they had already smashed that first cart into pieces. They should never have built another. For it is commanded in the Word of God that the Levites, the sons of Kohath, should bear the Ark upon their shoulders (Num. 7:9).

How dreadful it is that today men have tried to make the Ark of God ride on their new carts. Instead of keeping to the pattern clearly given in the Word, man-made carts, man-made methods, man-made offices and organizations, which cannot be found in the Bible, have been substituted for the pure pattern of the Word of God. One of the heartaches of India, is all the "new carts" which have been imported from Western nations, all trying to carry along the work of the Church. May God in His grace have mercy upon us!

Two men, Uzza and Ahio, drove the new cart. Their names are very significant. Ahio means "brotherly" and Uzza means "strength." The shocking thing is that many of these man-made carts may look all sweet and brotherly. But they are really being driven by the strength of men—not motivated by the Power of the Spirit of God. As it was in the record of David's new cart, so it is today. The end result of man-made carts is stumbling, slipping, sliding, and finally death.

The Oxen Are Stumbling (verse 9)

Despite all the singing and shouting of verse 8 (to which we shall refer in more detail later) the pattern was not right. This man-made pattern could never be used of God to bring the fullness of the Power of His Presence to the city of David. The Bible says the oxen began to stumble. Friends, anything that is not according to the Word of God will stumble, and ultimately fall. It may last for some time. Men may drive it for some time. But it will never know the fullness of the blessing of the Presence of Christ.

The Strength of Man is Smitten (verse 10)

God wills that His Word bring life. Anything not according to the Word of God will ultimately bring death. Man's strength, man's progress, may look inviting for a while, and even appear to be blessed of God, but will ultimately fail. Despite the fact that the oxen were stumbling and it was obvious God was not going to move in that way any more, Uzza thrust forth his hand to steady the Ark. He tried in his own strength to keep the man-made system going just a little while longer. God smote him dead.

What a lesson there is in this for us!

God will allow such disobedience and non-conformity to His commandments to go on for just so long—then comes judgment. Uzza decided that if this "revival" or move of God was going any further, he would have to use his strength to keep it going right. But they had come to the threshing floor of Nachon.[2] Now God was about to thresh this matter out! Nachon means "stroke," and with one stroke God showed His disapproval of any man-made carts. It was as if God said, "You've gone as far as you're going under this present man-made system. If you desire to have the Living Presence of God to any greater degree than you have now, you will have to come into a new order. You will have to put away these man-made carts, and come and move with the Spirit in the way I have already ordained in My Word. For all your organized machinery and zealous efforts are useless unless they are according to the pattern of My Word."

God fulfilled His Word. While the judgment of Uzza may seem harsh, the judgment was according to the Word of God. Firstly, it was expressly commanded to the Kohathites that they were to carry the Ark on their shoulders by use of the staves provided:

---

2 Marginal rendering; see also 2 Sam. 6:6.

The Oxen are Stumbling

"But they shall not touch any holy thing, lest they die" (Num. 4:15).

Thus in touching the Holy Ark of God Uzza deliberately disobeyed the commandment of God, and God fulfilled His Word.

There are many lessons for us in this incident. The five main ones are:—

(1) The holy things of God are not to be touched by the hands of man. While it is an unpleasant thing to think of, many a tragic end has come to Christians, even preachers, who have dared touch the holy things of God, or speak against His anointed servants:

"Touch not Mine anointed, and do my prophets no harm" (Psalm 105:15).

(2) Laxness and over-familiarity with the things of God are very dangerous. One of the dangers of this new move of God is that it does, at times, when not united with reverence and holy fear of God, lead to lightness and frivolity which God will judge. Uzza was one of the sons of Abinadab in whose house the Ark of the Lord had dwelt in Kirjath-jearim. Thus the saying, "familiarity breeds contempt" came to pass. Yes, we may come boldly to the Throne of Grace. We may enjoy the Presence of God. But let our rejoicing and worship be tempered with a godly realization of the Majesty of Jehovah.

(3) Judgment begins in the house of God. How often we need to be reminded of this all important truth:

"For the time is come that judgment must begin at the house of God." (1 Pet. 4:17).

(4) Man cannot, by his own strength, bring the Power of the Presence of God to Zion:

"Not by might (army), nor by power, but by My Spirit, saith the Lord of hosts" (Zech. 4:6).

(5) The danger of not doing things according to the pattern of the Word of God. The Scripture that commands:

"According to all that I show thee, after the pattern . . . even so shall ye make it" (Exod. 25:9),

should be a constant reminder to us in all we do. For only that which is according to the pattern of the Word of God will ever know the fullness of the Power of His Presence.

David confessed later on:

"The Lord our God made a breach upon us, for that we sought Him not after the due order" (1 Chron. 15:13).

The Amplified Bible brings this solemn truth to us thus:

"The Lord our God broke forth upon us, because we did not seek Him in the way He ordained!"

Here David owns that Uzza died not only for his own sin, but for the sin of which all were guilty; carrying the Ark of the Covenant in a new, man made cart.

Obededom's Blessing (verses 11-14)

Before he understood the significance of the death of Uzza and admitted his mistake, David was displeased at the death of Uzza and did not, for a time, continue to bring the Ark of God back to Zion. Rather, he took it to the house of Obededom, the Gittite. There he left the Ark of the Covenant for three months.

How often the moving of the Holy Spirit is hindered by our failure to "bring back the Ark of His Presence" in the way He has ordained. There is an even greater significance in this. **David had not yet prepared the Tabernacle in which the Ark of God was to dwell!**[3] David could have built all the new carts he wanted. Many Uzzas could strive in their own strength to help the work of God along. The people could shout and sing before God as much as they liked—but until the Tabernacle of David was pitched, the Ark of God would never return to Zion. We shall see something more of the significance of this preparation in our next chapter.

---

3   See 1 Chron. 15:1.

In the meantime, "the Ark of God remained with the family of Obededom in his house for three months" (verse 14). As long as the Ark of God was in his house, "the Lord blessed the house of Obededom, and all that he had." The Presence of "God, the Lord, that dwelleth between the cherubims" (verse 6), was dwelling in his house. Thus, his house, his family, and everything that he had was blessed of the Lord.

What a happy and blessed home it was! Obededom was blessed in his work. Obededom prospered. Above all this, he had intimate fellowship and communion with Him that dwelleth between the cherubim. Who would refuse the Ark of God today, and all the blessings the fullness of His Presence and Power brings?

Conform to His Word

When we read this chapter, we see it is little wonder that David cried, "How shall I bring the Ark of God to me?" (verse 12). So many are crying the same today. "Lord, how can we see your work go forward in this place?" "Lord, how can we experience a revival here?" One thing is sure, the answer is not in any new cart. God will not conform to the notions and ideas of men. He would conform us to His Own Word, and revive and refresh us with the Power of His Presence.

The new cart will not work. Can't you see the oxen are stumbling?

Chapter Fifteen
PREPARING A PLACE

1 Chronicles chapter 15

We trust the reader will appreciate that the Restoration of the Tabernacle of David is an almost inexhaustible subject. The first reference to it is most probably in the book of Exodus,[1] and the subject continues right throughout the Bible to the book of Revelation.[2] In such a small volume as this, we can merely give some of the main thoughts and keys to further study. Be assured you will be abundantly blessed and rewarded as you continue your own studies.

Time and space forbid us to dwell on the details of I Chronicles chapter 14, except to refer to verse 15. This verse, speaking of the "sound of going in the tops of the mulberry trees" (together with a song containing the same words), has often been associated with the "old-time Pentecostal" revival. But seen here in its context, we see that it speaks of movement and victory preceding the return of the Ark of the Covenant to the Tabernacle of David on Mount Zion—an altogether new move of God's Spirit.

---

1   In Exodus 15:17 the promise of God is:
"*Thou shalt bring them in, and plant them in the mountain of Thine inheritance, in the place, O Lord, which Thou hast made for Thee to dwell in, in the Sanctuary, O Lord, which Thy hands have established.*"
This appears to be a clear reference to Mount Zion and the Tabernacle of David. No other mountain is spoken of as the "mountain of Thine inheritance" except Mount Zion, and it is clear from our previous chapters that the Lord was in Zion. This verse also alludes to the Restoration of the Tabernacle of David, speaking of "the Sanctuary, O Lord, which Thy hands have established." The only Sanctuary, the only Tabernacle God Himself has ever promised to build is the restored Tabernacle of David. (See also Psalm 78:54).

2   In Revelation 13:6 we read that the beast, to which the dragon gave power, blasphemed the Tabernacle of God —the restored Tabernacle of David.

Preparing a Place (verse 1)

"And David made him houses in the city of David, (Zion*) and prepared a place for the Ark of God, and pitched for it a Tent (or Tabernacle)" (1 Chron. 15:1).

Evangelist Billy Graham has often said:

"It is strange that we prepare for everything except meeting God."[3]

Unfortunately, this is not only true outside the Church of Jesus Christ. It is tragically true of those inside the Church also.

The Bible teaches there will be no revival without preparation. There will be no Restoration of the Tabernacle of David in the Church without preparation. There must be a deep spiritual preparation done in our hearts by the Holy Spirit. Then, we shall meet God, and have communion with God, in an altogether new way.

In our previous chapters, we have noticed some of the preparation which took place for the return of the Ark of His Presence to Zion. There was a realization of need for more of God. There was a realization that the fullness of the Glory of God had departed. There was a lamenting, a longing, a hunger, a thirst after the living God. There was a coming together of the people. But here in I Chronicles 15:1, we read:

"David . . . prepared a place for the Ark of God, and pitched for it a Tent."

Let us again emphasize the preparation that took place before the return of the Presence of God; the return of the Ark of God and the great revival followed. And so it must be today. There is no quick and easy way to Power with God. There are no short cuts to revival. There must be the same preparation. David pitched his Tent in preparation for the return of the Ark. But today, a greater than David, even the Lord Himself has promised to build again the Tabernacle of David in our hearts and churches if we will but let Him do this new thing in us. Oh, may we be ready!

---

3   *The Quotable Billy Graham* (Murray Publishing Company).

Preparing a Place

Now David was willing to do things according to the Word of God (see verse 2). He is acting in faith—preparing this place, believing God will help him bring back the Ark. This act in faith is the response to the desire of his heart to see the fullness of the Power of God restored to his people. God help us to act in this same way today.

Return to the Pattern (verse 2)

"Then David said, None ought to carry the Ark of God but the Levites: for them hath the Lord chosen to carry the Ark of God, and to minister unto Him for ever" (1 Chron. 15:2).

During the time the Ark of God was in the house of Obededom, David must have spent some time with the Word of God. He reads in the book of Numbers how God commanded the Ark of the Covenant should be moved. Reading in the book of Deuteronomy he finds:

"The Lord separated the tribe of Levi, to bear the Ark of the Covenant of the Lord" (Deut. 10:8).

"The priests the sons of Levi, which bare the Ark of the Covenant of the Lord" (Deut. 31:9).

What a lesson to learn from David here! He is king of Israel. Again and again he has been hailed as the mighty victor. The people had rejoiced in his name as he returned from his battles (e.g. 1 Sam. 18:6, 7). But despite this, he swallows his pride, humbly admitting his wrong. His desire was correct. His ambitions were pure. He was doing the right thing. But in the wrong way! Thus he admits "none ought to carry the Ark of God but the Levites." Now he is willing to change his methods, and return to the pattern of the Word of God.

If mighty King David can do this, why can't we? Why can we not read the Word of God, find out God's methods and pattern, and return to them?

David pitched a Tent, or Tabernacle, for the Ark of the Covenant. The Psalms open up in a new way when we realize that the Tabernacle of David was the Tabernacle, the Temple, God's House, the Sanctuary, which is spoken of, many times, with so much affection. To understand this is to understand one of the keys to the Psalms, and to the Restoration of the Tabernacle of David.

Yes, David admitted he was wrong. No matter how wonderful his new cart was, it just would not work. God would not allow it to bring about the Restoration of the Power of His Presence. It stumbled and fell, causing death.

There seems to be coming a division in the Church of Jesus Christ. When I speak of division, 1 am not talking of a man-made division. I am referring to spiritual division. On one hand, there seem to be those perfectly satisfied with the way things are. Although the Ark of the Presence of God is not in Zion, at the most all they do is copy the Philistines, and endeavour to build even bigger and better carts. Despite the fact that through the centuries of Church history many lives have been lost in the battle for freedom from "the Philistines," they now want to copy "the Philistines," joining with them.

However, there are those who have seen the folly of the new carts of men. They are longing for revival. Like David they are returning to the Word of God. They are humble enough to admit that the new carts of men don't work. They are preparing to return to the pattern. With this return to the Word of God the saying is being fulfilled, "They that stumbled are girded with strength" (1 Sam. 2:4).

Now David is prepared to have the Levites carry the Ark of God upon their shoulders, by the staves which God has provided. There is an interesting and important allegory here. For the Bible says, "the government shall be upon His (Christ's) shoulder" (Isaiah 9:6). For us to enter the fullness of what God is bringing us back into, the Lord is restoring the Scriptural pattern of church government to the Body of Christ. The five ministries, and elders and deacons, are being restored according to the pattern of God's Word. Is this the kind of government you have in your church? "Shoulder" government, or "new-cart" government? Let us return to the pattern of the Word of God.

Spiritual Unity (verse 3)

"And David gathered all Israel together to Jerusalem, to bring up the Ark of the Lord unto his place, which he had prepared for it" (1 Chron. 15:3).

We have already dealt with this subject in a previous chapter. Let us add here, this was a unity with preparation and purpose—a spiritual unity with a spiritual purpose. But more than this, with a spiritual preparation also. Likewise, today, any unity of believers which is not coupled with spiritual preparation and expectancy is doomed to failure.

The Plurality of Ministry (verse 4)

"And David assembled the children of Aaron, and the Levites" (I Chron. 15:4).

Now David was returning to the pattern of the Word of God. Not a new cart, but God-anointed ministries will now bring the Ark of God to Zion in the God-appointed way. Not, as before, just one or two trying to bring the Presence of God, but all chosen ministries working together for the Glory of God. Not just one man taking the whole service from opening hymn to benediction, but all the ministries permitted to take their part.

David called for Zadok and Abiathar the priests, and for the Levites Uriel, Asaiah, Joel, Shemaiah, Eliel, and Amminadab. Each one of the names of the Levites who were called upon to carry the Ark has special significance here. Uriel means "God is Light." Asaiah means "Jehovah is Doer" or "Jehovah has made." Joel means "Jehovah is God," or "Jehovah is Mighty." Shemaiah means "Jehovah has heard." Eliel means "God is God," or "To whom God is Strength." And Amminadab means "My people are willing." What a gathering! No one is moving in his own strength, or in a one-man ministry, but all are moving together and depending on God for strength and light. These are ministries who are willing to take their place in the Body of Christ, and yet also willing to recognize the ministry given to their brother.

Notice also the Levites named, along with the priests Zadok and Abiathar, make a group of eight. Eight, as we have seen, is the number which speaks of resurrection life and a new beginning. As we see God restoring the plurality of the ministry in the Body of Christ, we will see Christ Himself manifest His resurrection life in His Body in the way He has ordained in His Word. Each one was a chief in his own right, and no doubt had a tremendous ministry and much experience. But God brought them to the place where they confessed they needed one another. No one man can carry the Ark of God alone. No one man, such as Uzza, gets the glory, for all are working together in harmony according to the pattern of the Word.

Praise God, for today He is restoring the truth:

"And He gave some, apostles; and some, prophets; and some, evangelists; and some, pastors and teachers; For the perfecting of the saints, for the work of the ministry, for the edifying of the body of Christ:

Till we all come in the unity of the faith, and of the knowledge of the Son of God, unto a perfect man, unto the measure of the stature of the fullness of Christ... which is the Head....

From whom the whole body fitly joined together and compacted by that which every joint supplieth, according to the effectual working in the measure of every part, maketh increase if the body unto the edifying of itself in love" (Eph. 4:1 1-16).

As we build again according to the pattern of the Word, this Scripture is being fulfilled in the Church. This is true of local assemblies where God-given travelling ministries to the Body of Christ are allowed to visit, and the local church is operating according to the pattern of God-given elders and deacons.

When the Ark was carried according to the pattern of the Word of God, an altogether new move of the Power of His Presence began. Why? Because they were obeying the Word of God:

"And the children of the Levites bare the ark of God upon their shoulders with the staves thereon, as Moses commanded according to the Word of the Lord" (1 Chron. 15:15).

Notice also that each of the Levites had their hands full of staves. They were not busy pulling swords and jabbing each other! The work at hand was so important they had no time for minor differences of opinion on how the various groups under their jurisdiction were to be run. They were intent on one thing—to move together, acting according to the Word of God. If some had pulled one way, and others had pulled the other way, again the Ark would have stumbled and disaster resulted. But now they are gathered together in a spiritual unity with a spiritual purpose. God is manifesting the Power of His Presence among them. There is true unity, love, and worship. Preachers, when will we stop "driving the oxen," and commence to flow together in the God-ordained way? Which one of these eight men was named the "chief carrier"? Which one held the most important part of the stave? What does it matter? They had heard the Word of the King, direct from the Book.

Let us then come together in love taking hold of our section of the staves. Multitudes are desperately waiting for the return of the Ark of God to Zion, so that they may have an opportunity to hear the Gospel of Christ, before it is too late.

The Urgency of This Hour (verses 5-11)

As we have briefly seen, all of the names of these ministries have a definite meaning applicable to the Restoration of the Tabernacle of David. In the same way, the numbers also in these verses have important truths for us today. We can only consider one of them here.

As all Bible scholars know, the numbers given in the Bible do not just "happen to be there." Bible numerics is an engrossing and rewarding study. Certain numerals have a distinguished place in the Word of God. Upon investigation it is found they have a most significant meaning for interpretation of scripture, and are inseparably linked with themes that wind, as unbroken wires in a cable, through the whole Bible.

"Of the sons of Kohath; Uriel the chief, and his brethren an hundred and twenty" (1 Chron. 15:5).

In the Bible the number 120 speaks of "the end of all flesh," or, "the bringing in of a new era." A brief look at the following verses will show this:

"And the Lord said. My spirit shall not always strive with man, for that he also is flesh: yet his days shall be an hundred and twenty years" (Gen. 6:3).

God did away with sinful flesh by the flood which followed this solemn announcement, and brought in a new era.

"And Moses was an hundred and twenty years old when he died: his eye was not dim, nor his natural force abated" (Deut. 34:7).

When Moses died, Israel entered into a new era of history as they marched forward into the promised land.

In 2 Chronicles 5:11-14 we read that 120 priests sounded with trumpets in the temple of Solomon, and the Glory of God so filled the temple the priests could not stand to minister. A new era of the Presence of God was ushered in.

We read there were 120 disciples gathered together in the upper room, continuing with one accord in prayer, when the Holy Spirit was poured out at the commencement of this new era of the Holy Spirit (Acts 1:15). Many other references could be listed.[4]

What is God saying to us in all this? Simply that the number 120, speaking to us of the end of that which is of the flesh, of the strength, struggling and striving of man, is vitally connected with the Restoration of the Tabernacle of David. God uses this number to warn of the urgency of this hour in which we live. It is later than we think. God is restoring the Tabernacle of David now.

Have we prepared our hearts for the return of the Power of His Presence?

---

4 E.g. 2 Chron. 3:4; 7:5; Dan. 6:1; John 4:35. It is also interesting to note that when the number of the end of flesh, 120, is multiplied by the number 50, the number of the year of Jubilee, the number 6,000 is the result. As we have already seen, a day with the Lord is as 1,000 years, and the 6,000 years are the first 6 days of God's redemptive week. Thus we see in God's week there are 120 Jubilees before the last "day," the 1,000-year Millennium.

Chapter Sixteen
SANCTIFY YOURSELVES

1 Chronicles chapter 15 (continued)

"*Sanctify yourselves, both ye and your brethren, that ye may bring up the Ark of the Lord God of Israel unto the place that I have prepared for it*" (1 Chron. 15:12).

The place was prepared but the people weren't. Thus the commandment, "Sanctify yourselves." When the people were sanctified, and began to carry the Ark of the Covenant in the Scriptural way to the Tabernacle David had prepared for it, they rejoiced greatly in the Power of His Presence.

If they were going to bring up the Ark of the Covenant—the Power, the Glory, and the Presence of Almighty God—to Zion, it was absolutely essential for them to be sanctified. For God commands:

"*Be ye clean, that bear the vessels of the Lord*" (Isaiah 52:11).

Those who took part in David's Tabernacle were commanded to be sanctified. All who would take part in the Restoration of David's Tabernacle must also be sanctified, for it is written:

"*Lord, who shall abide in Thy Tabernacle? who shall dwell in Thy holy hill (Zion)? He that walketh uprightly, and worketh righteousness*" (Psalm 15:1, 2).

Again it is written concerning the Tabernacle of David:

"*Who shall ascend into the hill of the Lord? or who shall stand in His holy place? He that hath clean hands, and a pure heart*" (Psalm 24:3, 4).

The command of God to live a sanctified life is so urgent, that no Christian can afford to take lightly this vital truth. Hear the Word of God:

"This is the will of God, even your sanctification" (I Thess. 4:3).

"The works of the flesh. . . they which do such things shall not inherit the kingdom of God" (Gal. 5:19-21).

"Holiness (or sanctification[1]), without, which no man shall see the Lord" (Heb. 12:14)..

Our reaction to these solemn warnings determines our eternal destiny. A person who has accepted Christ as Saviour, but has not experienced sanctification, lives in a most dangerous position. May these words drive us to prayer: "**Sanctification** without which no man shall see the Lord."

What Is Sanctification?

What is Sanctification? The word simply means "to be separated," or "set apart." Not a "holier-than-thou," "I will not have anything to do with you" way of life. Not a drab legal "I must not do this", "I must do that" experience. Not a proud "I am separated from the world" testimony. But a joyous, triumphant liberty, which knows the Power of God within, is greater than all the sin and temptation without. The separation taught in the Bible is deeply spiritual, and intensely practical.

We can say on the negative side of Sanctification, the Christian is separated from the power of sin. The believer's heart is washed from all known sin, by a deep inner cleansing of the Blood of Christ. In Sanctification, he is then set free from the very power of sin, by allowing the Cross of Christ to operate in his life. Not a theory. Not merely a doctrine. Sanctification is a blessed, liberating reality. Hallelujah!

On the positive side of Sanctification, the believer is separated unto God, to live daily in the victory of the Cross of Christ.

---

[1] The Greek word *hagiasmos*, which literally means separation, or setting apart, is translated in the New Testament 5 times as "holiness," and 5 times as "sanctification."

Separated *from* sin.

Separated *unto* God.

Blessed Sanctification! True holiness! But the full will of God for your Sanctification is only possible in the Power of the Spirit-filled life.

I recall a statement I once read which illustrates that the baptism in the Holy Spirit and Sanctification are not one and the same experience. Think on this:

Sanctification separates the soul *to* God.

The baptism in the Holy Spirit fills the soul *with* God.

Separated to God. Filled with His fullness. We need **both** experiences to satisfy the soul and fit us for heaven. **Both** experiences are needed to transform weak, frustrated Christians into New Testament disciples.

So great is the importance of Sanctification whole volumes could be written about it. But here we wish to emphasize that only Sanctified Christians are taking part in the Restoration of the Tabernacle of David.[2]

In the broadest sense of the word, Sanctification begins when we first accept Christ as Saviour, and goes on until we are finally taken into the presence of the Lord for evermore. At least, it should do.

However, the Bible uses the word *Sanctification* in a much narrower sense than this. It speaks of the crisis of heart-cleansing—a definite experience of being set free from the power of sin and self— followed by growing in grace, and in the beauty of this experience.

All three persons of the Godhead have a part to play in a true experience of Sanctification. As we yield to their invitation to enter into the joyous experience of knowing we are sanctified, we find in our hearts a love for the Father, Son, and Holy Ghost, we never knew was possible before. Of course, we do not come to each Person of the Trinity, and expect three distinct experiences. When you accepted Christ as your Saviour and were

---

[2] Because of the utmost importance of this vital subject, much of the teaching here is repeated from Chapter 6 of the author's book, *You Shall Receive Power*.

born again, it was one experience, but all three Persons of the Godhead were vitally concerned for your salvation, and were working in you. God our Father gave His Son, and called you to Himself. The Lord Jesus, Who had shed His Blood on the Cross for you, came into your heart and washed away your sins. The Holy Spirit convicted you of your sins, revealed Christ and His Power to save. He did a miracle in your heart. You were "born of the Spirit."

God the Father in Sanctification

May God help us see the tremendous need for us to be Sanctified, as He sees it! God the Father calls us to Sanctification. He calls us to make a total dedication of all that we have, and are, to Him: our desires, ambitions, thoughts, plans, friends, families, minds, bodies, and souls. Our all. In His love and concern for us, He wants to "sanctify us wholly," as it is written:

> *"The God of peace himself sanctify you wholly; and may your spirit and soul and body be preserved entire, without blame at the coming of our Lord Jesus Christ" (1 Thess. 5:23,* American Standard Version*).*

> *"Jude, the servant of Jesus Christ, and brother of James, to them that are sanctified by God the Father . . (Jude 1).*

God the Son in Sanctification

> *"But of Him are ye in Christ Jesus, who of God is made unto us ... Sanctification" (? Cor. 1:30).*

God the Son, our Lord Jesus Christ, not only shed His Blood on the Cross of Calvary, but took our sinful nature, (that root of sin governing us), to the Cross. Bible commentators point out, that in the book of Romans, from chapter 1 to 5:11, the Apostle Paul speaks of sins (in the plural). But from chapter 5:12 to the end of Romans, Paul teaches not how we may be forgiven from our sins, but how we may be delivered from sin—the sinful nature that seeks to rule us, and hold us in bondage to ourselves.

The Lord Jesus did not die on the Cross only that we might be forgiven. He died to make us holy. "To be made holy" is another meaning of the word, "Sanctification." God's commandment "Be ye holy; for I am holy" (1 Pet. 1:16) is not in the Bible to frustrate us. The exhortation to "be holy in all your conduct and manner of living" (1Pet. 1:15) is given to be obeyed! Indeed, God warns us, that without holiness, no man shall see the Lord (Heb. 12:14).

It is impossible for the believer to be set apart from the world, the flesh, sin's dominion, the old man, the self life, and all else that hinders him from enjoying Sanctification, until he sees himself identified with Christ in His work of atonement. The truth of our **identification** with Christ, is one of the most encouraging and life-giving teachings in the Word of God. The Bible says we suffered with Christ. We were crucified with Him. We died with Him. We were buried with Him. We were made alive with Him. We rose with Him. We ascended with Him, and are seated with Him now in heavenly places. This is what God says concerning the spiritual state of the true believer in His Son.

Let us look particularly at the death of our Lord upon the Cross for us. Watchman Nee forcibly clarifies this great truth:

I received forgiveness from the **sins** I have committed,

> forgiveness for what 1 have *done*,
>> by the power of the **Blood** of Christ.

But, I receive *deliverance* from **sin**, the sinful, self-governed nature of mine,

> deliverance from what I *am*,
>> by the power of the **Cross** of Christ.

To see this great truth, is to enter into an altogether new realm of Christian living. Longings for holiness fill the heart of every sincere believer. But so often every effort to live a holy life is met with defeat, confusion, and frustration. We feel deceived and bound by our own sinful nature. Like Paul, looking back to the time when sin still had him bound, we confess:

"For I fail to practice the good deeds I desire to do, but the evil deeds that I do not desire to do are what I am ever doing" (Romans 7:19,

Amplified Bible).

In desperation we cry:

"O unhappy and pitiable and wretched man that I am! Who will release and deliver me from the shackles of this body of death?" (Romans 7:24, Amplified Bible*).*

Take heart! Be encouraged! Hear the triumphant shout which follows:

"O thank God!—He will! through Jesus Christ, the Anointed One, our Lord!" (Romans 7:25, Amplified Bible).

Yes! It is gloriously possible, through Jesus Christ our Lord, to be delivered from the power of sin. Not through our efforts at holy living; not by our stuggling and striving to be holy; but through what He has *already done* for us on the Cross of Calvary. Praise His Holy Name.

Jesus did suffer on the Cross, and shed His Blood to wash away our sins. "Christ died *for* our *sins*, according to the Scriptures" (1 Cor. 15:3). However, the Bible teaches that Christ also died, not only *for* our sins, but to *take away sin* (singular) ; to take away the sinful nature out of the hearts of all who will come to Him for Sanctification. Consider these verses:

"Behold the Lamb of God, that taketh away the sin of the world" (John 1 :29).[3]

"Now once at the end of the ages hath He been manifested to put away sin by the sacrifice of Himself" (Heb. 9:26)."

It is failure to see this two-fold work of Christ on the Cross that has led to so many weak and defeated Christian lives. Yet this two-fold work— forgiveness from sins, and deliverance from sin— is taught both in the Old Testament propheticaliy, and in the New Testament experientially. Many examples could be given but we will consider only the Day of Atonement here.

---

3 The marginal rendering is also significant:— "Behold the Lamb of God, that beareth away the sin of the world," alluding to the scapegoat which was used to bear away the sins of the people on the Day of Atonement, (see Lev. 16).

The Day of Atonement

The Day of Atonement is a beautiful picture of what the Lord Jesus did for us on the Cross. The writer of Hebrews makes clear reference to this when he says:

"For the bodies of those beasts, whose blood is brought into the sanctuary by the high priest for sin, are burned without the camp.

Wherefore Jesus also, that he might sanctify the people with his own blood, suffered without the gate" (Heb. 13:11, 12).

On the Day of Atonement, having offered a sacrifice for himself and his house, the high priest came to the door of the tabernacle of Moses; (see Leviticus 16:1-10). At the door of the tabernacle were two he-goats. They were the sin offering for the people. Two goats, but one offering. These two goats were presented before the Lord at the door of the tabernacle. One goat was slain, shedding its blood for the sins of the people. The second goat, also to "make an atonement" with the Lord, was called the "scapegoat"—"the goat for going away"[4] or "taking away." In type, burdened with the sin and guilt of the people, it was "let ... go for a scapegoat into the wilderness."

To illustrate completely the work of Christ on the Cross for us, two goats were needed.[5] For, as we have already seen, there was a two-fold work of Christ on the Cross, because of the two-fold nature of sin in us—sins, the wrongs we have done; sin, the sinful nature in us. The Blood cleanses us from sins; the Cross delivers us from sin.

Knowing This

Now we can understand Romans 6:6,7:

"Knowing this" (God wants us to **know** and experience this truth), *"that our old man was crucified with Him, that the body of sin might be* **destroyed***, that henceforth we should not serve sin."*

---

4   *Analytical Concordance to the Holy Bible* by Dr. Robert Young.
5   We see this two-fold sacrifice again in the sacrifice of the two doves in the law of the cleansing of the leper in Leviticus, chapter 14.

This verse is speaking of the second part of the two-fold work of Christ on the Cross for us. What a transformation there would be in every Christian, if they would take God at His word here, and act as though it were true! Our old man was nailed to that cruel Cross on Golgotha's hill nearly 2000 years ago, that "the body of sin"— the very sinful nature, the sin principle at work within us—might be destroyed. We need no longer serve sin. Instead, we yield ourselves gladly to God, for His service. Be well assured, "No man can serve two masters"(Matt. 6:24).

"For he that is dead is freed from sin"

Freed from the power of sin! No longer enslaved to sin! No longer captive to self! No longer a servant of the old man! Free! Is not this what the heart longs for? It is yours, because of what the Lord Jesus Christ has done for you. When the realization of what the Lord has done for us dawns upon the soul, it revolutionizes the whole life.

"For sin shall not have dominion over you" (Rom. 6:14).

Sin shall no longer reign. Christ shall reign as Saviour, Lord and King. May the Lord lead us afresh to Calvary, and reveal the glorious truth of His twofold work in His atoning death for us. Then, of a truth, "Sin shall not have dominion over you." We are made "more than conquerors through Him that loved us" (Romans 8:37).

What tongue can tell, what pen describe the blessing of feeling clean within in the Presence of a Holy and Righteous God! Can any words convey the joy of coming reverently, yet boldly before Him, without the sense of guilt, sinfulness, and shame? *"Hearts sprinkled and purified from a guilty, evil conscience" (Heb. 10:22,* Amplified Bible). *"Free from sin . . . servants of righteousness"* (Rom. 6:18). *"Partakers of His holiness"* (Heb. 12:10).

God the Holy Spirit in Sanctification

The Bible teaches that the Holy Spirit, together with the Father and the Son, desires that we be sanctified, and leads us into this blessed, holy experience. Many Scriptures illustrate this:

> *"I should be the minister of Jesus Christ to the Gentiles, ministering the Gospel of God, that the offering up of the Gentiles might be acceptable, being sanctified by the Holy Ghost"* (Rom. 15:16).
>
> *"We are bound to give thanks to God always for you, brethren beloved of the Lord, because God hath from the beginning chosen you to salvation through sanctification of the Spirit and belief of the truth"* (2 Thess. 2:13).
>
> *"Elect according to the foreknowledge of God the Father, through sanctification of the Spirit, unto obedience and sprinkling of the blood of Jesus Christ"* (1 Peter 1:2).

The Holy Spirit definitely operates in our Sanctification. One of the greatest ministries of the Holy Spirit, is to take the glorious truths about the Lord Jesus Christ, and make them real and living to us.[6] The Holy Spirit reveals the truth of our identification with Christ on the Cross. He so anoints this to us, we know that what Jesus has done is an accomplished fact.

When we receive Christ as our Saviour, all His holiness is readily available to us. But, as yet we have not received it. This is called *Positional Sanctification*. Positional Sanctification can be illustrated thus: the Bible says that the Lord Jesus bore the sins of the whole world when He shed His Blood on the Cross. Salvation is readily available to every person on earth. But for millions it is only "Positional Salvation"—they are in a position where they can be saved. But they are not saved, until they personally receive Christ as their Saviour.

In just the same way, every true believer in Christ is in a position where he may be sanctified. But how many have *experienced* His holiness in their hearts?

After receiving Christ as their personal Saviour, most honest Christians become dissatisfied with their spiritual lives. The Holy Spirit is leading them on. For it is not the will of God that we live lives of failure and defeat,

---

6   See John 16:13, 14.

sin and unrighteousness. "This is the will of God, *even your sanctification*" (1 Thess. 4:3). When the Spirit reveals to us that Christ can and will take away our sinful nature and give us victory over sin, we fall to our knees, asking the Lord to cleanse and deliver us. This is termed Critical Sanctification. That is, it happens in our hearts as a crisis, as a definite experience. We arise cleansed, victorious, and free.

Walk in the Spirit

But let it not be thought that our Sanctification is now complete. Let us not be deceived into thinking that we can never sin again. After our initial experience in our crisis of Sanctification, we need the Cross of Christ to operate **daily** in our lives, to keep us free from sin. This is known as *Progressive Sanctification.* **This** is where the need for the baptism with the Holy Spirit comes in. It is the Holy Spirit Who gives us Power to lead a sanctified, pure and holy life, and to "grow in grace" (2 Pet. 3:18).

In his sermon on "The Holy Ghost," Wesley emphasizes this important truth:

"The title Holy, applied to the Spirit of God, does not only denote that He is Holy in His own nature, but that He makes us so."

The baptism, or fullness of the Spirit gives the believer Power to live the Christian life after he is born again. Similarly, the baptism in the Holy Spirit gives Power to live a sanctified, holy life. It is not a "once for all" experience that enables us to live a victorious Christian life. It is a daily, hourly walk in the Spirit. Anything less will lead to frustration, defeat, and even tragedy. Well has David McKee pointed out:

"If we walk in the Spirit, we shall not fulfil the lusts of the flesh. Amen! But if we take a holiday in the Spirit, we shall. If our lives are controlled by the Spirit of God, we shall not serve sin. But if some part of our life is not controlled by the Spirit of God, we have no choice —we shall inevitably serve sin.

"And this is New Testament Sanctification. Not only the negative cleansing of our hearts by faith, but the positive filling of our temples by the Spirit of Jesus, the Holy Ghost Himself.

"In Acts 1 5:8 and 9, we read; 'And God, which knoweth the hearts bare them witness, giving them the Holy Ghost, even as he did unto us; and put no difference between us and them, purifying their hearts by faith.'

"He purified their hearts by faith, giving them the Holy Ghost to fill what He had purified. And in the measure in which they retained that fullness, in that measure they remained sanctified . . .

"When I think that all Satan needs is one part of your life unsurrendered, to spoil the whole; then I suggest to you that you are called to a Spirit-filled life by the very demand of your own nature. There is no satisfying experience of Sanctification which stops short of being completely at the disposal of the sanctifying Lord by His Spirit."[7]

Are *You* Sanctified?

Positional Sanctification through that which Christ has done for us on the Cross of Calvary.

Critical Sanctification through our experience of His cleansing and delivering power.

Progressive Sanctification through the fullness of the Spirit, giving us Power to live holy and victorious lives, day by day.

Is this your experience? Dear friend, are you sanctified? It is not enough to hope so, or to think so. It is not enough to have wept at an altar. If you are living a Sanctified life, you know it! There is victory in your life, and assurance in your heart.

Possibly the most dangerous state to be in, is to be a carnal Christian. A Christian still dominated by sin. A Christian still ruled by self. May God help us see the seriousness of this! God specifically warns us concerning the works of the flesh:

"I warn you beforehand, just as I did previously, that those who do such things shall not inherit the kingdom of God" (Gal. 5:21).

---

[7] Rev. David McKee of the Irish Presbyterian Mission, in his message The Call of God to the Spirit-filled Life, used by his permission.

May our hearts be so gripped with the urgency to be Sanctified, that we will confess our need before Him, and receive His full salvation. There is no other way, but His way.

Oh! Be encouraged today! You need not doubt or fear a moment longer. God, in His great love, wants to sanctify you.

Sins can be forgiven. *Sin*—your sinful nature— can never be forgiven. It must be taken away. See your old man, your self life, your sinful nature nailed to the Cross. Thank the Lord Jesus that He is willing and able to bear your sin away. Sanctification is yours.

"Reckon ye also yourselves to be dead indeed unto sin" (Rom. 6:11).

It will mean repentance. It will mean a crisis. It will mean allowing Him to nail your all to His Cross. Crucifixion is painful. Nevertheless, death is sweet release from bondage to sin.

"For ye are dead, and your life is hid with Christ in God" (Col. 3:3).

But there is more in Romans 6:11 than reckoning yourself dead unto sin. Reckon yourself also:

"...alive unto God through Jesus Christ our Lord."

Now you may share in His Resurrection Power also. After His death, our Lord Jesus Christ was made alive, and rose triumphant from the dead. And all who allow Him to take away their sin by the power of His Cross, may share in His resurrection Power and glory. We are "quickened together with Him" (Col. 2:13), and "risen with Him" (Col. 2:12). How beautifully Romans 5:10 also illustrates this:

"For if, when we were enemies, we were reconciled to God by the death of His Son, much more, being reconciled, we shall be saved by His life.*"*

"Saved by His life"! *The Amplified Bible* rendering is lucid here:

*"It is much more certain, now that we are reconciled, that we shall be saved, **daily delivered from sin's dominion through His resurrection life.**"*

Washed in His Blood. Delivered from sin. Filled with His Spirit. Daily delivered from sin's dominion by His resurrection life. Sanctified wholly. This is God's will for His children.

How is God restoring the Tabernacle of David? With a sanctified people.

Chapter Seventeen
PRAISE THAT PLEASES

1 Chronicles chapter 15 (continued)

"And David spake to the chief of the Levites to appoint their brethren to be the singers with instruments of musick, psalteries and harps and cymbals, sounding, by lifting up the voice with joy" (1 Chron. 15:16).

The new move of God was going ahead "according to the Word of the Lord" (verse 15). Now we enter into yet another essential truth concerning the Restoration of the Tabernacle of David.

God is restoring the Tabernacle of David. "I will build it as in the days of old" (Amos 9:11), is His promise. And we see today, that this Last Day move of the Spirit of God is accompanied, as in David's Tabernacle, with new and continual expressions of praise and worship to the Lord.

A Joyful Noise (verse 16)

Now that David had returned to the pattern of the Word of God, the time had come to appoint singers and musicians **to worship and praise God.**

One of the foremost themes of the Bible, is that man was made to worship and praise God. As the late Dr. Tozer has expressed this truth in his booklet, *WORSHIP: The Missing Jewel in The Evangelical Church*:

> "We were created, and after the Fall redeemed, that we might be worshippers of the Most High God...God made us to be worshippers. That is the purpose of God in bringing us into the world."

Yes, worship is much more than the keeping of a form or ceremony. It is more than singing a hymn. It is more than making a noise. True worship and praise is "awesome wonder and overpowering love" in the Presence of our God, and expressing this love we feel in our hearts for Him in "some appropriate manner"—that is, in one of the Biblical methods given us to praise and worship God.

David appointed singers and musicians to praise and worship God. And the keynote of their praise was joy. "Sounding, by lifting up the voice with joy."

The Bible is insistent on this truth—the Good News of God's love, in both Old and New Testaments, is always accompanied by joy. For example, when Philip preached the Gospel of Christ in the wicked city of Samaria, the Lord confirmed the Word with mighty signs, wonders, and miracles. Many turned to the Lord, "and there was great joy in that city" (Acts 8:4-8).

We are commanded to:

*"Rejoice in the Lord **always**: and again I say, Rejoice" (Phil. 4:4).*

It is obvious from Scripture, that this joy is expressed with noise—"by lifting up the voice with joy," as they did when they went down to Obed-edom's house to bring back the Ark of God to Zion. This was not the morbid formality so often seen in much of Christian worship today. This was a joyful expression of the Life of Him who was anointed with the oil of gladness above His fellows (Psalm 45:7).

Many of our friends might say they have the joy of the Lord in their hearts and want to keep it there. But this is in direct contradiction to the Word of God. For the Bible teaches that joy in the heart will be manifested by praise on the lips! The Bible says:

"Blessed is the people that know the joyful sound: they shall walk, O Lord, in the light of Thy countenance" (Psalm 89:15).

Indeed, seven times in the Psalms we are commanded with the words: "Make a joyful **noise** unto the Lord."[1]

In all these verses, together with Psalm 89:15, the Hebrew word means to shout! Do you obey this Biblical commandment?

---

1   Psalm 66:1; 81:1; 95:1; 95:2; 98:4; 98:6; 100:1.

Commenting on this sixteenth verse of 1 Chronicles, Matthew Henry uses the term "every possible expression of joy." Truly, there is no joy which can compare with the joy of the Lord. We should indeed praise and worship Him with every possible expression of joy.

One other important point should be noted here. This rejoicing, and audible praise and worship, commenced **before** the Restoration of the Ark of the Covenant to its proper place in the Tabernacle of David. As soon as the place and people were prepared, and the Bible pattern and order restored, the people began to enter into an altogether **new** experience of demonstrative praise and worship to their God.

The worship in the tabernacle of Moses, as we have seen, was mostly silent. Only the gentle tinkling of the bells on the borders of the priest's garments could be heard. But here was something new. David longed after God. God had revealed to him his need for the Presence of the Ark of the Covenant. As soon as the people began to move with God, even **before** the Ark of God was restored in all its fullness, they began to show their gratitude to God for the blessing of His Presence by doing a new thing—loudly praising and worshipping Him.

This teaching runs right through the Old and New Testaments. For example, Joshua and his people blew their trumpets, and shouted with a great shout, before the city of Jericho was taken. But their shouting helped them win the victory, as the walls fell down. "Shout, for the Lord hath given you the city" was the commandment of God to His people (see Joshua chapter 6).

Gideon worshipped God **before** He revealed His Presence to the host of the Midianites (Judges 7:15). When he and his three hundred men shouted, before the battle, they won the victory.

The men of Judah "gave a shout" **before** the victory, and the Bible teaches that as they shouted God smote their enemies, and delivered them into their hands" (2 Chron. 13:15-16).

Jehoshaphat "appointed singers unto the Lord, and that should praise the beauty of holiness, as they went out before the army, and to say. Praise the Lord; for his mercy endureth for ever." This was **before** the battle even started. But what was the result?

"And when they began to sing and to praise, the Lord set ambushments against the children of Ammon, Moab, and mount Seir, which were come against Judah; and they were smitten" (2 Chron. 20:22).

When Jonah found that prayer was insufficient, he began to praise the Lord, and said:

"I will sacrifice unto thee with the voice of thanksgiving."

The result?

"And the Lord spake unto the fish, and it vomited out Jonah upon the dry land" (Jonah 2:9-10).

Paul and Silas, deep down in the inner dungeon, their backs bleeding and their feet firmly bound, began at midnight to sing "praises unto God: and the prisoners heard them." **Before** they were free they worshipped God. But there is power in praising God, and God sent an earthquake, setting the prisoners free. The jailer was converted to Christ and his family formed a nucleus for the Philippian Church (Acts 16:19-34).

Many other examples could be given of this Bible teaching—we must commence praising God, even before we see the fullness of that which we desire. And we praise Him with praises which can be heard!

Verses 17 to 24

There are many blessed truths in these verses, but we have space for only a few brief observations here.

Verse 17: Here we read of Asaph. How many of us have been blessed again and again by the Psalms of Asaph, without realizing that they were written at the Tabernacle of David? For Asaph recorded the prophecies and songs in the Spirit which were given before the Ark. These are preserved for us today in the book of Psalms.

For example, Asaph wrote:
"Out of Zion, the perfection of beauty,
God hath shined" (Psalm 50:2).

May we too in these days of Restoration sing the same Psalms "by lifting up the voice with joy" (verse 16).

Verse 18: Here we have a list of those who sang "the second degree." In the Hebrew language "second" means "a copy or double." The word "degree" means "a going up, or ascent." And so we see in verse 18 the list of singers who sang a higher part or harmony to the melody.

Verse 19: Here we have a list of those who not only sang, but they also "were appointed to sound the cymbals of brass."

Some years ago I played in a Broadcasting Symphony Orchestra in New Zealand. Whenever the music reached a particular climax, or an exciting passage was being played by the orchestra, one player clashed brass cymbals together. It certainly had the desired effect of conveying that something important was happening in that music.

Cymbals resounded heralding the most exciting event in Old Testament History—the restoring of the Ark of God to Zion.

Verse 20: Here we have listed for us those who were to play on psalteries. These instruments were actually harps, which resembled guitars. They were plucked with the fingers, and had a superior tone which was the result of them having a rounded back, similar to the string instruments we saw in the string bands in the Scandinavian churches.

These psalteries were set to "alamoth." This term is derived from the Hebrew word *alamah* which means "a virgin," and has reference to the higher pitch of her voice when compared with that of an adult man's voice. A modern day equivalent of *alamoth* would be "soprano," or "treble." At least one psalm (Psalm 46) was written especially for this treble voice. Some translate *alamoth* as "psalms of the virgins which danced" or "praised God with the dance." As we have already seen, it was not uncommon for Old

Testament women to rejoice before the Lord, praising Him with dancing.

Verse 21: Here we have a list of those who played "with harps on the Sheminith to excel." *Sheminith* means the "eighth note," or the "octave." In comparison with the *alamoth*, these sang eight notes lower and could be compared today to the bass voice. Both Psalms 6 and 12 were especially dedicated to the *Sheminith*.

Verse 22: In the *Amplified Bible* version this verse reads:

"Chenaniah, leader of the Levites in singing, was put in charge of carrying the Ark and lifting up song. He instructed about these matters, because he was skilled and able" (I Chron. 15:22).

Let us carefully note here, that **there is a direct relationship between the Ark of the Covenant and the noise of song, praise and rejoicing.** Every part of the Ark and its contents, as we have seen, speaks of the Lord Jesus Christ. By the Power of the Spirit, Who is given to glorify Christ (John 16:14), the Presence of Christ is being restored today to His people. The Ark of the Covenant and its contents are being restored today in spiritual application. As a direct result of this Restoration, there is praise, worship, song and rejoicing in the Church as never before. The Ark of the Covenant is also called "The Ark of thy Strength"(Psalm 132:8). And directly related to strength is joy. For the Bible says:

"The joy of the Lord is your strength" (Neh. 8:10).

So we could go on. Verse 24 tells us others "did blow with the trumpets before the Ark of God." The essential point is this—they brought the "Ark of the Covenant of the Lord out of the house of Obededom **with joy**" (verse 25).

We have already seen God helps and blesses those who rejoice before Him. Thus, it is written in the next verse (verse 26) God helped them as they brought up the Ark of the Covenant of the Lord with joy.

Verse 28: God here gives a clear picture of the exact manner in which the Ark of the Lord came to the Tabernacle of David:

*"Thus all Israel brought up the Ark of the Covenant of the Lord with shouting, and with sound of the cornet, and with trumpets, and with cymbals, **making a noise** with psalteries and harps."*

Yes, dear friend, they "were making a noise." There was no "let us now wait upon God in silence." While it may upset some of us a little, this is the exact way in which God has promised to restore the Tabernacle of David in the day in which we live. Loud praise and worship is not for a fanatical few. It is for all who will bring up the Ark of God. It is for all who long for the Power of His Presence.

Continual Praise

Moving on for a moment to chapter 16 of I Chronicles, we see they brought the Ark of God and put it in the middle of the Tent David had pitched for it. The journey of the Ark to Zion had finished. But the praise and worship did not finish! The rejoicing did not stop with the bringing up of the Ark to Zion. In 1 Chronicles 16:6 we read that they sounded and played and praised God the Lord "**continually** before the Ark of the Covenant of God."

There was continual praise. It was non-stop. It was 24 hours a day, 7 days a week. It made no difference whether it was day or night.

They praised God all day continually:

"My tongue shall speak ... of thy praise all the day long" (Psalm 35:28).

They praised God night continually:

"Behold, bless ye the Lord, all ye servants of the Lord, which by night stand in the house of the Lord.
Lift up your hands in the sanctuary, and bless the Lord.
The Lord that made heaven and earth bless thee out of Zion" (Psalm 134:1-3).

Without doubt, the Tabernacle of David was the noisiest place on earth! The place where people gathered together to meet with God and to worship Him—church, if you like. And today God is restoring this noisy

Tabernacle according to His own promise!

"Continually" is the word. David's Psalms (given by the Spirit at the Tabernacle of David), are filled with this blessed truth:

"I will bless the Lord at all times: His praise shall **continually** *be in my mouth" (Psalm 34:1).*

Not only in his heart, but also in his mouth!

"Let them shout for joy, and be glad, that favour my righteous cause: yea, let them say continually. Let the Lord be magnified, which hath pleasure in the prosperity of his servant" (Psalm 35:27).

But today, the Greater Ark of the New Covenant, our Saviour Jesus Christ is returning in all the Power of His Presence in revival in these last days. And the New Testament commandment concerning praise is this same word—"**continually**"!

"By Him therefore let us offer the sacrifice of praise to God **continually**, *that is, the fruit of our lips giving thanks to His Name" (Heb. 13:15).*

This is a New Testament commandment to New Testament Christians.

Why, even before they received the Holy Spirit, the early disciples "were **continually** in the temple, praising and blessing God" (Luke 24:53).

Continual praise and worship. This is the praise that pleases our God.

Praise That Pleases

In Revelation chapter 4, we read of those who praise and worship God in heaven. Then in verse 11, we see a direct connection between worship and pleasing God:

"Thou are worthy, O Lord, to receive
glory and honour and power: for thou hast
created all things, and for thy pleasure they are
and were created" (Rev. 4:11).

Do we not all want to please God? Then let us praise Him according to His Word, for this is well pleasing in His sight.

Praise that Pleases

How did the people bring the Presence of God to the Tabernacle of David? What did they do?

They lifted up their voices.
They sang with all their might.
Some sang high piercing notes.
Others sang deep and low.
There was dancing before the Lord.
They blew loud-sounding trumpets.
They clashed cymbals of brass.
They strummed guitars.
They shouted the high praises of God.
They rejoiced greatly before the Lord.

Why?

Because the Power of the Presence of God was with them.

The Ark of God is coming. Do you worship God "continually"? Does God receive pleasure from the continual praise of your lips?

This is praise which pleases.

Chapter Eighteen
PRAISE YE THE LORD

Time and again the Bible commands us to praise God. Both Old and New Testaments agree that God's true people are a praising people. Peter teaches that God brought us to Himself to praise Him;

"But ye are a chosen generation, a royal priesthood, an holy nation, a peculiar people; that ye should shew forth the praises of him who hath called you out of darkness into his marvellous light" (1 Pet. 2:9).

Paul also teaches:

"We should be to the praise of His glory, who first trusted in Christ" (Eph. 1:12).

As we have already seen, a loud demonstration of praise and worship took place as the Ark of God, the Power and Presence of God, was on its way to David's Tabernacle. This praise and worship continued when the Ark of the Covenant was set up in the Tabernacle of David. We are commanded over and over again to praise God. God is restoring the Tabernacle of David just as He did in Bible days, with praise, with worship, and rejoicing before the Lord. Because of this, we must be clear about what the Bible teaches concerning praise today.

Most Christians will say, "Oh, but I do praise God. We sing hymns in our church. I thank God daily for His blessings." While these are both good and commendable, the Bible teaches there is much more to praising God than this.

How many of us really **do** what the Bible commands us to do in praising God? Yet the Bible commands: *"Be ye doers of the word, and not hearers only, deceiving your own selves" (James 1:22).*

Are we doers of the word when it comes to praising God? Do you do all that God commands when praising Him? Do you use the Bible methods of praise in your church? We will study God's commandment to "Praise Ye the Lord" under our four headings:—

    I.   **WHEN** should we praise God?

   II. **WHERE** should we praise God?

  III. **HOW** should we praise God?

  IV. **WHY** should we praise God?

Let us now answer these questions from the Word of God.

I. WHEN SHOULD WE PRAISE GOD?

We have already seen the answer to this question in our last chapter. The Bible commandment is; "continually." There is no room for doubt, argument, or error here:

> "Let all those that seek thee rejoice and be glad in thee: and let such as love thy salvation say **continually**, Let God be magnified" (Psalm 70:4).

> "My praise shall be **continually** of thee" (Psalm 71:6).

Again King David says:

> "Blessed—happy, fortunate and to be envied — are those who dwell in Your House and Your Presence (the Tabernacle of David); they will be singing Your praises all the day long" (Psalm 84:4, Amplified Bible).

The New Testament clearly links the fullness of the Spirit, rejoicing in the Lord, and continual praise;

> "Be filled with the Spirit;
>
> Speaking to yourselves in psalms and hymns and spiritual songs, singing and making melody in your heart to the Lord;
>
> Giving thanks **always** for all things unto God and the Father in the Name of our Lord Jesus Christ" (Eph. 5:18-20).

To those who know the rich blessing of praising God, this is not vain repetition. It is a blessed, continual overflowing of the Rivers of Living Waters from within (John 7:38-39). Shall we not then obey God:

*"By Him (the Lord Jesus) therefore let us offer the sacrifice of praise to God **continually**, that is, the fruit of our lips giving thanks to his Name" (Heb. 13:15).*

II. WHERE SHOULD WE PRAISE GOD?

(1) In the Congregation (in Church)

"I will declare thy name unto my brethren: in the midst of the congregation will I praise thee" (Psalm 22:22).

"I will give thee thanks in the great congregation: I will praise thee among much people" (Psalm 35:18).

"Praise ye the Lord (margin. Hallelujah). Sing unto the Lord a new song, and His praise in the congregation of saints" (Psalm 149:1).

Many think we should enter mournfully into church, and into the Presence of God. However, the Bible teaches us exactly the opposite:

"Serve the Lord with gladness; come before His presence with singing. Enter into His gates with thanksgiving, and into His courts with praise: be thankful unto Him, and bless His Name" (Psalm 100: 2. 4).

Others say we should be quiet and silent in church. Sometimes this is called being "reverent." However, not one Scripture in the whole Bible can be found to support this idea! Rather, the Bible teaches the very opposite. The Bible teaches all should come into the house of God to worship and praise God together:

"I will bless the Lord at all times: his praise shall continually be in my mouth. O magnify the Lord with me, and let us exalt His Name together" (Psalm 34: 1, 3).

The New Testament also gives this same exhortation :

"Ye may with one mind and one mouth glorify God" (Rom. 15:6).

Blessed indeed are "the people who know the joyful sound" (Psalm 89:15) of seasons of praise and worship, where all the congregation "with one mouth" sing and shout their praises, glorifying the Lord.

(2) We Should Praise God in Our Homes;

"Let the saints be joyful in the glory and beauty (which God confers upon them); let them sing for joy upon their beds" (Psalm 149:5, Amplified Bible).

Actually, if we are really obeying the answer to our first question, and praising God continually, the answer to our second question will automatically be, "EVERYWHERE"!

(3) Before Unbelievers

Should we praise and worship God in front of those who do not know Jesus Christ as their Saviour? Some feel that loud and demonstrative worship will scare away those who are not familiar with it. But once again, the Bible teaches just the opposite:

"And he hath put a new song in my mouth, even praise unto our God: many shall see it, and fear, and shall trust in the Lord" (Psalm 40:3).

As the Amplified Bible translates the last part of this verse:

"Many shall see and fear—revere, and worship—and put their trust and confident reliance in the Lord."

Many other Scriptures could be listed commanding us to praise God before all people, with the resultant turning to the Lord of those who know Him not. When the Philippian jailer saw the results of two of his prisoners praising God, he and his household were converted to Christ, and followed Him through the waters of baptism! (Acts 16:25-34).

(4) We Should Praise God in the Harvest Fields

The Bible teaches we should praise God in every land where we minister the Gospel of Christ, encouraging all people to do the same. Here are just a few of the Biblical commands we could list:

"Make a joyful noise unto the Lord, all ye lands" (Psalm 100:1).

"I will praise thee, O Lord, among the people: and I will sing praises unto thee among the nations" (Psalm 108:3).

"O sing unto the Lord a new song: sing unto the Lord, all the earth. Sing unto the Lord, bless his name; shew forth his salvation from day to day.

Declare his glory among the heathen, his wonders among all people" (Psalm 96:1-3).

"Make a joyful noise unto the Lord, all the earth: make a loud noise, and rejoice, and sing praise" (Psalm 98:4).

Encouraging the people to whom we minister to praise the Lord focuses their attention on Jehovah, and His Son the Lord Jesus Christ. It is our solemn responsibility to teach people everywhere how to praise and worship God—using the Bible methods to express worship and adoration o the Lord.

(5) We should Especially Praise God at Zion, in the Tabernacle of David

The Bible exhorts all who dwell in Zion to worship God, making a joyful noise unto Him:

"Exalt the Lord our God, and worship at his holy hill" (Psalm 99:9).

"Praise thy God, O Zion" (Psalm 147: 12).

"Cry out and shout, thou inhabitant of Zion: for great is the Holy One of Israel in the midst of thee" (Isaiah 12:6).

"Great is the Lord, and greatly to be praised in the city of our God, in the mountain of his holiness.

Beautiful for situation, the joy of the whole earth, is mount Zion. . . .

Let mount Zion rejoice" (Psalm 48:1, 2, 11).

We are especially exhorted to worship God in "the House of the Lord"— the Tabernacle of David:

"Praise the Lord!—Hallelujah!

Praise the name of the Lord; praise Him, O you servants of the Lord! You who stand in the House of the Lord, in the courts of the House of our God,

Praise the Lord! For the Lord is good; sing praises to His name, for He is gracious and lovely!" (Psalm 135:1, 2. 3, Amplified Bible*).*

Oh, the blessings that are promised to those who experience the Restoration of the Tabernacle of David in their hearts! No wonder it is written:

"Blessed are they that dwell in thy House: they will be still praising thee" (Psalm 84:4).

Truly, those who know something of the return of the Power of the Presence of God to the Tabernacle of David, know how to praise and worship the Lord.

Praise Forever

Before leaving the subject of where we should praise and worship God, let us remember, if we think that loud, long praise and worship is not for us today, it will be much louder and much longer in heaven! There the praise sounds "as the voice of many waters, and as the voice of a great thunder." It is "with a loud voice" (Rev. 14:2, 7).

Some may object to loud "Hallelujahs" down here on earth. But what, I ask, will they do in heaven? For it is written:

"And 1 heard as it were the voice of a great multitude, and as the voice of many waters, and as the voice of mighty thunderings, saying. Alleluia: for the Lord God omnipotent reigneth" (Rev. 19:6).

"And again they said. Alleluia" (Rev. 19:3).

Surely those who are used to saying "Hallelujah" here below will feel more "at home" in heaven! We know that he who pitched the first Tabernacle of David will feel at home in heaven for he sang:

"1 will praise thee forever" (Psalm 52:9).

Chapter Nineteen

HOW SHALL WE PRAISE?

Let us now consider our third important question concerning worship and praise:—

III. HOW SHALL WE PRAISE GOD?

> *"Quicken thou me according to thy Word ... And quicken thou me in thy way" (Psalm 119:25, 37).*

The answer to the question, "How should we praise God?" is simply, "according to Thy Word... in Thy way." We are to praise and worship God, and rejoice before Him, in the way He teaches us in His Word.

When the Presence and Power of God comes among His people, there will always be manifestations of that Power and Presence. There will always be spontaneous worship and adoration of the Lord, as there was when the Ark of God came to the Tabernacle of David. And as the Ark of God returns to the Tabernacle of David which God is restoring, there are the same manifestations and the same praise and worship of God today. Some may call this praise and worship fanatical. Others may mock. (One actually did mock at the first Tabernacle of David—and deeply regretted having done so for the rest of her life). Yet others may even go so far as to call this heresy. The Apostle Paul testified:

> *"But this I confess unto thee, that after the way which they call heresy, so worship I the God of my fathers, believing all things which are written in the law and in the prophets" (Acts 24:14).*

Do all of us today believe all things written in the law and the prophets concerning worship? More than this—are we doing them?

Others may criticise believing and practising Biblical methods of praise and worship as emotionalism. That Biblical commandments and teachings should be criticised at all is serious enough. But he who can experience the Power and Presence of God's amazing love, and not have at times his emotions deeply stirred, must be, to say the least, of a very hard heart.

Billy Graham says of emotionalism;

"Some people accuse us of too much emotionalism. I say we have too little. This is why we are losing church people to other interests. We need not only to capture their minds, we've got to touch their hearts. We've got to make people feel their faith."[1]

TIME Magazine recently reported (September 27, 1968), under the headline, "That New Black Magic":

"As organized religion loses its appeal through its stuffiness and sterility, people seeking faith increasingly turn to mystical religions..."

In ten years of travelling for Christ through many lands, I have never yet seen a church which worshipped God in Spirit and in truth, practising the Biblical methods of praise and worship, with a decreasing membership.

"How should we praise God?" Here is a list of 14 Biblical ways by which we are exhorted to praise and worship God. Each one is a God-given expression of worship and adoration to the Lord.

(1) Praise God with Praise Which can be Heard

"O bless our God, ye people, and make the voice of his praise to be heard" (Psalm 66:8).

And how was the voice of His praise to be made audible? The answer is in verse 17:

"I cried aloud to Him; He was extolled and high praise was under my tongue" (Amplified Bible).

God commands us in His Word:

"Make a joyful noise unto the Lord . . . make a loud noise, and rejoice, and sing praise" (Psalm 98:4).

---

1   The Quotable Billy Graham (Murray Publishing Company).

David said that even when he was praying he "made a noise"(Psalm 55:2). How much more should our praise and worship be heard?

Thus we see it is not just a matter of worshipping God quietly in our hearts. The Bible commands that our voices be heard praising and worshipping the Lord.

(2) Praise God With Shouting

The Bible commands us to:

"Shout to God with the voice of triumph and songs of joy!" (Psalm 47:1, Amplified Bible).

Again the Bible commands:

"Let them shout for joy, and be glad, that favour my righteous cause: yea, let them say continually. Let the Lord be magnified" (Psalm 35:27).

Yet again it is written in the psalms of David:

"Let thy priests be clothed with righteousness; and let thy saints shout for joy" (Psalm 132:9).

Here again we see emphasized the transition from the legal and ceremonial to the spiritual. David is not so much concerned with the outward form of the priestly garments, but he is vitally concerned that the priests experience the righteousness of God in their lives. Also, he encourages the people to "shout for joy"—vastly different from the silent formality in the tabernacle of Moses.

It may not fit in with the mournful silence and decorum some feel should be seen in the house of God. However, the Bible teaches "**all** Israel brought up the Ark of the Covenant of the Lord with shouting" (1 Chron. 15:28). And God is restoring the Tabernacle of David with exactly the same expression of praise and worship—shouting.

(3) Praise God with Singing

"Sing praises to God, sing praises: sing praises unto our King, sing praises" (Psalm 47:6).

The book of Psalms was actually the "Hebrew Hymnal," the Book of Praises, hymns, or songs, designed to be set to music and used in the worship of God. A large number of these psalms, or hymns, are "songs of Zion"—songs given by the Spirit of God and recorded at the Tabernacle of David. But during the captivity, the people were not able to sing the joyful songs of Zion.² And so it is today. Those who are bound, who have not yet fully appreciated "the glorious liberty of the children of God"* are unable to worship God with spontaneous songs of praise and worship.

New Testament Christians are commanded:

"Be filled with the Spirit: Speaking to yourselves in psalms and hymns and spiritual songs, singing and making melody in your heart to the Lord:

Giving thanks always for all things unto God and the Father in the Name of our Lord Jesus Christ" (Eph. 5:18-20).

No doubt, in the early Church, the Old Testament Psalms were used. Several passages of the letters of Paul were used as hymns. Yet many songs were given spontaneously by the Spirit. As Arthur Way says in the preface to his popular translation, *The Letters of Saint Paul*:

*"Paul tells the Ephesian Christians to 'speak to one another in psalms, in hymns, in chants inspired by the Spirit.' Passages from the Psalms were sung by them no doubt. It is by no means certain that the 'Psalms' referred to are the Psalms of David and it can hardly be so in First Corinthians 14:26. The context shows that the composition of the psalms (or hymns) was one **manifestation of the Gifts of the Spirit.**"*

Paul also says:

"I will sing with my spirit—by the Holy Spirit that is within me; but I will sing (intelligently) with my mind and understanding also" (1 Cor. 14:15, Amplified Bible*).*

What tongue can describe with natural words that which is altogether supernatural? Here words fail us altogether. Who can ever forget being in

---

2   See Psalm 137.

a congregation with Spirit-filled sons and daughters of God, experiencing the singing lifted up by the Holy Spirit, where the words, melodies, and harmonies are all given by the Spirit. Most testify that in such times of worship they know the Presence of God in a very real and special way.

John Sherrill, well-known journalist, and a conventional Episcopalian, began, as a journalist, an objective investigation into the recurrence of "speaking with tongues" and other miraculous manifestations of the Holy Spirit in his own, and other historic denominations. (John and Elizabeth Sherrill were associated with David Wilkerson in the writing of the widely-read book *The Cross and The Switchblade*). He recalls the first time he heard singing in the Spirit:

> *"As the music continued, several people at the tables began to sing 'in the Spirit' Soon the whole room was singing a complicated harmony-without-score, created spontaneously. It was eerie but extraordinarily beautiful. The song leader was no longer trying to direct the music, but let the melodies create themselves: without prompting one quarter of the room would suddenly start to sing very loudly while others subsided. Harmonies and counter-harmonies wove in and out of each other."*[3]

We would in no wise belittle the inspired hymns of Wesley, Luther, Crosby, Alexander, and a host of others God has used to write words expressing our praise and worship to Him. But let us also remember that the Lord has provided two Spirit-inspired methods by which we may sing unto Him— with our understanding, and with our spirits. Let us then "Praise ye the Lord: for it is good to sing praises unto our God" (Psalm 147:1).

(4) Praise God With Thanksgiving

"I will praise the name of God with a song, and will magnify him with thanksgiving" (Psalm 69:30).

Thanksgiving is much more than saying grace at the meal table. The

---

3   *They Speak With Other Tongues*, by John L. Sherrill, (Hodder and Stoughton).

Bible says we are to magnify God with thanksgiving. Concerning thanksgiving, we may also note that God may be magnified with thanksgiving in unknown tongues, as the Holy Spirit gives utterance. The Bible teaches "if you bless and render thanks with (your) spirit (thoroughly aroused by the Holy Spirit)"—that is, by speaking in unknown tongues (verse 14)—you "to be sure . . . give thanks well" (1 Cor. 14:16, 17).[4]

(5) Praise God With a Joyful Noise

"Make a joyful noise unto God, all ye lands: Sing forth the honour of his name: make his praise glorious" (Psalm 66:1, 2).

Billy Graham's "Decision" Magazine recently published the following incident from the life of the famous composer, Franz Haydn:

"A friend once asked the great composer Haydn why his church music was always so full of gladness. He answered, 'I cannot make it otherwise: I write according to the thoughts I feel; when I think upon my God, my heart is so full of joy, that the notes dance and leap from my pen; and since God has given me a cheerful heart, it will be pardoned me that I serve Him with a cheerful spirit.'"

Let us heed God's invitation:

"O come, let us sing unto the Lord: let us make a joyful noise to the rock of our salvation" (Psalm 95:1).

How did David and his people bring the Ark of God to Zion? "With Joy" (1 Chron. 15:25). Because the very Presence of God dwelt between the cherubim of the Ark. Thus God was with them in the Power of His Presence, and as the Bible says,

"Thou wilt show me the path of life: in thy Presence is fullness of joy" (Psalm 16:11).

(6) Praise God With Crying out

"Cry out and shout, thou inhabitant of Zion: for great is the Holy One of Israel in the midst of thee" (Isaiah 12:6).

---

4   *Amplified Bible.* However, single or solitary outbursts in tongues must be interpreted, in the church, that the whole church may be edified.

How Shall We Praise?

It happened in Zion of old, and it happens in spiritual Zion today. When the Majesty and Greatness of the Presence of God is in the midst of His people. His people cry out their praises and worship to Him.

The famous evangelist, Charles Finney, testified that he "bellowed out," and "cried out" when he received his baptism in the Holy Spirit while alone in his law office on October 10, 1821. He says:

"I then received a mighty baptism of the Holy Ghost. Without any expectation of it, without ever having the thought in my mind that there was such a thing for me, without any recollection that I had ever heard the thing mentioned by any person in the world, the Holy Spirit descended upon me in a manner that seemed to go through me, body and soul. I could feel the impression like a wave of electricity, going through me. Indeed, it seemed to come in waves of liquid love. It seemed like the very breath of God. I can recollect distinctly that it seemed to fan me like immense wings. No words can express the wonderful love that was shed abroad in my heart. I wept aloud with joy and love: and I do not know but I should say, I literally bellowed out the unutterable gushings of my heart. These waves came over me, and over me, one after the other, until I cried out, 'I shall die if these waves continue to pass over me.' I said, 'Lord, I cannot bear any more.' Yet I had no fear of death...

"Thus I continued till late at night, when I received some sound repose. When I awoke in the morning the sun had risen, and was pouring a clear light into my room. Words cannot express the impression that this sunlight made upon me. Instantly the baptism that I had received the night before returned upon me in the same manner. I arose upon my knees in the bed and wept aloud with joy, and remained for some time too much overwhelmed with the baptism of the Spirit to do anything but pour out my soul to God. It seemed as if this morning's baptism was accompanied with a gentle reproof, and the Spirit seemed to say to me, 'Will you doubt? Will you doubt?' I cried, 'No! I will not doubt; I cannot doubt.'"

Would to God all who preach the Word today receive such a mighty baptism with the Holy Ghost and fire, and be as unashamed to cry out to God as Finney was!

(7) Praise God With Speaking in Tongues

When the one hundred and twenty were filled with the Spirit on the Day of Pentecost, they were heard praising the Lord in other tongues, telling forth "the wonderful works of God" (Acts 2:11). Peter's companions at Caesarea were convinced that Cornelius and his company had received the gift of the Holy Spirit "for they heard them speak with tongues, and magnify God" (Acts 10:46). And as we have already noticed, the Bible teaches the one who worships God in an unknown tongue speaks "unto God" and "givest thanks well" (1 Cor. 14:2, 17).

Jesus said speaking in new tongues was a sign all believers may enjoy. (Mark 16:17). How often those who love the Lord with all their hearts, have been at a loss for words to express their love, praise, and adoration to Him. Then the Holy Spirit takes over, and the spirit of the believer who has received the baptism with the Holy Ghost praises God. In this way the believer "who speaks in a strange tongue edifies and improves himself" (1 Cor. 14:4, *Amplified Bible*). For praise is born in the heart, and expressed with the tongue.

"Praise ye the Lord. I will praise the Lord with my whole heart" (Psalm 111:1).

"My tongue shall speak . . . Thy praise" (Psalm 35:28).

(8) Praise God With Laughter

"When the Lord turned again the captivity of Zion, we were like them that dream.

Then was our mouth filled with laughter, and our tongue with singing: then said they among the heathen. The Lord hath done great things for them.

The Lord hath done great things for us; whereof we are glad" (Psalm 126:1, 2, 3).

How Shall We Praise?

Laughter in church? Why, say some, the very thought seems sacrilegious. And yet some Christians will laugh at ridiculous, trivial amusements, and think nothing of it. The greatest joy in all the world is the joy which Jesus gives—the joy of the Lord. And they laugh, whose heart He makes merry.

One of the greatest outpourings of the Holy Spirit ever to take place in India occurred more than sixty years ago at Kedgaon, 30 miles from Poona.

As the Holy Spirit fell at Ramabai Mukti Mission, literal fire was seen.[5] Hundreds were baptized with the Holy Ghost and fire according to the promise of the Lord, and hundreds more were saved. Scriptural manifestations of the Power of God were witnessed, including shaking, dancing before the Lord, speaking with tongues, laughter, praise and worship, and many more. As always, when one section of God's Church receives an outpouring of the Spirit, there were criticisms at the manifestations of the Power of God. Writing in defence of these, Ramabai refers to praising God with laughter:

"On the day of Pentecost the manifestations were so great that the people mocked, saying, 'These men are full of new wine.' We are told in these days to suppress all manifestations of the Spirit as they are not proper... A young woman in church was on her knees between the pews, when with closed eyes, her mouth was filled with laughter and praise, because of the joy the Lord had poured out upon her. An elder sitting along the same pew saw this and arose demanding that it be stopped, as this was not proper behaviour in the house of God. If these manifestations of the Holy Spirit had been stopped on the day of Pentecost, the crowds of people would not have come together to enquire what had happened, and 3,000 people would not have been converted that day."[6]

---

5 For a fuller description of the revival at Kedgaon, see Chapter 14, "It Happened in India" of the author's book. *You Shall Receive Power.*

6 *The Baptism of the Holy Ghost and Fire*, (Printed at the "Mukti Mission" Press) 1906, by Pandita Ramabai.

Make no mistake about it. The Restoration of the Tabernacle of David is a restoration of joy. How many of us need such a restoration. We should pray with David:

"Restore unto me the joy of thy salvation; and uphold me with thy free spirit" (Psalm 51:12).

Again David said:

"Because Thy loving-kindness is better than life, my lips shall praise thee...my mouth shall praise thee with joyful lips" (Psalm 63:3, 5).

Is this your experience too?

(9) Praise God with Musical Instruments

As the Ark of the Covenant returned to the people of God, they praised God with almost every musical instrument available. So many Scriptures show we are commanded to praise God with musical instruments (for example, read Psalm 150). And the Bible teaches the musical instruments are to be played "with a loud noise":

"Rejoice in the Lord, O ye righteous: for praise is comely for the upright. Praise the Lord with harp: sing unto him with the psaltery and an instrument of ten strings.

Sing unto him a new song; play skilfully with a loud noise" (Psalm 33:1, 2, 3).

(10) Praise God by Bowing and Kneeling Before Him

"O come, let us worship and bow down: let us kneel before the Lord our maker" (Psalm 95:6).

This theme is seen also throughout the New Testament. For it is written, "At the Name of Jesus every knee should bow" (Phil. 2:10). Paul testified, "I bow my knees unto the Father of our Lord Jesus Christ" (Eph. 3:14). We are commanded to strengthen "the feeble knees" (Heb. 12:12). The Bible teaches kneeling is not just for praying, but also for praising, and giving God thanks.[7]

---

7   E.g. see Dan. 6:10

(11) Praise God By Falling Prostrate Before Him

"And Ezra blessed the Lord, the great God. And all the people answered. Amen, Amen, with lifting up their hands: and they bowed their heads, and worshipped the Lord with their faces to the ground" (Neh. 8:6).

This is not an uncommon sight today where the Power of God's Presence is manifested. Indeed, It has been an act of worship whenever God has moved by His Spirit in a mighty way. For example, John Wesley records in his Journal:

"We were present at our love-feast in Fetter Lane with about sixty of our brethren. About three in the morning as we were continuing instant in prayer, the power of God came mightily upon us, insomuch that many cried out for exceeding joy, and many fell to the ground. As soon as we were recovered a little from that awe and amazement at the presence of His Majesty, we broke out with one voice, 'We praise Thee, O God, we acknowledge Thee to be the Lord.'"[8]

Would these early Methodists with their emotional response to the moving of the Holy Spirit in their midst at three o'clock in the morning, be welcomed to some of our dry, formal one-hour services today?

(12) Praise God with Clapping of Hands

"O clap your hands, all ye people; shout unto God with the voice of triumph" (Psalm 47:1).

We clap our hands in appreciation of many things. A good item, a welcome, a good performance in a sporting event. Why then, be embarrassed to all clap hands together unto the Lord as an expression of our appreciation of Him? The Bible commands us to clap our hands unto the Lord.

(13) Praise God With the Lifting up of Hands

"Thus will I bless thee while I live: I will lift up my hands in thy name" (Psalm 63:4).

As we have already seen, when Ezra praised God, "All the people an-

---

8   *John Wesley's Journal*, Vol. I. Mon. Jan. 1, 1739 (emphasis ours).

swered. Amen, Amen, with lifting up their hands" (Neh. 8:6).

There was the lifting up of hands towards the Tabernacle of David:

"I lift up my hands toward the oracle of thy Sanctuary" (Psalm 28:2, marginal rendering).

In the New Testament we read that it is the will of God to "lift up holy hands, without wrath and doubting" (1 Tim. 2:8).

Again, it is written:

"Wherefore lift up the hands which hang down" (Heb. 12:12).

The *Amplified Bible* renders this verse:

"So then, brace up and reinvigorate and set right your slackened and weakened and drooping hands."

The Lord Jesus lifted up His hands upon the Cross of Calvary for us. Shall we not obey God's Word and lift up our hands in worship to Him? God commands us:

"Lift up your hands in the Sanctuary, and bless the Lord" (Psalm 134:2).

(14) Praise God With the Dance

"Praise Him with the dance" (Psalm 150:4).

Contrary to what some think, there are many references, in both Old and New Testaments, to rejoicing, praise, and worship being expressed in dancing. Dr. Robert Young's *Analytical Concordance to the Holy Bible* lists twenty-seven such references. While it is, as one writer has termed it, "the most extreme form of worship," dancing before the Lord is nevertheless a very blessed and Scriptural method of demonstrating our adoration of God. Only a few examples can be given here.

Moses sang the song of praise for the deliverance of the people from Egypt through the Red Sea (in which incidentally, is probably the first reference to the Tabernacle of David on Zion— Exod. 15:17). After this, his sister Miriam, together with all the women, praised God with dancing:

How Shall We Praise?

"And Miriam the prophetess, the sister of Aaron, took a timbrel in her hand; and all the women went out after her with timbrels and with dances.

And Miriam answered them. Sing ye to the Lord, for He hath triumphed gloriously; the horse and his rider hath He thrown into the sea" (Exod. 15:20, 21).

Gideon and his three hundred men knew the value of praise. For when they cried aloud and shouted, breaking their pitchers and blowing their trumpets, the enemy was dismayed. Gideon and his men pursued the Midianites to Abel-meholah, and it was there the enemy was defeated. Abel-meholah means "**the meadow of the dance.**"

One of King Solomon's twelve officers appointed over his food was to supply provisions for one month of the year from Abel-meholah, the meadow of the dance (1 Kings 4:7, 12). And today, dancing before the Lord is part of the table spread for us by the Greater than Solomon, the Lord Jesus Christ.

Elisha the prophet, who received the double portion of the Spirit of Elijah, was born at Abel-meholah, the meadow of the dance (1 Kings 19:16). God grant that today many more Elishas be born in the revival times of praise and worship, including dancing before the Lord.

When the tabernacle of Moses was at Shiloh, the daughters of Shiloh came "out to dance in dances" at certain feast days unto the Lord. "The children of Benjamin . . . took them wives, according to their number, of them that danced" (Judges 21:19-23). At certain times of the year, during the feasts unto the Lord, dancing was an integral part of rejoicing before Him in praise and worship. And today, "the people who know the joyful sound (who understand and appreciate the spiritual blessings symbolized by the feasts)"[9] also know the blessing of dancing before the Lord in expression of their love and praise to Him.

Dancing before the Lord was a customary part of victory processions

---

9   Psalm 89:15, *Amplified Bible.*

in the Old Testament. For example, when David was victorious over the Philistines:

"And it came to pass as they came, when David was returned from the slaughter of the Philistine, that the women came out of all cities of Israel, singing and dancing, to meet king Saul, with tabrets, with joy, and with instruments of musick" (1 Sam. 18:6).[10]

Turning to the New Testament, we read the father commanded music and dancing and making merry at the return of his prodigal son (Luke 15:22-25). Let us be careful not to react as the prodigal elder brother did!

But so many of us today could be described in the words of our Lord:

"We have piped unto you, and ye have not danced" (Matt. 11:17).

Dr. Edwin Orr has said in his book. *Full Surrender*:

"Now I share with Dr. Ironside, the view, that if a Christian is happy and feels like dancing, there is no reason why he should not go to his room or another suitable place and dance before the Lord"[11]

The Preacher declares:

"There is ... a time to mourn, and a time to dance" (Eccles. 3:1, 4).

Do you dance before the Lord with joy?

The Meaning of Dancing

The various Hebrew and Greek words from which our English word "dance" comes, have various shades of meaning which explain to us what this dancing before the Lord is. They are to keep festival, to turn, twist; to move round; to lift up the feet; to skip and leap.

---

10 See also 1 Sam. 21:11 and 29:5.
11 From *Full Surrender* by J. Edwin Orr (Marshall, Morgan 8s Scott). It was in Dr. Orr's meetings in St. Paul's Presbyterian Church, Christchurch, New Zealand, in 1956, that the author first clearly came to understand the fullness with the Spirit is a second operation of the Spirit, as distinct from conversion. It was a joy and a blessing to have him stay in our home here in India 10 years later. There are many other "suitable places" where we may dance before the Lord; for example, the house of God.

How Shall We Praise?

When the lame man was healed at the gate of the temple in Acts chapter 3, he entered into the temple walking, and leaping, and praising God (Acts 3:8). The crippled man at Lystra also leaped when he was healed (Acts 14:10). Look up all the references to leaping in the Bible. You will find this an interesting and rewarding study.

The great English translator of the Bible, William Tyndale (who was later arrested and burned at the stake for his reformer's zeal), defined the Gospel thus:

"EUAGELIO (that we call Gospel) is a Greek word, and signifieth good, merry, glad and joyful tidings, that maketh a man's heart glad, and maketh him sing, dance and leap for joy."[12]

Above all, hear the words of Jesus:

"Rejoice ye in that day, and leap for joy: for, behold, your reward is great in heaven: for in the like manner did their fathers unto the prophets" (Luke 6:23).

There it is. The commandment of our Master. The Lord Jesus also said we were to love God with all our strength. And it takes all our strength to leap and dance before Him in worship, adoration and praise. (Mark 12:30).

The Restoration of Praising God With the Dance

When the people of God were in captivity, the prophet Jeremiah lamented:

"The joy of our heart is ceased; our dance is turned into mourning" (Lam. 5:15).

But the Lord revealed by His Spirit that there was coming a day of Restoration. Concerning this day of Restoration, God said:

"In the latter days ye shall consider it (Amplified—understand this)" (Jer. 30:24).

Then the Lord speaks of the wonderful rebuilding of which we have spoken so much:

---

12   As quoted in *Decision* Magazine, May 1968.

THE POWER OF HIS PRESENCE

"*At the same time (the latter days— chapter 30:24) saith the Lord . . .*
"*Again I will build thee, and thou shalt be built, O virgin of Israel: thou shalt again be adorned with thy tabrets, and shalt go forth in the dances of them that make merry. . .*
Then shall the virgin rejoice in the dance, both young men and old together: for I will turn their mourning into joy, and will comfort them, and make them rejoice from their sorrow" (Jer. 31:1, 4, 13).

Dancing before the Lord is a direct result of this Last Day Restoration Revival—an expression of rejoicing in the Lord, praising God for all His goodness. This is particularly true of the Restoration of the Tabernacle of David in these Last Days.

When the Power of the Presence of God above the Ark of the Covenant came to Zion, David danced before the Lord:

"*David danced before the Lord with all his might*" (2 Sam. 6:14).

Despite all the blessings of God he had experienced, David had mourned and lamented after the fullness of the Power of His Presence. When he brought up the Ark of God to Zion, he testified that God turned his mourning into dancing:

"*Thou hast turned for me my mourning into* **dancing**: *thou hast put off my sackcloth, and girded me with gladness:*
To the end that my tongue[13] *may sing praise to thee, and* **not be silent**. *O Lord my God, I will give thanks unto thee forever*" (Psalm 30:11, 12).

And those who would take part in the Restoration of the Tabernacle of David, the children of Zion, are commanded to praise God with dancing:

"*Let the children of Zion be joyful in their King.*
Let them praise His name in the dance" (Psalm 149:2, 3).

---

13   Marginal rendering.

Chapter Twenty

WHY SHOULD WE PRAISE?

Why should we praise God? The Bible gives many reasons why we should praise God, and why we should use the Scriptural ways to praise Him. Here are just a few.

IV. WHY SHOULD WE PRAISE GOD?

(1) Because God Commands it in His Word

"Praise the Lord! for it is good . . . praise is becoming and appropriate" (Psalm 147:1, Amplified Bible*).*

God, in His Word, commands us to praise Him. Is this not good enough reason? Dare we disobey His Word? And to those who only want to seek God quietly, the Bible teaches that praise is an essential part of seeking God:

"They shall praise the Lord that seek Him" (Psalm 22:26).

(2) Because God Comes to Dwell in the Praises of His People

"But thou art holy, O thou that inhabitest the praises of Israel" (Psalm 22:3).

Here is one of the essential keys concerning the teaching of praise and worship. When God's people begin to praise and worship Him using the Biblical methods He gives, the Power of His Presence comes among His people in an even greater measure.

(3) Because There is Power in Praising God

The Bible teaches there is a distinct and direct connection between praise and Power or strength:

"Blessed are they that dwell in thy house: they will be still praising thee. Blessed is the man whose strength is in thee; in whose heart are the ways of them...

They go from strength to strength, every one of them in Zion appeareth before God" (Psalm 84:4, 5, 7).

The man who has his heart set on praising God in the Bible way, also has his strength in the Lord. Jesus made this clear by what He said when He rode into the city of Jerusalem.

As the Lord Jesus began His descent from the Mount of Olives, riding the colt into Jerusalem, the Bible says "the whole multitude of the disciples began to rejoice and praise God with a loud voice for all the mighty works that they had seen" (Luke 19:37). The Scripture records there were only two kinds of people present—those who were praising God with a loud voice, and the Pharisees who were trying to silence the loud praises. (We have the same two kinds of people with us as the Ark is being restored to Zion). The Lord Jesus answered the displeasure of the chief priests, scribes, and Pharisees by quoting Psalm 8:

"Have ye never read, Out of the mouth of babes and sucklings thou hast perfected praise?" (Matt. 21:16).

However, when we turn to Psalm 8:2, we read:

*"Out of the mouth of babes and sucklings hast thou ordained **strength**."*

Thus the Lord Himself teaches that perfect praise gives strength. Let us then heed God's commandment:

"Awake, awake; put on thy strength, O Zion" (Isaiah 52:1).

Not only this, the Lord teaches us that this rejoicing and praising with a loud voice is **perfected praise!** This certainly gave the scribes and Pharisees something to think about. This is not an emotional outlet for these particular people because it suits their make-up. This is not childish babbling. According to the words of Jesus, this loud noise, this rejoicing and praising God is "perfected praise."

Why Should We Praise?

Thus, there is a direct relationship between praise and strength. The Lord will "send thee help from the Sanctuary, and strengthen thee out of Zion," the place of continual praise, worship and rejoicing (Psalm 20:2). The Bible says, "The joy of the Lord is your strength" (Neh. 8:10). Luke records the disciples "were continually in the temple, praising and blessing God" (Luke 24:53). He also said they "returned to Jerusalem with great joy" (verse 52). Luke ends his Gospel with the disciples worshipping and praising God, and begins the Acts of the Apostles with them being filled with the strength and Power of God (Acts chapter 2).

Time and again praise brings victory, power, deliverance, and blessing. We have already noted the Biblical examples of Joshua, Gideon, the men of Judah, Jehoshaphat, Jonah, Paul and Silas. All experienced the Power of praise to win the victory, to deliver them, to bless them. And today we may still "triumph in thy praise" (Psalm 106:47).

It was in the Tabernacle he built on Mount Zion that David understood the end of his enemy:

"I went into the Sanctuary of God; then understood I their end...
Thou castedst them down into destruction" (Psalm 73:17, 18).

Yes! There is Power and strength in praising God. How many Christians are robbing themselves of so much blessing, victory, strength, power and deliverance, because they do not praise God in the Bible way.

(4) Because Praise Glorifies God

"Whoso offereth praise glorifieth me: and to him that ordereth his conversation aright will I shew the salvation of God" (Psalm 50:23).

It is the desire of every true son and daughter of God to glorify their heavenly Father. The Bible says that praising God is one of the ways we may glorify Him.

(5) Because it is a Good Thing to Praise the Lord

"It is a good thing to give thanks unto the Lord, and to sing praises unto thy name, O most High" (Psalm 92:1).

Contrary to what some people imagine, the Bible teaches it is a good, healthy spiritual exercise to worship and praise God in the Scriptural methods. One world-famous churchman once remarked that the Biblical manifestations were "ultimately healthy."

(6) Because Praise is Right

"Rejoice in the Lord, O ye righteous: for praise is comely (becoming, appropriate, proper and right) for the upright" (Psalm 33:1).

The Bible leaves us in no doubt as to what we should do. The Bible teaches that the right thing for those who know the righteousness of Christ in their hearts, is at all times, to praise, rejoice before, and worship the Lord.

(7) Because Praise Purifies

"As the fining pot for silver, and the furnace for gold; so is a man to his praise" (Prov. 27:21).

The Bible says the Lord is

"...like a refiner's fire...and He shall sit as a refiner and purifier of silver; and He shall purify the sons of Levi, and purge them as gold and silver, that they may offer unto the Lord an offering in righteousness" (Mal. 3:2, 3).

When God is sincerely worshipped in spirit and in truth, and the Power of His Presence is manifested in the hearts of His people, the refining fire of His Spirit works as a purifier making holy those whose hearts are fixed on Him, by praise and worship.

Thus we see some of the answers to the questions, WHEN, WHERE, HOW, and WHY we should praise God. The lists of reasons could go on. But these given from the Word of God should suffice. We are often challenged to examine our prayer life. This is good and right. But today God calls us to examine our **praise** life.

Do you praise God in the Biblical ways—as He has commanded you?

Chapter Twenty-one
ALL THAT IS WITHIN ME
1 Chronicles chapter 15 (continued)

"All that is within me, bless His Holy Name" (Psalm 103:1).

What is meant by the Biblical commandment to "bless His Holy Name"? What is the deep significance of praise and worship? The ultimate purpose of praise and worship is much more than the fourteen outward manifestations and expressions of adoration to our God. That in all things, all the glory might be rendered unto God, is a vital purpose of praise and worship. "That in all things He might have the preeminence," is the Word of God (Col. 1:18). "Do all to the glory of God" (1 Cor. 10:31)."

True praise and worship is also the acknowledgment and acceptance of God's will without question:

"If any man be a worshipper of God, and doeth His will, him He heareth" (John 9:31).

The Bible teaches that God Himself, the very Person of our Lord, must be the centre of existence for those who are His true children:

"For of Him, and through Him, and to Him, are all things: to whom be glory for ever. Amen" (Rom. 11:36).

To worship the Lord in the God-given ways is to bow in submission to the will of God, and acknowledge Him as Lord of all (Phil. 2:9-11). Apart from understanding the end results of praise and worship, it is not for us to ask why God has chosen these ways to worship Him:

"For my thoughts are not your thoughts, neither are your ways my ways, saith the Lord.

For as the heavens are higher than the earth, so are my ways higher than your ways, and my thoughts than your thoughts" (Isaiah 55:8, 9).

How true these verses are to any of us concerning our praise and worship. For so few seem to worship God in the ways He has laid down for us in His Word. We cannot rationalize and think these things out. If we wish to experience the Presence of His Power in the Restoration of the Tabernacle of David, it is for us, with child-like faith, to act upon His Word, and praise Him according to His ways. For, to know God is to love Him, and to love Him is to praise Him.

Spirit, Soul and Body

The Bible teaches man is a triune being—spirit, soul and body. The Bible also teaches God wills the spirit, soul and body of every believer be strong, sound and complete:

"May your spirit and soul and body be preserved sound and complete and found blameless at the coming of our Lord Jesus Christ, the Messiah" (1 Thess. 5:2, Amplified Bible).

The *Living Letters* renders these words:

"May your spirit, and soul and body be kept strong and blameless until that day when our Lord Jesus Christ comes back again."

The following verse says:

"Faithful is He that calleth you. Who also will do it" (1 Thess. 5:24).

Yes, God wants us to be strong, sound and complete in spirit, soul and body. As we have seen from God's Word, there is a direct relationship between our strength and our praise life. Those who are taking part in the Restoration of the Tabernacle of David are thus commanded:

"Awake, awake; put on thy strength, O Zion" (Isaiah 52:1).

As we have seen, there is strength in praising and worshipping God. Indeed, Jesus said that loud praise is strength, and perfected praise. If we would know the wholeness God desires for our spirit, soul and body, every part of our being—spirit, soul and body—must praise and worship Him.

All that is Within Me

Spirit, soul and body can be briefly defined:

(1) **Spirit** (Greek *pneuma*) is the "refined and higher part of man." It is the eternal, God-conscious spirit in man. The believer's spirit has been renewed in Jesus Christ, and "the Spirit Himself beareth witness with our spirit, that we are the children of God" (Rom. 8:16).

(2) **Soul** (Greek *psuche*) is between the spirit and body of man. The soul is the nature, character, and force of a man. The Greek word has the sense of "animal soul." It is the seat of the personality— will, mind, emotions, intellect. It is conscious of deeper things than can be experienced by the five senses, and craves higher ideals than the natural realm can supply.

(3) **Body** (Greek *soma*) is made of flesh, bone, blood, etc. and is formed to house both the spirit and the soul. The body reacts to the outside world via the five senses.

We can, therefore, observe:

(1) the spirit is God-conscious;

(2) the soul is self-conscious;

(3) the body is sense-conscious.

(1) The Spirit is to Worship God

All true praise, worship, and rejoicing before the Lord originates in the spirit:

*"For we are the circumcision, which worship God in the **spirit**, and rejoice in Christ Jesus, and have no confidence in the flesh" (Phil. 3:3).*

Mary praised God in her song of thanksgiving:

"My spirit hath rejoiced in God my Saviour" (Luke 1:47).

Note carefully what the Lord Jesus Himself taught concerning true worshippers:

"But the hour cometh, and now is, when the true worshippers shall worship the Father in spirit and in truth: for the Father seeketh such to worship Him. God is a spirit: and they that worship Him must worship Him in spirit and in truth" (John 4:23, 24).

To use the words of David:

"I will praise Thee, O Lord my God, with all my heart: and I will glorify Thy Name for evermore" (Psalm 86:12).

Yes, David worshipped God with all his heart. But notice *how* he expressed this praise and worship to God from his heart. Do we worship God with all our hearts in the same way today? We are commanded to.

(2) **The Soul is to Worship God**

Time and again David says, "Bless the Lord, O my soul" (Psalm 103:1). Again he says, "Hallelujah.' Praise the Lord, O my soul" (Psalm 146:1).

(3) **The Body is to Worship God**

Here we emphasize a very important distinction. The Bible clearly says that flesh is to praise God:

*"My mouth shall speak the praise of the Lord: and let **all flesh** bless His Holy Name for ever and ever" (Psalm 145:21).*

"I cried unto Him with my mouth" (which is flesh), *"and He was extolled with 'high praise'* (Amplified Bible) *with my tongue"* (which is flesh) *(Psalm 66:17).*

"I will greatly praise the Lord with my mouth" (which is flesh) *(Psalm 109:30).*

"O clap your hands" (which are flesh) *"all ye people" (Psalm 47:1).*

"Thus will I bless thee while I live: I will lift up my hands" (which are flesh) *"in Thy Name" (Psalm 63:4).*

The list could be multiplied many times.

However, we should be very careful to note that the Bible commands us to worship God *with* our body (which is flesh), but not *in* (motivated by) the flesh. **Only that which has its origin in the spirit is spiritual.** This cannot be over-emphasized.

All that *originates* in the soul is carnal, soulish.

All that *originates* in the body is fleshly, sensual.

Praise that pleases God is manifested *through* the soul and body of the

worshipper, but its *origin* is the Spirit of God moving upon the human spirit which has been renewed in Jesus Christ.

It is possible for Christians to praise for emotional pleasure, but the gratification of this desire only brings spiritual weakness and instability. On the contrary, however, praise and worship which originates, not in the soul, but in the spirit, and is motivated by the Holy Spirit of God, brings as we have already seen from the Bible, strength, and power.

The New Testament also teaches that we are to "glorify God in your body" (1 Cor. 6:20). But the previous verse speaks of our body being the temple of the Holy Spirit. It must be the Holy Spirit in us, making real the Power of His Presence. As we shall see in our next chapter, this does not mean that we sit idly waiting for a mighty move of the Holy Spirit to shake us and make us praise God in the Biblical ways. God does not force us to obey Him. But God will make real the Power of His Presence in the midst of those who praise and worship Him, by the Power of His Holy Spirit.

According to the Word of the Lord

> "And the children of the Levites bare the ark of God upon their shoulders with the staves thereon, as Moses commanded according to the word of the Lord.
>
> "And David spake to the chief of the Levites to appoint their brethren to be the singers with instruments of musick, psalteries and harps and cymbals, sounding, by lifting up the voice with joy.
>
> "Thus all Israel brought up the Ark of the Covenant of the Lord with shouting, and with sound of the comet, and with trumpets, and with cymbals, making a noise with psalteries and harps" (1 Chron. 15:15, 16, 28).

We are now in a position to return to another important aspect of the Tabernacle of David. We want to note the difference between the praise we read of in 1 Chronicles 13:8, and 1 Chronicles chapter 15.

We note that in 1 Chronicles 13:8 "David and all Israel played before God with all their might, and with singing, and with harps, and with psalteries, and with timbrels, and with cymbals, and with trumpets." While all this is commendable, the fact is that they could have rejoiced before the Lord and worshipped and praised Him for years, but they would never have known the fullness of the Power of His Presence. The Ark of the Covenant would never have come to the Tabernacle of David, despite all the praise. This brings us to emphasize yet again, that true worshippers not only praise God in Spirit but also "in truth (John 4:23-24). Jesus said, "Thy Word is truth"(John 17:17).

As we have seen, the people were not acting according to the Word of the Lord. As David confessed later, "We did not seek Him in the way He ordained" (1 Chron. 15:13, *Amplified Bible*). However, God did reveal the truth of the vital connection between praise and the Word to David:

"In God I will praise His Word" (Psalm 56:4, 10).

When the people began to act "according to the Word of the Lord," God was well pleased with their rejoicing, praise and worship.

There is only one safeguard to keep praise and worship from the soulish realm, and that is the Word of God. For it is written:

"For the Word of God is quick, and powerful, and sharper than any two-edged sword, piercing even to the dividing asunder of soul and spirit, and of the joints and marrow, and is a discerner of the thoughts and intents of the heart" (Heb. 4:12).

Without the sharp two-edged sword in operation, people just do not know the difference between soul and spirit. Thus they do not know whether they are worshipping God in the soulish or spiritual realm. But here we read of the separating power of the Word of God to take the parts of the whole being of man, and separate them, even as the Old Testament priest flayed and divided limb from limb the animal of the burnt offering.

The return to the pattern of the Word of God brought true worship and praise in the bringing back of the Ark of God to Zion. In like manner, the "sword of the Spirit, which is the Word of God" (Eph. 6:17) divides, and shows the believer the difference between his soul and his spirit, enabling him to worship God from his spirit through his soul and body.

Let All Things Be Done

This Last Day Restoration of the Tabernacle of David is a Restoration of all things. Furthermore, as we saw from the book of Jeremiah, this includes the Restoration of the Bible methods of praise and worship.

When faced with the Scriptural challenge to worship God in the Bible way, many are quick to quote 1 Corinthians 14:40, "Let all things be done decently and in order." With this command we most heartily agree. But let it be emphasized that this verse specifically commands, **"Let all things be done."** We should be careful to let God be the judge of that which is decent and in order. By this, 1 mean that which man often calls indecent and out of order, God calls decent and perfectly in order. David's wife called his dancing before the Lord indecent. But God did not. If Scriptural manifestations of rejoicing and praise and worship are used, how can man say that these are not decent and in order?

When the Spirit of God is outpoured upon man, and the Power of His Presence experienced. Biblical manifestations of His Power, and praise, are always witnessed. We have already mentioned the great outpouring of the Holy Spirit at Raimabai Mukti Mission in 1905. Here we share more of Pandita Ramabai's own testimony concerning the things which happened;

"The Holy Spirit has been poured out on many Indian churches, as on us at the beginning. Praise God! He is teaching the Indian Christians to know and understand spiritual things. Many are being anointed with the spirit of intercessory prayer, spending hours, lost to time and surroundings, pleading for the unsaved. Young men and women are receiving the GIFTS of the Spirit, speaking with tongues, interpreting tongues previously unknown to them; the sick are being healed, and unclean spirits cast out in answer to prayer. Where the Holy Spirit's work is not interfered with through some Uzzah putting his hands to the ark to steady it; where there is continued prayer, and faithful teaching of the Word, the people go on to experience repentance unto salvation, also repentance unto the baptism of the Holy Ghost and fire, and to receive power in prayer, and gifts of the Holy Spirit. Revivals

have come to those missions where the Word of God is honoured, and taught in simplicity, the minds of the people not having been filled with doubts...

"If we read the history of great revivals we shall find that perhaps without exception they have been accompanied with manifestations of the Holy Spirit. The Word of God also shows us that such manifestations have existed from the beginning. David danced for joy before the Ark of God. Ezekiel and Philip were caught away by the Holy Spirit. Paul saw a great light, heard a voice, fell suddenly while his whole body trembled, so mighty was the power of conviction that came upon him. On the day of Pentecost the manifestations were so great that the people mocked, saying, 'These men are full of new wine.'...

"In Assam and India trembling under the power of conviction, loud crying in prayer, the pouring forth to God in loud confession of sins of a lifetime, sudden falling on the ground, writhing, being twisted and violently thrown down when an unclean spirit has been cast out as the person has cried for deliverance, have been frequent scenes. Joy unspeakable, filling faces with glory, has been manifested by singing, clapping the hands, shouting praises, dancing...

"...but we have seen over and over again during the past fifteen months, that where Christian workers have suppressed these manifestations, the Holy Spirit has been grieved, the work has stopped, and no fruit of holy lives has resulted. Who are we to dictate to an all-wise God as to how He shall work in any one?"

Concerning her own experience, Ramabai writes:

"The writer testifies that she herself has, in the silence of the midnight hour, alone in her room without a sound in the house, been shaken from her innermost being, until her whole body was convulsed, and filled with joy and consciousness that the Holy Spirit had taken possession of every part of her being. No one had greater prejudice against religious excitement than she, but every time she put her hands upon the work at Mukti to suppress joy or strong conviction, or reproved persons being strongly wrought upon physically in prayer, the work *of revival stopped, and she had to confess her fault before it went on again. We have learned that God's ways are past finding out, as far above ours as the heavens are above the earth."* [1]

One wonders with what impact this mighty revival would have swept across India if the Biblical manifestations of the Power of God's Presence had been permitted to continue and develop. For that which appears to be "apparent confusion" is, as Ramabai has said, not confusion in the eyes of the Lord who ordained all these things.

"Let all things be done." Do you let all things be done in your church? Are all things done in your life?

Do you praise God with everything that is within you?

---

[1] From *The Baptism of the Holy Ghost and Fire*, Second Edition ("Mukti Mission" Press) 1906, by Pandita Ramabai.

Chapter Twenty-two

THE SACRIFICE OF PRAISE

1 Chronicles chapter 15 (continued)

Some of our readers may find it difficult at first to commence to worship God in the Biblical way. But in the ways of God, there seems to be a definite link between taking what appears to be a foolish step, which God has commanded, and receiving Power and blessing from Him. At God's command Moses lifted up his rod over the Red Sea and the waters parted. Joshua and his people marched around Jericho for seven days, shouted, and the walls fell down. Gideon's three hundred men conquered the host of Midian, armed only with pitchers, lanterns and trumpets. The blind man was commanded to wash, and he began to see. Peter was commanded to go and catch a fish, to find money to pay his taxes. Illustrations could be multiplied.

Billy Graham says concerning this paradox, that the secret lies in overcoming self-consciousness and self-will sufficiently to perform the task. Most people find it extremely difficult to get out of their chairs and walk forward in his large meetings. But this seemingly foolish step brings power with it.

Many Christians feel that praising and worshipping God, and rejoicing before Him in the Biblical way seems foolish, even embarrassing. But God's ways are not our ways. Who are we to dare doubt that which God has commanded in His Word? Who are we to question God? Should we not rather be acting on His Word than presumptuously questioning it? Some will excuse themselves by saying, "I don't feel like it." Others say they are waiting for God to move them. But would the same people wait until God moves them not to steal? Would the same people wait for God to move them before they tell the truth? The same God Who gives us clear commandments not to steal and to tell the truth, also gives the commandment to praise.

We are to praise. *We* are commanded to act upon the Word—to praise and worship God. Then, as we have seen, if we truly love the Lord, the Holy Spirit will give us strength to worship Him according to His Word. We do not need to fear we will be acting of ourselves, or "of the flesh."

Nevertheless, for many to worship God in the Scriptural manner will be a sacrifice—a sacrifice of praise. And this is exactly what God commands us to offer' unto Him.

The Meaning of Sacrifice

We have seen the Bible meaning of praise. But what is meant by a "sacrifice of praise"?

In the books of Moses we read of the animal sacrifices offered to God. However, the Lord Jesus Christ offered Himself on the Cross of Calvary for our sins. Now we no longer need to sacrifice animals to the Lord.

The Bible does not record that any sin offerings were offered in the Tabernacle of David. Rather, he says:

"I will praise the name of God with a song, and will magnify Him with thanksgiving.
This also shall please the Lord better than an ox or bullock that hath horns and hoofs" (Psalm 69:30, 31).

Just as an act of sacrificing an animal was made under the law, so we are commanded under grace, to make an act of the sacrifice of praise. The Greek word for sacrifice, *thusia*, according to *Vine's Expository Dictionary of New Testament Words*, "primarily denotes the act of offering." This is the word used in Hebrews 13:15 where we are commanded to offer the sacrifice of praise continually," and in 1 Peter 2:5 in which we are commanded

The Sacrifice of Praise

to offer unto God "spiritual sacrifices." Thus we see, this "sacrifice of praise" is not some vague thought or state of mind, but a definite act of worshipping and praising God in the Bible way.

The definition of "sacrifice" found in Webster's Dictionary is also very applicable and meaningful for us here:

"*Sacrifice*—the act of giving up something one has or wants, for the good of others; to make an offering to God; to give up, lose, renounce, or destroy for a cause."

We have (or want) popularity. Our Christian friends think of us as good, balanced, "normal" Christians, in the usual rut. But Jesus said, "Woe unto you, when all men shall speak well of you!" (Luke 6:26). Is it not better to give up our position and popularity, and begin to offer to God the sacrifice of praise in the Bible way, despite what others will think and say about us? What greater cause is there for which to lose your self-consciousness, renounce your self-will, and destroy your pride, than the praise and glory of God!

The Results of the Sacrifice

We have already noticed the great blessings which accompany those who praise and worship God—the Power of His Presence, deliverance, victory, to mention but a few. Let us just here remind ourselves again of Jonah.

As you remember, Jonah was swallowed by a great fish, and was inside the fish for three days and three nights. The second chapter of the book of Jonah opens with Jonah praying unto the Lord. But nothing happened. Then Jonah begins to praise God:

> "But as for me, I will sacrifice to You with the voice of thanksgiving; I will pay that which I have vowed. Salvation and deliverance belong to the Lord!" (Jonah 2:9, Amplified Bible).

See the miraculous result of the sacrifice of Jonah's voice of thanksgiving:

"And the Lord spoke to the fish, and it vomited out Jonah upon the dry land" (verse 10).

Yes, there is great deliverance and blessing for those who will obey God's commandment to offer unto Him the sacrifice of praise.

It is most doubtful that Paul and Silas, their backs bleeding, their bodies hurting, felt very much like praising God in the inner prison at midnight. But when they prayed and sang loud praises to the Lord, not only the prisoners heard them, but the Lord who dwells in the praises of His people heard them. The Lord came down and loosed all the prisoners, and gave salvation to the jailer and his whole household. This was the foundation of the Philippian church. When other things fail, try praising God!

Restoration of the Sacrifice of Praise

God revealed to Jeremiah there was to be a great Restoration in the Last Days. We are taught this also includes a Restoration of the sacrifice of praise—praises which can be heard in the House of the Lord:

*"Thus saith the Lord: Again there shall be **heard** in this place . . . The voice of joy, and the voice of gladness, the voice of the bridegroom, and the voice of the bride, the voice of them that shall say. Praise the Lord of hosts; for the Lord is good; for His mercy endureth for ever: and of them that shall bring the sacrifice of praise into the House of the Lord" (Jer. 33:10, 11).*[1]

Notice that the sacrifice of praise is with the voice of joy and gladness. It

---

[1] Notice there are five voices promised here. The number five in the Bible speaks to us of the Gospel, God's grace, atonement, and its outworking. For example, the five "I wills" of Satan (Isaiah 14:12-17); Eve sinned through the five senses (Gen. 3:1-6); the five pillars into the Holy Place (Exod. 36:38); the redemption money was five shekels of silver (Num. 3:47); David chose five stones as he went to slay Goliath (1 Sam. 17:40); the Lord did five things to His vineyard' (Isaiah 5:2): the five-fold Name of Messiah (Isaiah 9:5); the five voices restored (Jer. 33:11); five signs following (Mark 16:16, 17); five ministries in the Church (Eph. 4:11); five types chosen by God (1 Cor. 1:27, 28); Christ bore five bleeding wounds in His body on the Cross; etc. There are scores more of examples in the Bible.

is not some sad, dismal, heartbreaking sacrifice. But as David said, "sacrifices of joy" (Psalm 27:6) which are to be offered unto God in the Tabernacle of David.

The Sacrifice of Praise in the Tabernacle of David

Today God is restoring the Tabernacle of David. The Bible teaches that the sacrifice of praise was intimately connected with the Tabernacle of David, and thus is also being restored in this day. David said:

"For in the time of trouble He shall hide me in His pavilion: in the secret of His Tabernacle shall He hide me; He shall set me up upon a rock.

And now shall mine head be lifted up above mine enemies round about me: therefore will I offer in **His Tabernacle sacrifices of joy** (margin—shouting); *I will sing, yea, I will bing praises unto the Lord" (Psalm 27:5, 6).*

In his psalm which opens with the words, "I love the Lord," David says:
"I will offer to Thee the sacrifice of thanksgiving, and will call upon the Name of the Lord" (Psalm 116:17).

Again let us emphasize that in the list of offerings and sacrifices at the Tabernacle of David there is no mention of sin offering. This indicates that a people cleansed from sin will take part in the promised Restoration of David's Tabernacle. However, while there were no sacrifices for sin, there were sacrifices of praise! Hear the oft-repeated cry of the Father Heart of God:

"Oh that men would praise the Lord for His goodness" (Psalm 107:21).

How are we to do it? The answer is in the next verse:
"And let them sacrifice the sacrifices of thanksgiving, and declare His works with rejoicing" (Psalm 107:22).

Those who take part in the Restoration of the Tabernacle of David, and know the Power of His Presence in the way He has promised, will be a people who praise and worship God—a people not ashamed to offer to the Lord their continual sacrifices of praise.

Turning again to the New Testament, we are told by the Apostle Peter that God is building a spiritual House upon Zion which shall show forth the praises of God:

"Ye also, as lively stones, are built up a spiritual house, an holy priesthood, to offer up spiritual sacrifices, acceptable to God by Jesus Christ.

"Wherefore also it is contained in the scripture. Behold, I lay in Zion a chief corner stone, elect, precious: and he that believeth on Him shall not be confounded.

But ye are a chosen generation, a royal priesthood, an holy nation, a peculiar people; that ye should shew forth the praises of Him who hath called you out of darkness into His marvellous light" (I Pet. 2:5, 6, 9).

Yes, it may cost you something to offer to God your sacrifice of praise. Your concern about what people will think of you—your self-consciousness (which is more soulish and carnal than praise), your pride—all of these must go before you can worship God in the Bible ways.

Start now. Offer to God your sacrifice of praise—and from now on let it be "continually":

"By Him (Jesus) therefore let us offer the sacrifice of praise to God continually, that is, the fruit of our lips giving thanks to His name" (Heb. 13:15).

Chapter Twenty-three
SKEPTICS BEWARE!

1 Chronicles chapter 15 (concluded)

The closer the Ark of the Covenant came to Zion, the more enthusiastic became the expressions of praise, worship, and rejoicing before the Lord. And so it is today. As the Lord restores the Power of His Presence to His Zion on earth in these last of the Last Days, Christians are worshipping the Lord as He was worshipped at the first Tabernacle of David.

David—Prophet, Priest and King (verse 27)

"David was clothed with a robe of fine linen, as were the Levites who bore the Ark, and the singers, and Chenaniah, director of the music of the singers. David also wore an ephod (a priestly upper garment) of linen" (1 Chron. 15:27, Amplified Bible*).*

We have already seen something of the uniqueness of King David's position in Old Testament history. By the Power of the Spirit of God, David, as it were, "looked beyond the veil," and entered, in a type, into much New Testament blessing in his life and ministry.

The Bible says in our verse above that "David was clothed with a robe of fine linen." The priestly garment of fine linen speaks of the righteousness of Christ. Thus David, in a type, was clothed with the righteousness of Christ, for it is written of the Bride of Christ:

"And to her was granted that she should be arrayed in fine linen, clean and white: for the fine linen is the righteousness of saints" (Rev. 19:8).

Christ Jesus Himself is our righteousness:

"But of Him are ye in Christ Jesus, who of God is made unto us wisdom, and righteousness" (1 Cor. 1:30).

1 Chronicles 15:27 goes on to say:

"David also had upon him an ephod of linen."

The ephod was a white linen cape, hanging to the front and back, the two pieces of which were joined with an onyx stone on each shoulder. It was, originally, to be worn by the high priest (Exod, 28:4; Lev. 8:7). It was expressly commanded that the priests come only from the priestly tribe, the tribe of Levi (Num. 3:6, 7). But only the descendants of Levi through Kohath's grandson, Aaron, could be priests. The priesthood was hereditary in the family of Aaron, and restricted to it. The other families of Levi's descendants, not descended from Aaron, were in charge of the sanctuary. But only the priesthood from Aaron's line ministered at the altar. In the sixteenth chapter of Numbers we read the awful judgment of God upon those who rebelled and dared to "seek the priesthood also" (Num. 16:10).

Furthermore, God's judgment was strong against another king who dared think he could minister in the priest's office. Speaking of King Uzziah, it is written:

"But when he was strong, his heart was lifted up to his destruction: for he transgressed against the Lord his God, and went into the temple of the Lord to burn incense upon the altar of incense" (2 Chron. 26:16).

But Azariah the priest, together with eighty more brave priests rebuked him, and God's judgment struck the king:

"And they withstood Uzziah the king, and said unto him. It appertaineth not unto thee, Uzziah, to burn incense unto the Lord, but to the priests the sons of Aaron, that are consecrated to burn incense: go out of the sanctuary; for thou hast trespassed; neither shall it be for thine honour from the Lord God.

Then Uzziah was wroth, and had a censer in his hand to burn incense: and while he was wroth with the priests, the leprosy even rose up

Skeptics Beware!

in his forehead before the priests in the house of the Lord, from beside the incense altar" (2 Chron. 26:18, 19).

Thus a man of the tribe of Judah, even though he was a king, was smitten with leprosy, and was cast out and "cut off from the house of the Lord" because he disobeyed God's commandment. Priests had to be from the tribe of Levi.

King Saul, of the tribe of Benjamin, presumed to exercise priestly ministry by offering a burnt offering (1 Sam. 13:9). God's Word of judgment immediately followed:

"And Samuel said to Saul, Thou hast done foolishly: thou hast not kept the commandment of the Lord thy God, which he commanded thee: for now would the Lord have established thy kingdom upon Israel for ever.

But now thy kingdom shall not continue: the Lord hath sought him a man after his own heart, and the Lord hath commanded him to be captain over his people, because thou hast not kept that which the Lord commanded" (1 Sam. 13:13, 14).

Again we see the priestly ministry must be carried out by the tribe of Levi only.

But here we see King David, not of the tribe of Levi, but of the tribe of Judah (a tribe commanded not to be priests), clothed with a priestly garment. Furthermore, this is not the first time David has broken the law concerning the priesthood. The Lord Jesus Himself referred to this unique place, this "prophetic experience" of David (Matt. 12:3-4).

Thus we see that David entered into something of the blessing of New Testament Christians—that of being both a king and priest unto God. This blessing and ministry of being a king and priest unto God runs right through the Bible. The Lord first promised it in Exodus 19:6:

"Ye shall be unto me a kingdom of priests."

We know the Lord Jesus Christ is King of kings and our Great High Priest. Of Him it is written,

"He shall be a priest upon His throne" (Zech. 6:13).

It is the will of God that we be like Jesus—indeed God says He has made us to be like His Son when we are cleansed in His precious blood:

"As He is, so are we in this world" (1 John 4:17).

*"Unto Him that loved us, and washed us from our sins in His own blood. And hath made us **kings** and **priests** unto God and His Father; to Him be glory and dominion for ever and ever. Amen"* (Rev. 1:5, 6).

*"Ye are a chosen generation, a **royal priesthood**"* (1 Pet. 2:9).

What a blessing it is to know that because of the cleansing blood of our Lord Jesus, we have become kings and priests unto God. It was at the return of the Ark of the Covenant David entered into this new blessing and ministry. And so it is today. As the Tabernacle of David is restored in the Church, the fullness of the truth of our position and ministry is coming to the fore again.

At his tabernacle on Zion, David also entered into his prophetic ministry. This we readily see from the Psalms given to him there by the Spirit of God. In fact, the Bible expressly says it was on the very day the Ark of God was set up in the midst of the Tent that David pitched for it, that he entered into his prophetic ministry in a new way. The Lord Jesus Himself referred to this prophetic ministry of David.

Because we see the foretaste of these blessings at the first Tabernacle of David, we may with great expectancy look forward to the fullness of their manifestation at the restored Tabernacle of David.

David Danced Before the Lord (verse 29)

"Thus all Israel brought up the Ark of the Covenant of the Lord with shouting, and with sound of the cornet, and with trumpets, and with cymbals, making a noise with psalteries and harps.

"And it came to pass, as the Ark of the Covenant of the Lord came to the city of David (Zion), that Michal the daughter of Saul looking out at a window saw king David dancing and playing" (1 Chron. 15:28, 29).

Skeptics Beware!

"And David danced before the Lord with all his might; and David was girded with a linen ephod. "So David and all the house of Israel brought up the Ark of the Lord with shouting, and with the sound of the trumpet.

"And as the Ark of the Lord came into the city of David, Michal Saul's daughter looked through a window, and saw king David leaping and dancing before the Lord" (2 Sam. 6:14, 15. 16).

Because the blessing of experiencing the Power of God's Presence was so great, as he brought up the Ark of the Covenant to Zion "David danced before the Lord with all his might." David was, in fact, worshipping the Lord with his whole spirit, soul and body. As we saw in Chapter 19 (All That is Within Me), this is God's will. David was fulfilling the first and great commandment. He danced before the Lord with all his might, because he knew God's commandment to love God with all his might:

"And thou shalt love the Lord thy God with all thine heart (spirit) and with all thy soul (soul) and with all thy might (body)" (Deut. 6:5).

Let us emphasize again, our spirit, soul and body are to be governed by the Word of God:

"Therefore shall ye lay up these my Words in your heart (spirit) and in your soul (soul), and bind them for a sign upon your hand (body)" (Deut. 11:18).

Indeed, those who obey this commandment are promised "days of heaven upon the earth" (Deut. 11:21).

"Thou shalt love the Lord thy God with all thy might." David was doing just that. "David danced before the Lord with all his might." Have you? Have you ever employed your whole spirit, soul and body to love and worship your God with all your might as the Bible commands?

Do His Will

Both Old and New Testaments teach that because of the anointing of God upon him, David was a man after God's own heart and fulfilled the will of God:

THE POWER OF HIS PRESENCE

> *"Then thou spakest in vision to thy holy one, and saidst, I have laid help upon one that is mighty; I have exalted one chosen out of the people.*
>
> *I have found David my servant; with my holy oil have I anointed him: With whom my hand shall be established: mine arm also shall strengthen him"* (Psalm 89:19, 20, 21).
>
> *"He raised up unto them David to be their king; to whom also He gave testimony, and said, I have found David the son of Jesse, a man after mine own heart, which shall fulfil all my will"* (Acts 13:22).

The Tabernacle of David was God's will. To bring back the Ark of the Covenant, the Power of His Presence, was God's will. And that David should express himself in such joyous demonstration of his praise and worship, was also God's will. Matthew Henry has these comments to make:

> *"(David) himself attended the solemnity with the highest expressions of joy that could be; he leaped for joy. His dancing was not artificial, by any certain rule or measure but was a natural expression of his great joy and exultation of mind."*[1]

There was only one person in the whole of Israel who did not understand or appreciate David's dancing before the Lord—his own wife Michal. The reason she did not share the enthusiasm, and enjoy the blessing of the return of the Power of God's Presence, was that she had disobeyed the commandment of the king. He had commanded that all Israel should gather together.[2] But Michal had failed to obey. She did not gather. Therefore, she missed the blessing of God's Presence, and the joyous blessings of praise and worship. Instead of gathering together with all the people at the king's command, she stayed home; she stayed in her own little corner, in her own house, and looked down from her window, haughtily criticizing and despising the joyous procession. She was on the outside looking in.

---

1   *Matthew Henry's Commentary on the Whole Bible* (Marshall, Morgan & Scott).
2   See 1 Chron. 13:2, 4, 5; 15:3.

Skeptics Beware!

Friend, here is a very important lesson for us today. You can only fully appreciate something when you are actually in it. You can only enjoy the blessing of praise and worship during the Restoration of the Tabernacle of David when you are experiencing the promised Restoration. As Jesus said, the joy of the blessing comes in acting on the Word, not looking down upon it, from the outside looking in, examining, rationalizing, and criticizing:

"If ye know these things, happy are ye if ye do them" (John 13:17).

"If any man will do His will, he shall know of the doctrine, whether it be of God" (John 7:17).

Here we can learn an important lesson from the Lord's parable of the prodigal son. At the feast of Restoration, where there was feasting, music, making merry, and dancing, it was the self-righteous elder brother who was the "prodigal." For the Lord said the elder brother "was angry, and would not go in" and enjoy the blessings of the rejoicing (Luke 15:28). Let us be careful, lest we too miss out.

Because Michal had failed to obey the king's command to gather together with Israel and take part in the blessing and praise and worship of the Lord, to her the noise of the procession was so much senseless babbling and carnal display. And yet while she criticised, the people were enjoying the fullness of the Power of the Presence of God. Friend, when you first see and hear people praising God in the Bible ways, it may seem to you to be excitement, vain repetition, fleshly display, irreverent, and whatever else you like to call it. But for those on the inside—for those who are experiencing praise—it is, according to the Word of God, good and pleasant, becoming and appropriate:

"Praise the Lord! For it is good to sing praises to our God, for He is gracious and lovely; praise is becoming and appropriate" (Psalm 147:1, Amplified Bible).

Billy Graham has this to say:

"Men and women of enthusiasm disturb the complacent, the smug, and the apathetic; and so the people with their heads buried in the sand pass judgment, calling them mad, beside themselves.

"The really sane people are often those at whom the world laughs and despises. As we look back on Christ we can see that it was He who was sane, and His critics who were mad."[3]

If there is anything the Church needs today, it is men and women of enthusiasm. Christians who have so experienced the Power of God's Presence in their lives, and so dedicated their all to Him, that they will enthusiastically enter into all God is doing today. Such enthusiasm is contagious, and will help bring about revival in the Church.

The Result of Michal's Folly

"And it came to pass, as the Ark of the Covenant of the Lord came to the city of David. (Zion), that Michal the daughter of Saul looking out at a window saw king David dancing and playing: and she despised him in her heart" (1 Chron. 15:29).

"Then David returned to bless his household. And Michal the daughter of Saul came out to meet David, and said. How glorious was the King of Israel to day, who uncovered himself today in the eyes of the handmaids of his servants, as one of the vain fellows shamelessly uncovereth himself!

And David said unto Michal, It was before the Lord, which chose me before thy father, and before all his house, to appoint me ruler over the people of the Lord, over Israel: therefore will I play before the Lord.

And I will yet be more vile than thus, and will be base in mine own sight; and of the maidservants which thou has spoken of, of them shall I be had in honour.

Therefore Michal the daughter of Saul had no child unto the day of her death" (2 Sam. 6:20-23).

In the moment of David's greatest triumph, his wife mocked him. In the light of all David meant to her, and all the love he had showered upon her, she should have known better. There are some important things we should note about David's wife Michal:

---

3   *The Quotable Billy Graham* (Murray Publishing Co.)

Skeptics Beware!

1) She was the King's daughter (1 Sam. 14:49; 18:20, 27; etc).

2) She was the bride of King David (1 Sam. 18:27).

3) She was the purchase of blood (1 Sam. 18:25-27).

4) She had loved her husband (1 Sam. 18:20). She had once almost risked her life to deliver him from his enemy (1 Sam. 19:12.)

5) How early David had loved her! He refused to be crowned king until she was restored to him 2 Sam. 3:13-14).

In Psalm 45, the psalm of the royal wedding, "A Song of loves" (see the title of the psalm), David speaks of his wife Michal thus:

"Hearken, O daughter, and consider, and incline thine ear; forget also thine own people, and thy father's house" (Psalm 45:10).

However, she did not heed King David's command to forget her father's house. For in her despising of David's praise and worship, she acts more like Saul's daughter rather than David's wife. David continues his Song of loves:

"So shall the king greatly desire thy beauty: for he is thy Lord; and worship thou him.

The king's daughter is all glorious within: her clothing is of wrought gold.

She shall be brought unto the king in raiment of needlework: the virgins her companions that follow her shall be brought unto thee.

With gladness and rejoicing shall they be brought; they shall enter into the king's palace" (Psalm 45:11, 13-15).

But Michal was anything but "glorious" when she mocked David for dancing before the Lord. She did not enter into the celebrations of the return of the Ark of the Covenant with "gladness and rejoicing" at all.

At the end of the psalm, Michal is promised children, fruitfulness and fame:

"Instead of thy fathers shall be thy children, whom thou mayest make princes in all the earth.

I will make thy name to be remembered in all generations: therefore shall the people praise thee for ever and ever" (Psalm 45: 16, 17).

But instead, the blessing was reversed and changed into a curse, and Michal chose barrenness and fruitlessness by her disobedience to the king's command, and her scorn of such a demonstrative celebration of his praise and worship.

But Psalm 45 does not only speak of King David and his marriage to Michal. The prophetic mantle of the Holy Spirit upon David was operating here, and he is foretelling a Greater King, a Greater Bride, the Greater Wedding—that of our Heavenly Bridegroom, Jesus Christ, and His Bride.

Michal is, without doubt, a picture of a true blood-washed child of God. Yet, despite all she was, she mocked her king and lord for his enthusiastic demonstration of praise and worship.

I wonder if it has occurred to those who mock and write books against Christians who worship God in the Bible ways, that they are speaking not against the worshippers themselves, but against the Holy Spirit who dwells within the worshippers. To do so—to speak against the work of the Holy Spirit in this way—is most dangerous (Matt. 12:31-32). Michal called David's dancing before the Lord an indecent display. (It should be noted here that David was fully covered and clothed. However, he had removed his royal garments to put on the priestly garment. We mention this because some critics have gone so far as to call dancing before the Lord immoral).

David answered his wife that his rejoicing "was before the Lord." He assured her that he would not cease his playing and laughter and dancing before the Lord, because he knew he was chosen of God, anointed of God, and in the perfect will of God. He was expressing his joy, praise and worship to His God Who was with him through the Power of His Presence. Because of God's goodness and mercy and blessing to him, David would sing, leap and dance before the Lord. Furthermore he says, that he "will yet be more vile than thus, and will be base in my own sight." David is willing to empty himself of all his self-consciousness and self-will. He does not care what people think of him. He does not care how he is reviled. He will humble himself before his God and worship Him in the Scriptural ways. God give us more Davids today, who think more of God than what others will think of them.

Because of her folly at daring to mock God's anointed for the way he had worshipped his God, the judgment would come upon her. Michal, in spite of her relationship with the king, becomes barren and fruitless to the day of her death.

The Michals of Today

What tragic judgment on the one who could have been the fruitful wife of David. Those of us living in the East appreciate the shame the woman who has not borne children has to bear. But it is no light matter to speak against the Power of the Presence of God, or the manifestations of His Power.

More tragic yet is that many in the Church today do not seem to have learned the lesson of Michal. They know great David's Greater Son, Jesus Christ. They know that they are purchased with blood. But still, like Michal, some fail to enter into this Last Day Restoration Revival, and look askance at any physical manifestations of the Presence of God. And the result of such an attitude has not changed.

This severe judgment of God on those who mock manifestations of His Presence has not been withdrawn. Because they despise and mock—even blaspheme Biblical manifestations of God's Presence (such as the gifts of the Holy Spirit and Scriptural praise and worship)—the critics, even though they know and love Christ have, like Michal, become barren, cynical, and fruitless. Rather than have their traditional tranquillity and solemnity disturbed by Scriptural outbursts of the Power of the Presence of God, they would rather, like Michal, stay in their own little corner, criticizing those who allow the Ark of God's Presence to show forth His glory in their midst.

Sons and daughters of Zion, fear not! Since the days when Cain slew Abel, since Noah was mocked, since Joseph was sold by his brethren, there have been those who would rather criticise the Ark than carry it—would rather mock those who allow Scriptural manifestations of God's Power than join them. Throughout the centuries, all who would allow God to move by His Spirit have been regarded with suspicion. Scores of examples could be given. Yet anyone willing to study Church history will find that physical manifestations of God's Power have been defended in the most unexpected quarters.

For instance, John Wesley was criticized by those within the Church, as is always the case, not by those outside it, for the physical outbursts which resulted from his preaching. Speaking of outcries, convulsions, dancing, visions, trances, and similar manifestations, he wrote in his *Journal*:

"The danger was to regard them **too little***, to condemn them altogether; to imagine they had nothing of God in them, and were a hindrance to His work. Whereas the truth is:*

" (1) God suddenly and strongly convinced many that they were lost sinners, the natural consequences whereof were sudden outcries and strong bodily convulsions;

"(2) to strengthen and encourage them that believe, and to make His work more apparent, He favoured several of them with divine dreams, others with trances and visions."

Dear reader, possibly the Biblical manifestations of speaking in tongues, shouting and praising God, dancing before the Lord, are strange to you. They could even seem utterly unacceptable. But those of us who have had the privilege of preaching Christ to people hearing of Him for the first time, have observed some of their reactions to the Gospel. These are possibly similar to your reactions today. While they have appreciated God's great love for them, it has been an immense shock for these people to think that God was born in a manger, suffered tiredness, hunger and thirst, and shed His Blood when nailed to a wooden Cross. Repulsive, unlovely, unacceptable—

Skeptics Beware!

these have been their first thoughts concerning many main points of the Gospel We so readily take for granted. But when the initial strangeness has worn off, what a blessing it has been to see these same ones responding to the moving of the Spirit and giving their lives to Jesus Christ as Lord.

And so it is with the physical manifestations of the Power of God in our lives and churches. Once the initial shock and strangeness has gone, these manifestations of God's Power are found to be of untold blessing. One wonders if Peter, Paul and Silas would not feel more at home in meetings where these physical manifestations are permitted (the type of meetings they were used to), than in some of today's staid formal services—so different from New Testament Christianity.

Despite all Scriptural exhortations to the contrary, some still want to be silent in their worship. But the Bible says:

"Thou hast turned for me my mourning into dancing: thou hast put off my sackcloth, and girded me with gladness;

*"To the end that my tongue[4] may sing praise to thee, and **not be silent**. O Lord my God, I will give thanks unto thee for ever"* (Psalm 30:11, 12).

The whole congregation is exhorted not to be silent:

"Blessed be the Lord God of Israel from everlasting to everlasting: and let all the people say. Amen. Praise ye the Lord. Hallelujah"[5] (Psalm 106:48).

Yet others say they would prefer to seek God quietly. Yet again the Bible commands those who are seeking God not to be silent:

"Let all those that seek thee rejoice and be glad in thee: let such as love thy salvation say continually. The Lord be magnified" (Psalm 40:16).

Yet another physical manifestation for seeking God is recorded in Psalm 143:6:

---

4   Marginal rendering
5   Marginal rendering

"I stretch forth my hands unto thee: my soul thirsteth after thee, as a thirsty land."

Others desire to have the Word of God without the praises. "We just want the Word," is sometimes heard. But the Bible teaches that praise and the Word of God are intimately connected. The Bible commands the children of Zion to:

"Let the high praises of God be in their mouth and a two-edged sword in their hand" (Psalm 149:6).

Our two-edged sword is, of course, the Word of God (Heb. 4:12, Eph. 6:17).

When David spoke of the "holy temple" of God, he was referring to the Tabernacle of David. Here is how he linked praise and the Word of God:

"I will praise thee with my whole heart: before the gods will I sing praise unto thee. I will worship toward thy holy temple, and praise thy name for thy lovingkindness and for thy truth: for thou hast magnified thy word above all thy name" (Psalm 138:1, 2).

Those who believe the Word of God praise the Lord:

"Then believed they His words; they sang His praise" (Psalm 106:12).

As we have already seen it is not enough to hear the Word—we must cu:t upon it also. We must praise and worship God, and rejoice before Him, according to His Own Word.

Skeptics Beware

Friend, I say this in love. If, in spite of all the evidence given in the Bible, you still do not want to obey God and worship Him in the Bible ways, do not criticise or mock those who do! It is very dangerous to criticise that which God is doing:

"Because they regard not the works of the Lord, nor the operation of His hands. He shall destroy them, and not build them up" (Psalm 28:5).

As Michal discovered, the shameful consequences of mocking demonstrations of praise, and physical manifestations of the Power of God's Presence, are very severe. If it is in the Word of God, do not criticise it. If you do understand it, leave it alone.

Skeptics—beware!

Chapter Twenty-four
THE PRAISE OF SACRIFICE
1 Chronicles chapter 16

"And it was so, that when they that bare the Ark of the Lord had gone six paces, he sacrificed oxen and fatlings" (2 Sam. 6:13).

"And it came to pass, when God helped the Levites that bare the Ark of the Covenant of the Lord, that they offered seven bullocks and seven rams" (1 Chron. 15:26).

"So they brought the Ark of God, and set it in the midst of the Tent that David had pitched for it: and they offered burnt sacrifices and peace offerings before God" (1 Chron. 16:1).

The Praise of Sacrifice (verse 1)

One of the great Biblical truths which has been to the forefront in this new move of God throughout the world is the truth of **praise**. As Christians are learning to praise God, they find His promise to "inhabit the praises of His people" operates in their lives, bringing freedom, blessing, deliverance, and a new vital sense of His Presence (Psalm 22:3).

The Lord is teaching us to offer to Him the **sacrifice of praise**. The Bible commands us, "By Him therefore let us offer the sacrifice of praise to God continually, that is, the fruit of our lips, giving thanks to His Name" (Heb, 13:15).

However, the Bible does not only teach us the "sacrifice of praise," but also the **praise of sacrifice**. This is altogether different. It is, unfortunately, a form of praise and worship very few Christians have experienced or know much about. It is the making of a sacrifice to God, which is itself praise and worship to Him. A sacrifice, the laying at His feet as dead and offering unto Him something which we love—something which is very precious to us—and by this sacrifice an even deeper worship springs from our hearts.

As we can clearly see from the above verses of Scripture, sacrifices and offerings were a very integral part of the restoring of the Presence of God to Zion. Yes, there was praise, worship, rejoicing before the Lord, and unspeakable joy—but there were also sacrifices and offerings made unto the Lord. Let us not lose sight of this important fact.

The sacrifices made by the people of Israel as they brought the Ark of the Covenant to Zion cost them something. In terms of time, the bringing up of the Ark was slowed down by the constant stopping to sacrifice to the Lord every six paces. But this is an unbreakable law of God—there is no blessing without sacrifice, and our sacrifices as an offering to the Lord are a vital part of our praise and worship.

There are many examples of this in the Bible. For example Hannah gave back to God in worship that which God had given her, her son Samuel (1 Sam. 2:20-28). Do we worship God in giving back to Him all He has given us?

Job was stripped of all he had. Yet the Bible says, he "fell down upon the ground, and worshipped," saying, "The Lord gave, and the Lord hath taken away; blessed be the Name of the Lord" (Job 1:20-21). Job also said that even if God would slay him he would continue to trust in God and maintain his worship and praise (Job 13:15).

David fasted and prayed for his little son's life. But God said "no" and the boy died. Yet the Bible says "David came into the House of the Lord and worshipped" (i.e. he worshipped in the Tabernacle of David—2 Sam. 12:15-20). Beloved, this is true worship—when we can worship God for His ways, even when they sometimes appear strongly against our ways.

One of the classic examples in the Bible of the praise of sacrifice is recorded in the life of Abraham. Abraham's son of promise was born. How precious he was to Abraham! Abraham loved him dearly.

But one day God said to Abraham,

The Praise of Sacrifice

"Take now" (not later!) *"thy son, thine only son Isaac, whom thou lovest, and get thee into the land of Moriah; and offer him there for a burnt offering upon one of the mountains which I will tell thee of"* (Gen. 22:2).

How can we ever imagine how Abraham felt! I can scarcely think how I would feel if God told me to offer one of my sons for a burnt offering. But Abraham, the father of faith, implicitly obeyed the Lord. His consecration was so deep, so sincere. He was willing even to sacrifice his precious dear one, the son of his love, Isaac. Abraham rose early and prepared quickly to obey God's commandment. After they had journeyed for three days, Abraham saw the place where he was to make his sacrifice. There he was to slay his son and offer him as a burnt offering to the Lord. He turned to his young men and said, "Abide ye here with the ass and I and the lad will go yonder and *sacrifice*." Is this what Abraham said? Surely it must be.

But look again! As Abraham went to sacrifice his beloved son unto the Lord, he said:

*"I and the lad will go yonder and **worship**"* (Gen. 22:5).

Worship! Praise! Yes, Abraham so loved his God that he considered the sacrifice of that which was most precious to him as worship!

Sacrifice and the Tabernacle of David

The Bible does not say that the sacrifices and offerings during the Restoration of the Ark of the Covenant to David's Tabernacle on Mount Zion were sin offerings. The Bible says they were peace offerings and burnt offerings. The people had already sanctified themselves (1 Chron. 15:12). They had, in a type, kept the Feast Day of Atonement.

At the end of every sixth step they took, David sacrificed oxen and rams. It is important to note that in the very next verse it is recorded David danced before the Lord with all his might.[1] Thus we see the rejoicing and the sacrifice were taking place at the same time! And it is true today, that the deeper our consecration, and the more complete sacrifice we have made

---

1   See 2 Sam. 6:13, 14.

of ourselves to the Lord, the greater will be our rejoicing in praise and worship.

The six paces speak to us of the first six days of God's week, which we have already considered. And even as at the end of the sixth step sacrifices and offerings were made, so at this end of the sixth day of God's week, we need to offer to Him the praise of sacrifice.

It is also recorded that each sacrifice consisted of **seven** bullocks and **seven** rams. We have already made reference to the significance of the number seven in the Bible, which speaks to us of completeness and perfection. Thus the sacrifices made unto the Lord during the bringing up of the Ark of God to Zion were complete and perfect. Likewise today, nothing but a complete and perfect consecration and sacrifice of all that we are and have to God is sufficient.

Sacrificing All

We are living in the Last Days. Jesus is coming again soon. Yet multitudes are still waiting for the Church to arise from slumber and selfishness to tell them of Jesus, His love and His salvation. Millions have yet to hear His Name for the first time. God calls us today as never before to offer to Him the praise of sacrifice—for us to make a sacrifice of our time, our ambitions, our wills, our finance—our **all** as an offering to the Lord.

So few of us seem to have ever given to the Lord that which we love. We give Him what we feel we can do without. We give Him what we want to give. And yet God so loves us, that He gave us the Son of His love for our salvation. "King David said, I will pay the full price... I will not...offer... offerings which cost me nothing" (I Chron. 21:24, *Amplified Bible*). Can we do less?

As you make this sacrifice to the Lord, you will enter into a new realm of praise—a new depth of worship you never dreamed was possible. It will hurt. It may break you. But remember,

The Praise of Sacrifice

"the sacrifices of God are a broken spirit: a broken and contrite heart, O God, thou wilt not despise" (Psalm 51:17).

No doubt you have offered to God the sacrifice of praise. Have you also offered to Him *the praise of sacrifice?*

Chapter Twenty-five
WHERE DO YOU WORSHIP?

1 Chronicles chapter 16 (concluded)

There are many precious truths in each verse of 1 Chronicles chapter 16—verses which tell how David's first Tabernacle was pitched, and what happened there. From the study of each verse we can find out how David's Tabernacle is being restored in these days. We can but briefly touch on them in this last chapter of this section.

Verse 2 tells us there came an end to the burnt offerings and the peace offerings. The Ark of the Covenant was at last set up in the middle of David's Tabernacle. The fullness of the Power of His Presence was restored to Israel. The people were blessed by the King. And friends, I am convinced the Bible teaches there is a Power and a faith, and a "salvation ready to be revealed in the last time" (1 Peter 1:5), which is greater than anything the Church has ever seen or known before. As we have already stressed, there is ample evidence in Scripture that the Bride of Christ shall be blessed by her King, and perfected, before He comes again.

"And when David had made an end of offering the burnt offerings and the peace offerings, he blessed the people in the name of the Lord."

Verse 3 is a beautiful type or picture of communion. Many Old Testament saints took "communion" in a figure. Melchizedeck ministered bread and wine to Abraham, and blessed him (Gen. 14:18-19). Again, Abraham "broke bread" with the three heavenly visitors (Gen. 18:1-8). And here at David's Tabernacle the king ministered to every man and woman in Israel "a loaf of bread and a good piece of flesh, and a flagon of wine."

The bread speaks to us of Jesus, who said "I am the Bread of Life...which came down from heaven" (John 6:35, 41). The flesh reminds us that "God was manifest in the flesh" (1 Tim. 3:16) in the body of His Son, Jesus Christ, and we have access unto God "by a new and living way, which He hath newly made for us, through the veil, that is to say. His flesh" (Heb. 10:20, *marginal rendering*).

The wine speaks to us of the blood of Christ, Who "took the cup, when He had supped, saying. This cup is the New Testament in my blood: this do ye, as oft as ye drink it, in remembrance of me" (1 Cor. 11:25).

Firstly then, by a spiritual experience of salvation and the new birth, we have been made partakers of the very life of Christ. Indeed, He said:

"Verily, verily, I say unto you. Except ye eat the flesh of the Son of man, and drink his blood, ye have no life in you" (John 6:53).

Secondly, we are reminded here of the breaking of bread, or communion service, in which we are told to eat of the bread, and drink of the cup, showing forth "the Lord's death till He come" (1 Cor. 11:26).

Verses 4-6 remind us again that the praise and worship did not stop with the setting up of the Ark of the Covenant in David's Tabernacle. When the Ark was fully set up the sacrifice ceased, but the praise most certainly did not. Praise, worship, giving thanks and praise with loud voice and musical instruments, psalteries, harps, cymbals, trumpets, was to continue without ceasing, night and day, every day! This is again emphasized in verse 37:

*"So he left there before the Ark of the Covenant of the Lord, Asaph and his brethren, to minister before the Ark **continually**, as every day's work required" (1 Chron. 16:37).*

From verse 7 onwards, we see the great ministry of the giving of the Psalms of praise on Zion. As the Spirit of God moved upon David to bring forth these inspired Psalms, Asaph recorded them, and these form many of the Psalms in our Bibles today. Let it be emphasized, that so many of the Psalms came forth by the Power of the Spirit of God at the Tabernacle of David.

Ceremony Replaced (verse 37)

Now we see what Matthew Henry has referred to as the early replacement of ceremonial formalities with spiritual worship. No sacrifices for sin were offered at the Tabernacle of David, because no brazen altar was there. No incense was burned at the Tabernacle of David, for there was no altar of incense there. However, as we have already seen, each piece of furniture in the holy place of the tabernacle of Moses has its spiritual fulfillment in the Ark of the Covenant. Despite the fact there were no altars, see how spiritual praise and worship took the place of the legal, traditional, ceremonial sacrifices:

"Let my prayer be directed before thee as incense; and the lifting up of my hands as the evening sacrifice" (Psalm 141:2, marginal rendering*).*

Thus we see that the lifting up of hands as a sacrifice of praise took the place of the evening sacrifice on the brazen altar. Prayer took the place of the incense burnt upon the altar of incense. Praise God, in this wonderful Restoration of the Tabernacle of David, old ceremonial, traditional forms are being replaced by spiritual acts of praise and worship.

Nothing Between (verse 37)

Let us also be careful to note in verse 37 that the ministry of praise and worship continued day and night *"before the Ark of the Covenant of the Lord."* Let us say it again. Let it sink deep into our hearts—there was **NO VEIL** before the Ark of the Covenant in David's Tabernacle as there had been in the tabernacle of Moses. There was nothing between the Lord and His people. They went right into the very Presence of the Almighty God.

As we saw earlier, in the tabernacle of Moses the people could not come and behold the Shekinah Glory of God. Only the high priest could come once a year, and then he had to bring blood to atone for the sins of the people. But we see so many New Testament blessings revealed to us in the Tabernacle of David. And this is one of them—not only was the veil rent in two. It was taken away! There was no veil. There was nothing between the Lord and His people. Hallelujah!

Now we can understand why David was able to say:

"I have looked upon you in the Sanctuary to see your Power and your glory" (Psalm 63: 2, Amplified Bible*).*

David beheld the Power and Glory of God who dwelt between the cherubim.

But not only did David and those who ministered before the Ark of the Covenant behold the Glory and Power of God. All the people of all the tribes were invited to worship God before the Ark of the Testimony at the Tabernacle of David. We are all familiar with Psalm 122. The House of the Lord, here, is the Tabernacle of David:

"I was glad when they said unto me. Let us go into the House of the Lord...

Whither the tribes go up, the tribes of the Lord, unto the Testimony of Israel (the Ark of the Covenant), to give thanks unto the Name of the Lord" (Psalm 122:1, 4).

"They have seen thy goings, O God; even the goings of my God, my King, in the Sanctuary.

The singers went before, the players on instruments followed after; among them were the damsels playing with timbrels.

Bless ye God in the congregations, even the Lord, from the fountain of Israel" (Psalm 68:24-26).

Yes, because there was no veil in the Tabernacle of David to hide the Glory of His Presence, the Shekinah Light shone from Zion far and wide:

"Out of Zion, the perfection of beauty, **God hath shined**" *(Psalm 50:2).*

What a tremendous blessing and encouragement it is to know that God is restoring the Tabernacle of David—the Tabernacle with no veil—in His Church during these Last Days. This is not a blessing for a select few. This is not an invitation just for those in the full-time work of God. Rather, **all** are invited to behold the Power of His Presence and to experience the Light and Glory of Him who said, "As long as I am in the world, I am the Light of the world" (John 9:5). And as the Power and Glory of His Presence shines through those believers who will come all the way to Zion, so shall be brought to pass that which is written, "Ye are the light of the world" (Matt. 5:14).

Abundant Blessing

Can we picture the scene on Mount Zion? God's people are experiencing the fullness of the Power of His Presence. There is liberty, praise, worship, righteousness, rejoicing, victory, safety and security. And this is that which God is restoring to His Church today. Blessed be His Name!

And what are the results of this Restoration? We have to leave the reader to study 1 Chronicles chapters 17 and 18. In chapter 17 David is assured that God is with him. He receives many promises of blessing from the Lord, and enjoys intimate communion with Him in prayer. In chapter 18, we see David enjoying victory over all his adversaries. This speaks to us of the complete victory the Lord has promised to those who follow Him:

"Behold, I give unto you power to tread on serpents and scorpions, and over all the power of the enemy: and nothing shall by any means hurt you" (Luke 10:19).

In I Chronicles 18:14 we see David reigning, reminding us of the kingly authority in this world of believers in Christ. These, together with all the other truths of these chapters, are wonderful to consider when again we realize that all these blessings are available for us today.

However, before we move on from chapter 16, there is just one more important fact I want us to consider.

The Tabernacle on Mount Gibeon (verse 39)

What blessings there were on Mount Zion! With the Power of God's Presence there in the Tabernacle of David, would anyone want to go back to the tabernacle of Moses with all its ritual and formality? Certainly the tabernacle of Moses was good in its day. But God has moved on. God has done a new thing. The Power of God's Presence is now in the Tabernacle of David. Surely, nobody could desire the old after seeing the manifold blessings of the new.

Five miles from Zion is the old city of Gibeon. Gibeon was one of the four cities of the Hivites, the inhabitants of which made a league with Joshua, thus escaping the fate of Jericho and Ai.[1] Gibeon lay within the territory of Benjamin. Together with its "suburbs" Gibeon was allotted to the priests, of whom it later became a principal city."[2]

But what is this we see on the Mount at Gibeon? A drab-looking tent. Its colour a dull bluish-grey. Sombre and melancholy. Silent. Why, it is the tabernacle of Moses! Even though the Tabernacle of David hais been completed, the tabernacle of Moses is still there, only five miles away.

The offerings to the Lord are sacrificed there every morning and evening. All the ritual and formality "that is written in the law" (verse 40) is still being performed. The tabernacle of Moses is still with us after all! The brazen altar is there. The laver is there. Going in past the first veil we see the table of shewbread, the candlestick, and the altar of incense. Passing through the second veil from the Holy Place into the Holy of Holies, we should be able to behold the dazzling Glory of God's Holy Presence—but He is gone! It is so very dark here! The Power of His Presence is not here! The Ark of the Covenant is no longer in the Holy of Holies! God has moved on! His fullness now dwells on Zion!

You may come to Gibeon. You may continually offer burnt offerings at the brazen altar. You may wash at the laver. You may eat at the table of shewbread by the light of the golden candlestick. You may offer incense on the altar of incense. But you will never find God's fullness there! God has moved on! For it is written:

---

1   See Josh. 9:3-15.
2   See Josh. 18:25; 21:17.

Where Do You Worship?

"I ... have gone from ... one tabernacle to another" (1 Chron. 17:5).

Of Gibeon it is written:

"The high place that was at Gibeon; for there was the tabernacle ... which Moses the servant of the Lord had made in the wilderness.

But the Ark of God had David brought up from Kirjath-jearim to the place which David had prepared for it: for he had pitched a Tent for it at Jerusalem (in Zion)" (2 Chron. 1:3, 4).

The tabernacle of Moses which was at Shiloh has now been shifted to Gibeon. But shifting the place, changing the name, making new appointments to serve at it, cannot help it at all. Because God's Glory has forsaken it and is no longer there:

"So that He forsook the tabernacle of Shiloh, the tent which He placed among men...

But chose the tribe of Judah, the mount Zion which He loved.

And He built His Sanctuary (David's Tabernacle) like high palaces, like the earth which He hath established for ever.

He chose David also His servant" (Psalm 78:60, 68-70).

The fullness of God's Presence is no longer in the old tabernacle of Moses, and all it represents. God has chosen the Tabernacle of David for the fullness of the Power of His Presence to dwell in Zion.

Where Do You Worship?

We do not wish to belittle in any way the tabernacle of Moses, with all its spiritual application and experiences. Even as David appointed ministers at both Zion and Gibeon, at both David's Tabernacle and Moses' tabernacle, so God has His ministries for both tabernacles today. At the tabernacle of Moses you may still enter into the outer court through the one door, speaking to us of the Lord Jesus Christ (John 10:9). You may still experience salvation and cleansing from sin here by the brazen altar which speaks of the Cross of Calvary, where Jesus shed His blood for our sins. You may still experience water baptism, and the "washing of water by the Word"

(Eph. 5:26) in the waters of the brazen laver. You may still enter into the Holy Place, and experience the light from the golden candlestick upon the Word of God on the table of shewbread. You may experience the anointing of the oil at the candlestick—the baptism and anointing of the Holy Spirit. You may still have sweet communion with the Lord in prayer at the altar of incense. But you can go no further.

Time and again we are exhorted to go on with God:

"Therefore leaving the word of the beginning of the doctrine of Christ, let us go on unto perfection" (Heb. 6:1, marginal rendering).

But we can readily see that it is impossible to go on unto perfection in the tabernacle of Moses. Even if we do go through the veil, there is darkness and emptiness and frustration in the Holy of Holies. God has moved on. Will you not go on five miles to Zion?[3]

Let us repeat again—all that was in the tabernacle of Moses has its fulfillment in, and is superseded by experiencing the fullness of the Power of God's Presence at the Ark of the Covenant in the Tabernacle of David on Mount Zion. All the blessings of the tabernacle of Moses at Gibeon are on Mount Zion, at David's Tabernacle—**and many more!**

Gibeon or Zion?

We all know that we can never hear the Word of God without having to make a decision. Today God calls each of us to make a decision—a decision which has far-reaching consequences for us all. A decision which for many of us is very difficult to make. A decision which if we choose aright, may cost us position, popularity, and friends. But if we make the wrong decision, choosing not to obey God, the consequences may be far worse.

God has promised to restore the Tabernacle of David in this day and age in which you and I live. How? In exactly the same way as the first Tabernacle of David was built three thousand years ago. With weeping. With sanctification. With loud praise. With sacrifice. With manifestations of

---

[3] We have already discussed the significance of the number five; see page 282.

the Holy Spirit and demonstrations of rejoicing before the Lord—just as at Zion.

Friend, what is your decision? Gibeon or Zion? Where will you worship?

"But you are come unto Mount Zion" (Heb. 12:22).

Have you?

Part V
WHY?

WHY is God restoring the Tabernacle of David?

Chapter Twenty-six
THE CHURCH RESTORED

We were going to move house. At long last we had seen a house we could rent. It was to be the first new house my wife and I had ever lived in. But the construction was not complete, so we could not yet move in. We had met the owner, and he was desirous we should live in his house. But, until the building was complete, it was impossible for us to live there.

The Lord is desiring to dwell, in all His fullness, in His house, the Church—here and now, before the Second Coming. But until the building is complete, He cannot come and dwell with us in all the fullness of the Power of His Presence.

Restoration BEFORE Revival

Thousands of sincere Christians throughout the world are earnestly praying for revival today. All of us praise God for the movings of His Spirit which have been witnessed in various places from time to time. But the revival for which we pray—the revival we so desperately need—will be nothing short of a world-wide outpouring of the Holy Spirit. This outpouring, when the fullness of the Spirit of God, the fullness of the Power of His Presence, will dwell in the Church, shall herald a far greater revival than has ever been experienced in history.

But it is impossible for God to dwell with us in all His fullness until the dwelling place is ready. As we have seen, David prepared a dwelling place, and he prepared the people—then he brought up the Ark of the Covenant, the Power of the Presence of God, to Zion. In like manner, we must seek

God for the Restoration first, then will come the revival. There must be a Restoration before the revival in all its entirety comes to the Church.

Why then is God restoring the Tabernacle of David? Apart from the very obvious reason that He has promised to do so, and the Scripture cannot be broken, an almost endless list of reasons could be given. Many of these reasons are evident from our previous chapters. However, we may summarize thus:

(1) **The Church Restored**—God is restoring the Tabernacle of David so that His Church might be restored in preparation for the coming Revival;

(2) **The Church Revived**—God is restoring the Tabernacle of David to revive His Church in preparation for the Great Harvest of souls He has promised in these Last Days;

(3) **The Church Reaping**—God is restoring the Tabernacle of David to bring about the Great Harvest in preparation for the Second Coming of Christ.

God is a God of order. God always works according to the pattern He has laid down in His Word. Both the Bible and history reveal a repeated cycle of events seen so often in Restoration Revivals which God has sent:—

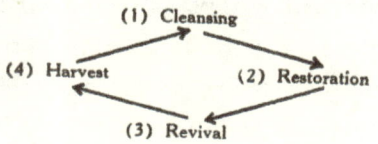

Despite all the confusion and calamities in these last of the Last Days, God is at work. He wants us to know what He is doing, and how He is doing it, so that we may flow in the perfect will of God. In the portion of Scripture in which God promises to build again the Tabernacle of David, He says also, "The Lord ... has been making these things known from the beginning of the world" (Acts 15:18, *Amplified Bible*). Praise God, He has not left us in darkness, but rather shares with us that which He is doing in these days.

Cleansing

We cannot over-emphasize the important part the cleansing of the Church has in the Restoration of the Tabernacle of David. Those who experience, in spiritual application, the Restoration of the Tabernacle of David and the spiritual experiences of Mount Zion, shall be holy, righteous, and cleansed. We have already seen that the commandment to those who were to bring up the Ark of God to Zion was, "Sanctify yourselves." And David continues this teaching in his Psalms:

"Lord, who shall abide in thy Tabernacle? who shall dwell in thy holy hill?

He that walketh uprightly, and worketh righteousness"
(Psalm 15:1, 2).

He will see that those who dwell in the Tabernacle of David, in God's holy hill, which is Zion (Psalm 2:6), shall be a righteous people.

Again David emphasizes the need for this cleansing in Psalm 24:

"Who shall ascend into the hill of the Lord? or who shall stand in His holy place?

He that hath clean hands, and a pure heart; who hath not lifted up his soul unto vanity, nor sworn deceitfully.

He shall receive the blessing from the Lord, and righteousness from the God of his salvation" (Psalm 24:3-5).

"But upon Mount Zion . . . there shall be holiness" (Obad. 17).

The Bride of Christ

The cleansing and holiness required by God for the Restoration of the Tabernacle of David is intimately connected with the preparation of the Bride of Christ. We see the Tabernacle of the Lord and the Bridegroom connected in the nineteenth Psalm:

"In them hath He set a Tabernacle . . .
Which is as a Bridegroom coming out of His chamber" (Psalm 19:4, 5).

We must emphasize that our heavenly Bridegroom, the Lord Jesus

Christ, is not going to marry a weak and defeated Bride tainted in any way by sin. Christ is coming again for a cleansed, victorious Bride:

"Christ also loved the Church, and gave Himself for it:
That He might sanctify and cleanse it with the washing of water by the word.
That He might present it to Himself a glorious church, not having spot, or wrinkle, or any such thing; but that it should be holy and without blemish" (Eph. 5:25-27).

These verses are referring to the preparation of the Bride of Christ before His Second Coming. The Bride which God presents to His Son Jesus Christ will not have a spot or a wrinkle or any such thing. She will "be holy and faultless" (Eph. 5:27, *Amplified Bible*).

Here in India, every father goes to much trouble to get the best bride possible for his son. You can read in the matrimonial columns of the newspapers long descriptions and qualifications the bride must have: "Wanted, for a tall handsome fair young man of 25 years, earning Rs. 500 per month, a tall, slim, fair, well-educated, home-loving girl, not less than 1 60 cms. in height from a well-placed family. . . etc. Apply in the first instance with photograph, full details and horoscope . ."

If fathers here on earth are so particular in choosing a bride for their sons, how much more will our Heavenly Father prepare for His Son a spotless Bride! In Revelation 19 we read that the Bride of Christ will be righteous, and a people who praise and worship God loudly (Rev. 19:1-9). Cleansing is an all- important part of the Restoration taking place in these days.

Put On Thy Beautiful Garments

Another picture of the beauty of the Bride of Christ is given to us in Isaiah 52:1:

"Awake, awake; put on thy strength, O
Zion; put on thy beautiful garments."

Even as Joseph, a type of Christ, gave his younger brother Benjamin (whose name means "son of the right hand") five changes of raiment, so the Bible teaches there are five "beautiful garments" for the Bride of Christ—salvation (Isaiah 61:10); righteousness (Isaiah 61:10); praise (Isaiah 61:3); humility (1 Pet. 5:5); and love (Col. 3:14).

Some today, who call themselves Christians are, as Micah prophesied, trying to pull off these robes God has provided (Micah 2:8). Let us then heed the commandment of the Lord to watch and keep our garments in these Last Days (Rev. 16:15). Remember also the fate of him who did not wear a wedding garment (Matt. 22:11-14).

Building An Habitation

After this cleansing, God now takes His cleansed people and builds them into an habitation for His Spirit. We have already looked at some of the exciting and descriptive shades of meaning of the original Greek and Hebrew words from which our English word "restore" is translated. Let us repeat again that Restoration means "a putting down again," "to make whole, complete," "to give, to cause to go up," "to build again," "to make thoroughly right." Just as the Ark of the Covenant, the Power of God's Presence, was brought to dwell in David's Tabernacle, even so shall the fullness of the Power of the Resurrection of Christ, by the Holy Spirit, come to dwell in the restored, rebuilt Tabernacle of David.

Let us also again emphasize that this is God's Building. The Lord says, **"I will build again** the Tabernacle of David" (Acts 15:16). Well did the Psalmist say:

"Except the Lord build the house, they labour in vain that build it" (Psalm 127:1).

The Lord's building is a solid building:

"They that trust in the Lord shall be as mount Zion, which cannot be removed, but abideth for ever" (Psalm 125:1).

Jesus said, *"I will build My Church"* (Matt. 16:18). Paul said, *"Ye are God's building"* (1 Cor. 3:9). Peter said, *"Ye also, as lively stones, are built up a spiritual house"* (I Pet. 2:5).

This, then, is the reason why God is restoring the Tabernacle of David—that He might dwell in the midst of His people by the Power of His Spirit in a new way, ushering in the fullness of this End-time Revival, and the Great Harvest preceding the Second Coming of our Lord Jesus Christ.

In the book of Ephesians, Paul also brings out this truth:

"(Ye) are built upon the foundation of the apostles and prophets, Jesus Christ Himself being the chief corner stone;
*In whom all the **building** fitly framed together groweth unto an holy temple in the Lord:*
*In whom ye also are builded together for **an habitation of God through the Spirit**" (Eph. 2:20-22).*

It is interesting to note that the Greek word used for "temple" in the above verse is not *hieron* ("a sacred, priestly edifice, temple"). The word *naos* is used, meaning "a dwelling place, inner sanctuary." The same Greek word is used in the well-known Scripture, 1 Corinthians 6:19:

"What? know ye not that your body is the temple (dwelling place, inner sanctuary) of the Holy Ghost?"

What a wondrous salvation is ours, that our God should desire to build us up into a place for the fullness of the Power of His Presence to dwell. David took the "inner sanctuary" (the Holy of Holies) to his Tabernacle on Zion. In these days His *naos*—the "dwelling place" of His fullness—will be the restored Tabernacle of David.

The Restoration of All Things

Here we must repeat that the Restoration of the Tabernacle of David includes "the complete Restoration of all that God spoke by the mouth of all His holy prophets" (Acts 3:21, *Amplified Bible*).

To meditate upon the significance of this statement staggers the imagination. We do not need to understand fully. But we do need to prepare for, to believe, and expect the Lord to fulfil His Own Word.

The Church Restored

All the prophets spoke of this great Restoration. One of the notable prophets of this Restoration is Joel. In Joel chapter 1 we read of the desperate need for this Restoration Revival. In chapter 2:1-17 we see the Restoration. In chapter 2:18-32 we read of the Revival. In the third chapter we see the Great Harvest. Joel chapter 1 corresponds to the loss of the Ark of the Covenant, the departure of the Glory of God from His people, and the resultant defeat and death. In the early verses of Joel chapter 2 we see the Restoration commences with lamenting and weeping, just as the building of the Tabernacle of David started with lamenting and crying after God. Then comes the blessed Restoration:

"And I will restore to you the years that the locusts have eaten" (verse 25).

Then the promise shall come to pass:

"Then I restored that which I took not away" (Psalm 69:4).

Reading on in Psalm 69, we find the Restoration includes praise and thanksgiving (verse 30), and dwelling in Zion (verse 35, 36). All that the enemy has tried to take away and destroy, God is restoring:—

God is restoring Bible sanctification;

God is restoring the baptism with the Holy Ghost and fire;

God is restoring the Spirit-filled life;

God is restoring the gifts of the Holy Spirit;

God is restoring the "principles of the doctrine of Christ," with a special emphasis on the "doctrine of baptisms" and "the laying on of hands," the others soon to be restored;

God is restoring locally-governed assemblies, with elders and deacons according to the Bible pattern;

God is restoring the five ministries given to the Church:

God is restoring love in the Body of Christ; God is restoring praise and worship in the Bible methods;

God is restoring unity, true Christ-centred unity, in the Church;

God is restoring the joy of the Lord to His people.

How encouraged we should be in these days! Hallelujah!

Restoration Through God's Word

The Restoration taking place today in preparation for the great revival is a Restoration according to the Word of God. It is a Restoration built by the Power of the Word of God. It is a Restoration of Bible-based doctrine:

"The law (or doctrine)[1] of the Lord is perfect, restoring the whole person; the testimony of the Lord is sure, making wise the simple" (Psalm 19:7, Amplified Bible).

David prayed for God's light (His Word[2]), and God's truth (His Word[3]), knowing these would lead him to Zion, and to the Tabernacle there:

"O send out Your light and Your truth; let them lead me, let them bring me to Your holy hill and to Your dwelling (*Hebrew*, Tabernacle[4])" (Psalm 43:3, *Amplified Bible*).

Notice in the next verse, David is assured that then he will rejoice and praise his God.

Yes, this Restoration is according to the Word of God, by the Power of the Word of God. Let us then bring our lives and churches into line with the Word. Let us allow the Word of God to operate, restoring all that God would build in us in these days, in preparation for the mighty revival commencing in these days.

Restoration for Protection

The Bible teaches that God is restoring the Tabernacle of David for the **protection** of His true sons and daughters:

"And the Lord will create upon every dwelling place of mount Zion and upon her assemblies ... a Tabernacle for a shadow in the day time from the heat, and for a place of refuge, and for a covert (or shelter) from storm and from rain" (Isaiah 4:5, 6).

---

1   *Authorized Version*, marginal rendering.
2   Psalm 119:105.
3   John 17:17.
4   See also *Authorized Version*.

The Church Restored

Before the Great Tribulation, there will be persecution, tribulation, and suffering for the true Church of God. As the early Church was persecuted for the miraculous resurrection life and Power of Christ working through it, so in these Last Days shall the restored Church which returns to the Bible ways be persecuted. True sons and daughters of God will not be recognized as real Christians. Then shall come to pass the following Scriptures in all their fullness:

"For unto you it is given in the behalf of Christ, not only to believe on Him, but also to suffer for His sake" (Phil. 1:29).

The Apostle Peter wrote:

"Beloved, think it not strange concerning the fiery trial which is to try you, as though some strange thing happened unto you:
But rejoice, inasmuch as ye are partakers of Christ's sufferings; that, when His glory shall be revealed, ye may be glad also with exceeding joy.
If ye be reproached for the name of Christ, happy are ye; for the spirit of glory and of God resteth upon you: on their part He is evil spoken of, but on your part He is glorified" (1 Pet. 4:12-14).

As we have seen the direct connection between the Restoration of the Tabernacle of David and the Restoration of joy, so we see here, and in other Scriptures, a similar relationship between persecution and joy. Notice that Peter says when we are reproached for the Name of Christ, the joy of the Spirit of God shall be our portion. Thus we can see in an even clearer way God's plan to restore the fullness of the Biblical methods of rejoicing in the Lord before this great persecution commences. Peter called it "exceeding joy." Speaking of persecution, the Lord exhorts us "to rejoice and be exceeding glad":

"Blessed (and happy and enviably fortunate and spiritually prosperous, that is, in the state in which one enjoys and finds satisfaction in God's favour and salvation, regardless of his outward conditions[5]), are they which are persecuted for righteousness' sake: for theirs is the kingdom of heaven.

---

5   *Amplified Bible.*

Blessed are ye, when men shall revile you, and persecute you, and shall say all manner of evil against you falsely, for my sake.
Rejoice, and be exceeding glad: for great is your reward in heaven: for so persecuted they the prophets which were before you" (Matt. 5:10-12).

What a blessing it is to know that God has a place where we may find protection from all fiery trials and persecutions—the Tabernacle of David on Mount Zion, representing for us such a deep spiritual experience of the Power of His Presence, that the joy of the Lord is our strength regardless of the persecution from the outside.

Those experiencing the blessings of Zion in their hearts will enjoy God's defence and help in the day of trouble:

"The Lord hear thee in the day of trouble: the name of the God of Jacob defend thee;
Send thee help from the Sanctuary (David's Tabernacle), and strengthen (margin—support) thee out of Zion" (Psalm 20:1, 2).

See God's protection in His pavilion, David's Tabernacle, for those who worship Him:

"Oh, how great is Your goodness, which You have laid up for those who fear, revere and worship You, goodness which You have wrought for those who trust and take refuge in You before the sons of men!
In the secret of Your Presence You hide them from the plots of men; You keep them secretly in Your pavilion from the strife of tongues" (Psalm 31:19, 20, Amplified Bible).

This same blessed protection from our enemies in the time of trouble, and the joy those who have experienced in their hearts the Restoration of the Tabernacle of David know, is also taught in Psalm 27:

"One thing have I desired of the Lord, that will I seek after; that I may dwell in the House of the Lord all the days of my life, to behold the beauty of the Lord, and to enquire in His temple.
For in the time of trouble He shall hide me in His pavilion: in the secret of His Tabernacle shall He hide me; He shall set me up upon a rock.

And now shall mine head be lifted up above mine enemies round about me: therefore will I offer in His Tabernacle sacrifices of joy (margin—shouting) ; I will sing, yea, I will sing praises unto the Lord" (Psalm 7:4-6).

Here are more verses for our meditation on the blessed protection of the Tabernacle of David:

"I will abide in thy Tabernacle for ever: I will trust in the covert of thy wings" (Psalm 61:4).

"There is a river, the streams whereof shall make glad the city of God (Zion), the holy place of the Tabernacle of the most High (David's Tabernacle).

God is in the midst of her; she shall not be moved: God shall help her, and that right early" (Psalm 46:4, 5).

"God is known in her palaces for a refuge. For, lo, the kings were assembled, they passed by together" (Psalm 48:3, 4).

Those who experience the fullness of the blessing of Zion in their hearts need not fear:

"Therefore thus saith the Lord God of hosts, O my people that dwellest in Zion, be not afraid" (Isaiah 10:24).

God's Word promises, *"The Lord shall comfort Zion"* (Isaiah 51:3).

Another precious promise concerning protection for Zion is found in Isaiah 31:4:

"For thus hath the Lord spoken unto me. Like as the lion and the young lion roaring on his prey, when a multitude of shepherds is called forth against him, he will not be afraid of their voice, nor abase himself for the noise of them: so shall the Lord of hosts come down to fight for mount Zion, and for the hill thereof."

The Bible says that our "adversary the devil, as a roaring lion, walketh about, seeking whom he may devour" (I Pet. 5:8). But those who have the spiritual experience of the blessings of Zion in their hearts need not fear, for the Lord has indeed promised to fight for them.

Again, speaking of those who dwell upon Zion, it is written, "They shall dwell safely, and none shall make them afraid" (Ezek. 34:28).

In the light of the speed with which we are approaching the end of this age, and the persecution God's saints must suffer, not one of us can afford to be without the blessing and protection of David's Tabernacle.

Ready for Revival

The Church restored will become the Church revived. When Zion is restored, Zion shall experience the revival so desperately needed. The time for God to work is come:

> *"Thou shalt arise, and have mercy upon Zion: for the time to favour her, yea, the set time, is come.*
> *When the Lord shall build up Zion, He shall appear in His glory"*
> *(Psalm 102:13, 16).*

Many of us have heard the well-known hymn, "Showers of Blessing":

> *There shall be showers of blessing.*
> *This is the promise of God,*
> *There shall be seasons refreshing.*
> *Sent from the Father above:*
>
> > *Showers of blessing.*
> > *Showers of blessing we need,*
> > *Mercy drops around us are falling.*
> > *But for the showers we plead!*

Yes, we have sung it. But how many of us have realized that God's promise of showers of blessing is directly given for the Restoration of the Tabernacle of David! For the Bible verse reads:

> *"And I will make them and the places round about my hill (Zion) a blessing; and I will cause the shower to come down in his season; there shall be showers of blessing" (Ezek. 34:26).*

First Restoration, then Revival. The Restoration of the Tabernacle of David is ushering in the greatest Revival the world has ever known.

Indeed, "there shall be showers of blessing," for "it is time for thee. Lord, to work" (Psalm 119:126).

Chapter Twenty-seven
THE CHURCH REVIVED

We shall never experience real Revival in the Bible sense of the word, unless we seek God for His promised Restoration. It is impossible for God's Spirit to indwell and revive in the measure He desires, any thing not built according to the pattern of His Word. David built a Tabernacle on Mount Zion for the return of the Presence of God. If there had been no preparation, no Tabernacle built, the Ark of God, the Power, the Presence, and Glory of God would have had no habitation.

The Meaning of Revival

The word "Revival" has, sad to say, fallen into misuse. Because of this, much of the impact and blessing of the word has been lost. For example, among some Christians it is used to describe a series of meetings—"the evangelist held a small revival in our church." Nothing could be further from the truth. In the Bible, the word "Revival" means much more than just a special evangelistic campaign!

The word occurs at least fifteen times in the Bible, but the Hebrew and Greek words from which our English word "Revival" is translated occur many more times. Because it is so important to understand what God means when He says "Revival," let us see some of the many meanings of this blessed and encouraging word:—

"to cause to live,"
"to keep or make alive,"
"to live again,"
"to cause to be whole, or recover,"

"to preserve, to preserve alive, or preserve life,"
"to repair,"
"to quicken,"
"to save, to save alive, or save lives,"
"to nourish,"
"to recover strength,"
"to bring back to normal condition."

Revival means the inflow of the life of a person with life to share, to a person in need of recovery.

These definitions describe the Revival we need. The Revival which God is sending. Blessed be His wonderful Name!

When at high school, I was active in swimming and life-saving. In life-saving, we were taught how to pull out of the water those in danger of drowning, and how to "revive" them by resuscitation. To revive a patient, the life-saver places his mouth on the mouth of the unconscious patient. He is almost lifeless, unable to breathe for himself. As the life-saver breathes his breath into the almost-drowned person the life of the life-saver is transfused into the patient, and the patient revives.

When we compare the New Testament Church with the near-lifeless Church of today, we all too readily recognise we need Revival. Much of the dynamic miracle-working Power of the Resurrection Life of Jesus Christ is lost. But after the promised Restoration, God will pour out His Spirit from heaven. Then the very life of God will be transfused into His children, reviving them to newness of life.

After Restoration—Revival

God has promised:

"And it shall come to pass afterward, that I will pour out my Spirit upon all flesh; and your sons and your daughters shall prophesy, your old men shall dream dreams, your young men shall see visions" (Joel 2:28).

The Church Revived

"I will pour out my Spirit." *"Afterward."* After what? *After* Restoration. *After* we have courage and humility to draw near to God with a deep sense of our hunger and need for Revival. *After* we "turn . . . to me with all your heart, and with fasting, and with weeping, and with mourning" (Joel 2:12).

After we "rend your heart . . . and turn unto the Lord your God" (verse 13).

Strong orders. Desperate words. Extreme measures. But God's commands to us!

"And also upon the servants and upon the handmaids in those days **I will pour out my Spirit**" *(Joel 2:29).*

"I will pour out my Spirit." "In those days." What days? In the days when we: "Let the priests, the ministers of the Lord, weep between the porch and the altar, and let them say,

Spare thy people, O Lord, and give not thine heritage to reproach, that the heathen should rule over them, or use a byword against them:' Wherefore should they say among the people, Where is their God?" (verse 17).

"Then" . . . when we have fulfilled these conditions . . . *"Then"* will the Lord be jealous for His land, and pity His people" (verse 18).

"Then" . . . we will "be glad . . . and rejoice in the Lord" for He will pour out the Rain of His Spirit upon us (verse 23).

"I will pour out my Spirit." "In those days." Rather, we can say, "In *these* days." Yes, these days in which you and 1 live. For Peter, explaining what was happening on the Day of Pentecost, says:

"This is that which was spoken by the prophet Joel; And it shall come to pass in the **last days**, *saith God, I will pour out of my Spirit upon all flesh"* (Acts 2:16, 17).

"This Jesus hath God raised up, whereof we all are witnesses. Therefore being by the right hand of God exalted, and having received of the Father the promise of the Holy Ghost, He hath shed forth this, which **ye now see and hear**" *(verses 32, 33).*

That which they could "see and hear" on the Day of Pentecost was God fulfilling His Promise to pour out His Spirit on all flesh. If Peter was living in the "last days," in which days are you and I living?

In the last chapter of his second letter, Peter describes the Last Days, the destruction of this world, and the Second Coming of Christ in detail. Exactly as he prophesied, scoffers, even in these last days have come saying,

"Where is the promise of His coming? For since the fathers fell asleep, all things continue as they were from the beginning of the creation" (2 Pet. 3:3, 4).

For years skeptics have questioned, "How can the heavens pass away with a great noise, and the elements melt with fervent heat? How can the earth and the works therein be burned up?" But now, scientists (if not the Church!), proclaim there is nuclear power to do just this! Now politicians (if not Christians!), know that Peter's prophecy is a dreadful and frightening possibility.

We need make no apology for being alarmists. God has commanded us to

"blow ye the trumpet in Zion, and **sound an alarm** *in my holy mountain: let all the inhabitants of the land tremble: for the day of the Lord cometh, for it is nigh at hand"* (Joel 2:1).

Bible prophecies are being fulfilled before our very eyes at an alarming rate. Jesus Christ is coming soon. If Peter was living in the Last Days, it is no overstatement to say we are living in the last of the Last Days! "Behold, the bridegroom cometh!" Do you have sufficient oil of the Spirit in your lamp?[1]

The Two Rains

Here we must emphasize again that the prophesied "showers of blessing" are promised to those taking part in the Restoration of the Tabernacle of David and experiencing the spiritual blessings of Zion in their hearts:

---

1 See Matt. 25:1-13.

The Church Revived

"And I will make them and the places round about my hill (Mount Zion) a blessing: and I will cause the shower to come down in his season; there shall be showers of blessing" (Ezek. 34:26).

To further understand this Revival, this outpouring of the Holy Spirit on all flesh, let us remember there were two rains in the agricultural year of Israel. This is first mentioned in Deuteronomy 11:1 3 and 14:

"And it shall come to pass, if ye shall hearken diligently unto my commandments which I command you this day, to love the Lord your God, and to serve Him with all your heart and with all your soul.

That I will give you the rain of your land in his due season, the first rain and the latter rain, that thou mayest gather in thy corn, and thy wine, and thine oil."

In the third month of the year, around the time of the Old Testament Feast of Pentecost, the first, or former rain fell. Then four long months went by. This was known as the dry period. There was no rain. None had fallen since the rain in the Feast of Pentecost. As the dry hot summer came to its end, the watchers would anxiously scan the heavens for the sign which announced the coming rains.

The sun had set—and as they continued to scan the heavens, the watchers saw the appearance of three stars in the darkening skies. These were called the pointers. Together with these pointers they saw the top of the crest of the new moon. To those carefully looking for the second, or latter rain, these were the signs. The rains were coming!

The signal was given. The sound of the trumpets was heard. The rains were coming. The old dry spell was over and the new day was dawning. Soon the summer fruits would be harvested. God's people would gather together to keep the first part of the Feast of Tabernacles, the Feast of Trumpets. This would be followed by the Feast Day of Atonement and the Feast of Tabernacles.

The Two Harvests

This has a striking parallel in the history of the Christian Church. Just as the rain fell first at Pentecost in Old Testament Israel, so it fell in the history of spiritual Israel, the Church (Gal. 6:16). On the day of Pentecost in Acts chapter 2, the "Former Rain" of the Holy Spirit fell upon the waiting disciples. They were filled with the Spirit. They were filled with joy, comfort, and great boldness in the face of tremendous opposition. Signs and wonders accompanied their witness. There was a great harvest of souls.

While the Lord was never left without a witness, it is an historical fact that a dry and barren season followed. By and large, the Feast of Pentecost was not kept: precious few were filled with the Spirit. Historians call this The Dark Ages.

But then signs—pointers of the coming Latter Rain began to appear. In 1519 Martin Luther, the first great leader of the Protestant Reformation, openly denied the Pope's supremacy and infallibility. (Would to God there were more Luthers in the Protestant Ecumenical Movement today!) Then followed Calvin, Knox, Wesley, Booth and many others ... all who experienced showers of Rain of the Holy Spirit upon their outstanding witness and ministry ... until at the commencement of this century, in many countries, there were spontaneous outpourings of great magnitude and power. In Wales, Sweden, India, Africa, America and many other places, the Holy Spirit of God began to fall "on all flesh" in a new way. There was a Restoration of New Testament Power and gifts of the Holy Spirit, and a great harvest of souls. The Latter Rain[2] outpouring of the Holy Spirit had commenced! And, blessed be God, it has not stopped. It will increase in intensity until the coming of the Lord:

---

2   We want to emphasize that when we speak of the "Latter Rain", we are referring to a Bible Truth, and not any group or organization of that name.

It is interesting to note that the term "Latter Rain" is mentioned nine times in the Bible; it will be remembered that there are nine fruit of the Spirit listed in Galatians 5:22, 23; and nine gifts of the Spirit in 1 Corinthians 12:8-10; etc.

"Be patient therefore, brethren, unto the coming of the Lord. Behold, the husbandman waiteth for the precious fruit of the earth, and hath long patience for it, until he receive the early and latter rain" (James 5:7).

How loving, patient, and long-suffering is our Heavenly Husbandman! Let us *"Ask ye* of the Lord rain in the time of the latter rain" (Zech 10:1); an enduement with Power that will enable every one of us to "put ye in the sickle, for the harvest is ripe" (Joel 3:13), and bring in the harvest of sheaves for the Lord (see Psalm 126:5-6).

Actually Israel had two harvests in the year. The first was a harvest of grains, *"corn."* The second a harvest of fruits—especially grapes and olives, *"wine* and *oil."*[3] The first harvest was watered by the former rain of Pentecost, the second watered by the latter rain of Tabernacles. In many scriptures, the Lord speaks of corn, wine and oil together, symbolizing the fullness of harvest, and harvests' blessings. Repeated continual harvests are promised in conjunction with the Restoration of David's Tabernacle.

The Three-fold Outpouring

Many teach we cam expect an even greater outpouring of the Spirit on all flesh in these days of the Latter Rain, than the early Church experienced in the Former Rain. Referring to Elisha's plea to Elijah ("I pray thee, let a double portion of thy spirit be upon me"—2 Kings 2:9), they speak of the "double-portion blessing." But it is clear from the Scripture that the latter rain was already a "double-portion," a two-fold harvest. However, God has promised us the Former and the Latter Rain in the **one month**— in the time when the Lord is doing this "new thing" —restoring the Power of His Presence:

"Be glad then, **ye children of Zion***, and rejoice in the Lord your God: for He hath given you the former rain moderately, and He will cause to come down for you the rain, the former rain, and the latter rain in the first month"* (Joel 2:23).

---

3   See Deut. 11:14, Joel 1:10, 2:19, 2:24; etc.

James tells us that Jesus will not come again until the Church "receive the early and latter rain" (James 5:7).

Could it be, that we are about to receive the two-fold blessing of the latter rain, plus the blessing of the former rain in this day? A **three-fold** anointing and enduement with Power, to fit the Church for the stupendous task of giving a holy testimony in the midst of evil forces such as have never been seen before. A Power for witnessing "to every creature" the Resurrection Power of our Lord Jesus Christ. To prepare the Church, sanctified, cleansed, and washed, to be presented, a glorious, spotless Bride, holy and without blemish, to the Heavenly Bridegroom, Jesus Christ, at His Coming. Let us be careful not to limit the Holy One of Israel.

The teaching of the three-fold, or treble blessing runs right throughout the Bible. It is possibly first alluded to in Genesis chapter 49, when Jacob tells his sons "that which shall befall you in the last days" (verse 1). Reuben was Jacob's firstborn. As such he was entitled to a double blessing, which was his birthright. As the firstborn, he would also be successor to his father as head of the family or tribe. But Reuben forfeited all these blessings because of his sin. A closer examination of Scripture reveals in actual fact he lost a threefold, a treble blessing. E. Bendor Samuel, quoting from the *Ancient Jerusalem Targum*, relates that this blessing is thus paraphrased:

"Reuben, my firstborn art thou, my strength and the beginning of my sorrow. To thee, my son Reuben, would it have pertained thee to receive three portions above thy brothers, the priesthood, birthright, and kingdom, but because thou hast sinned, the birthright is given to Joseph, the kingdom to Judah, and the High Priesthood to Levi."

Thus we see Reuben lost the three-fold blessing of the Lord—the birthright, the kingdom, and the priesthood—through sin. Let us not lose the three-fold blessing of God which He has promised to us—this three-fold outpouring of Rain showers of His Spirit in these days of the glorious Restoration of the Power of His Presence.

Christ's Resurrection Life

As we read the book of the Acts of the Apostles, there is one thing that stands out above all others. During the first outpouring of the Holy Spirit—the Former Rain—the New Testament Christians manifested the Resurrection Life of Christ. Just as Jesus had promised them, they did exactly the same works He did (John 14:12). They healed the sick, raised the dead, cast out devils, set people free, and saw multitudes accept Christ as their Lord and Saviour. The Resurrection Life of Christ flowed through them, doing the same things He did when on earth.

In this Last Day outpouring we are commencing to see the same thing, and will continue to see it in an even greater and mightier measure as the Tabernacle of David is restored. These are indeed Revival days. We have already stressed that all the prophets spoke of this Last Day Restoration Revival. It is written in the book of Hosea:

"After two days will He revive us: in the third day He will raise us up, and we shall live in His sight.

Then shall we know, if we follow on to know the Lord: His going forth is prepared as the morning; and He shall come unto us as the rain, as the latter and former rain unto the earth" (Hos. 6:2, 3).

Both Old and New Testaments teach "that one day is with the Lord as a thousand years" (Psalm 90:4; 2 Pet. 3:8). In verse two of Hosea 6 the prophet is speaking about the fifth and sixth days of God's Week—the two thousand years of this Gospel Dispensation. The third day is, of course, the one thousand years' reign of Christ upon the earth.[4] The prophet then goes on to tell us that at the end of this Second Day, when God revives us, we shall see the Latter and the Former Rain at the one time, just as the Lord promised in Joel 2:22, and James 5:7.

---

4   The Lord Jesus also referred to this when He said, "Behold, I cast out devils and I do cures today and tomorrow, and the third day I shall be perfected (I finish, complete, My course—*Amplified Bible*)" (Luke 13:32).

During this tremendous outpouring of the Spirit the world is going to witness the greatest demonstration of the Resurrection Life of Christ ever seen. And the Church is going to know the blessing of being "daily delivered from sin's dominion through His Resurrection Life" (Romans 5:10, *Amplified Bible*).

The Revival God has promised will be essentially "Christ-glorifying." No one group, or man, or denomination, or doctrine, will be exalted. But rather, the Power of the Holy Spirit will glorify the very Person of Christ, revealing the Power of His Resurrection Life:

"He will honour and glorify Me, because He will take of (receive, draw upon) what is Mine and will reveal (declare, disclose, transmit) it to you.

Everything that the Father has is Mine. That is what I meant when I said that He will take the things that are Mine and will reveal (declare, disclose, transmit) them to you" (John 16:14, 15, Amplified Bible).

The return of the Ark of the Covenant to the people of God at David's Tabernacle was the Restoration of the Power of His Presence. And with the Restoration of the Power of His Presence came the Restoration of the Reviving Power of God's Life. Praise God indeed, for He is restoring David's Tabernacle in Revival Power today!

Revival and David's Tabernacle

Those entering into the Restoration of David's Tabernacle share the blessings promised in Ezekiel 34:26:

"And I will make them and the places round about my hill (Mount Zion) a blessing: and I will cause the shower to come down in his season; there shall be showers of blessing."

Furthermore, the promises of Revival in the Bible are always connected with the rejoicing or some other aspects of the blessing of the Tabernacle of David, on which God has promised to pour out His Spirit:

The Church Revived

"And it shall come to pass in that day... I will pour upon the house of David... the Spirit" (Zech. 12:9, 10).

David prayed:

"Wilt Thou not revive us again: that Thy people may rejoice in Thee?" (Psalm 85:6).

Without Revival, they could not enter into the full experience of rejoicing in the Lord. Then David is assured:

"Though I walk in the midst of trouble. Thou wilt revive me" (Psalm 138:7).

Habakkuk's prayer for revival was "set to wild, enthusiastic and triumphal music" (Hab. 3:1). He prayed:

"O Lord, revive your work in the midst of the years, in the midst of the years make yourself known!" (Hab. 3:2, Amplified Bible).

Let us pray for revival in our day with the same enthusiasm. And not only pray, but allow God and ask Him to restore the Tabernacle of David, and all it represents, in our lives and churches. For nothing short of this outpouring from heaven will prepare us to reap the coming great harvest.

Chapter Twenty-eight
THE CHURCH REAPING

Both Old and New Testaments make it clear that God is not only restoring the Tabernacle of David to bless His people, but also to make them a blessing, and use them for His glory:

"And I will make them and the places round about my hill (Zion) a blessing" (Ezek. 34:26).

In the Scriptures which promise us the Restoration of the Tabernacle of David, we are also promised a great harvest of souls—the Church reaping multitudes for the Lord in phenomenal numbers.

The Plowman Shall Overtake the Reaper

"In that day will I raise up the Tabernacle of David that is fallen, and close up the breaches thereof; and I will raise up his ruins, and I will build it as in the days of old:

That they may possess the remnant of Edom, and of all the heathen, which are called by my name, saith the Lord that doeth this.

Behold, the days come, saith the Lord, that the plowman shall overtake the reaper, and the treader of grapes him that soweth seed; and the mountains shall drop sweet wine, and all the hills shall melt" (Amos 9:11-13).

The above verses clearly show the direct relationship between the Restoration of the Tabernacle of David, and the great harvest of souls. Verse 12 tells that they who would take part in the Restoration of David's Tabernacle shall possess those who know not Christ. In verse 13, we are told "the days come, saith the Lord, that the plowman shall overtake the reaper, and the treader of grapes him that soweth seed."

Jesus said the seed is the Word (Matthew 13:19). The sower is he that sows the Gospel seed, that preaches the Good News of salvation through Jesus Christ. Usually, in both the spiritual and the natural, it takes time from the sowing of the seed until the ripening of the fruit. The seed is sown, watered, nurtured. After a long time the vine finally gives forth its fruit. But here we read, in conjunction with the Restoration of the Tabernacle of David, that one shall be sowing seed, and another shall be immediately behind plucking the fully mature and ripened grapes!

"The plowman shall overtake the reaper" speaks of the abundance of repeated harvests. Commenting on this verse, Matthew Henry says:

> " 'The plowman shall overtake the reaper,' that is, there shall be such a plentiful harvest... The hills that were dry and barren shall be moistened and shall melt with the 'fatness or mellowness' (as we call it) of 'the soil.' This must be understood of the spiritual blessings with which all those are blessed who are in sincerity added to Christ and His Church; they shall have the bread of life, to 'strengthen their hearts,' and the wine of divine consolations to 'make them glad—meat indeed' and 'drink indeed'—all the benefit that comes to the souls of men from the word and Spirit of God. When great multitudes were converted and when the preachers of the gospel were 'always caused to triumph in' the success of their preaching, then the 'plowman overtook the reaper.'"[1]

"All Men Seek for Thee"

> *"After this I will return, and will build again the Tabernacle of David, which is fallen down; and I will build again the ruins thereof, and I will set it up:*
>
> *That the residue of men might seek after the Lord, and all the Gentiles, upon whom my name is called, saith the Lord, who doeth all these things" (Acts 15:16, 17).*

Here is an amazing fact. Not only will the restored revived Church be

---

[1] *Matthew Henry's Commentary on the Whole Bible* (Marshall, Morgan & Scott).

busy seeking lost souls for the Lord—the lost souls will be seeking Christians to ask them about the Lord! Even today there is an encouraging, yet alarming world-wide hunger in those **outside** the Christian Church to hear the Gospel. While some Christians may not like to admit it, the fact is, "the multitudes in the valley of decision"(Joel 3:14) *want* to hear about Christ and His saving love. The words of Mark 1:37—" All men seek for Thee"—are as true today as when Simon Peter uttered them nearly two thousand years ago. This new hunger to hear the Gospel pin-points our responsibility to obey the Great Commission as possibly nothing else does. Disobedience here is sin. Let us be even more personal. If you and I, as believers in the Lord Jesus Christ, do not go and tell others of His Atoning Death and Triumphant Resurrection, *who will*? As that great missionary statesman, A. B. Simpson, founder of the Christian and Missionary Alliance has said:

> *"Disobedient Christians will be overtaken with an awful shame and loss at the judgment of believers when they find themselves excuseless for their past disobedience."*

He goes on to quote the words of an old Muslim woman to a Christian in Bengal:

> *"How long is it since Jesus died for sinful people? Look at me; I am old; I have prayed, given alms, gone to the holy shrines, become as dust from fasting, and all this is useless. Where have you been all this time?"*[2]

Other new Christians have asked, "What about my father? My grandfather? You say God is 'not willing that any should perish" (2 Pet. 3:9), but somebody was willing for them to perish. Where were you Christians during their time?"

How well I remember, not long after I had become a Christian, finding enough courage to invite one of my friends to a Gospel Meeting. His reply? "I have been waiting for you to ask me." And I thought he wasn't interested in the Gospel! This young man accepted Christ as his Saviour and Lord, and later became the national youth leader in his denomination.

---

2 In "The Eternal Question Still Remains Unanswered," from *Herald of Faith*.

Yes, this hunger after God is not only inside the Church—it is everywhere! And God wants to "satisfy the longing soul, and fill the hungry soul with goodness"(Psalm 107:9).

While it may be difficult for some of us to imagine, the Bible teaches that in these Last Days there is coming upon the earth an unprecedented hunger for the Word of God. This hunger for God's Word is foretold in the chapter preceding the promise of the Restoration of David's Tabernacle:

"Behold the days come, saith the Lord God, that I will send a famine in the land, not a famine of bread, nor a thirst for water, but of hearing the words of the Lord:

And they shall wander from sea to sea, and from the north even to the east, they shall run to and fro to seek the word of the Lord, and shall not find it.

In that day shall the fair virgins and young men faint for thirst"
(Amos 8:11-13).

Will you and I be able to meet the needs of those who seek the Word of the Lord?

"Come to The Tabernacle of David"

The Bible teaches that when the reviving Power of God's Presence returns to His Church, and the Tabernacle of David is restored to His people, multitudes from all nations shall run to these Spirit-filled, rejoicing Christians, seeking the way of salvation:

"And it shall come to pass in the last days, that the mountain of the Lord's House (David's Tabernacle) shall be established in the top of the mountains, and shall be exalted above the hills: and all nations shall flow unto it.

And many people shall go and say. Come ye, and let us go up to the mountain of the Lord (Zion), to the House of the God of Jacob; and He will teach us of His ways, and we will walk in His paths: for out of Zion shall go forth the law, and the word of the Lord from Jerusalem"
(Isaiah 2:2, 3).

It is obvious these verses shall be fulfilled just prior to the Second Coming of Christ, because the following verse (verse 4) plainly speaks of the Second Coming of Christ, and His reign upon the earth.

We have already seen that Isaiah chapter 4 is speaking about Zion, and David's Tabernacle there. Another beautiful picture of this astoundingly great harvest and the fruitfulness of Zion, and her assemblies, is given in Isaiah 5:1:

"Now will I sing to my well-beloved a song of my beloved touching his vineyard. My well-beloved hath a vineyard in a very fruitful hill."[3]

The Lord Jesus teaches us the vineyard is the Church (Matt. 21:33), and here in Isaiah 5:1 He is the "well-beloved." In this verse then, we see Zion spoken of as "a very fruitful hill." Those who take part in the glorious Restoration of the Tabernacle of David and the subsequent Revival, will indeed be fruitful for their Lord, fulfilling His desire, that they "should go and bring forth fruit" (John 15:16).

So many Scriptures could be given showing the essential connection between the Restoration of the Tabernacle of David in Zion (that part of His Church which seeks Him with all their heart, and obeys His commandments), and the great harvest of souls among the heathen. We have room for only one more here:

"You (Lord) will arise and have mercy and loving-kindness for Zion, for it is time to have pity and compassion for her, yes, the set time is come—the moment designated.
So the nations shall fear and worshipfully revere the name of the Lord, and all the kings of the earth Your glory" (Psalm 102:13, 15, Amplified Bible).

Here we see the pattern of God—revival for His people and the turning of the heathen to the Lord for their salvation.

The Church Reaping

With the Power of the Spirit and the manifestation of the Resurrection

---
3   Notice in the following verses the Lord did five things for His vineyard.

Life of Christ received at the outpouring of the Early Rain, the early Church "turned the world upside down" (Acts 17:6). In the face of terrifying opposition, in which they were stoned, beaten, thrown to lions, mercilessly tortured and killed; without riches, organisation, security or recognition, their efforts at preaching the Gospel were accompanied with triumphant success! The harvest of souls they reaped was nothing short of phenomenal—three thousand were converted to Christ in one day; five thousand on another; multitudes on another. And yet, in those days, it was a crime to be a Christian—a crime for which there was no apology accepted, no trial allowed, and no forgiveness granted. Despite the religious freedom in these days the results of our puny efforts can in no way be compared with the impact the first century Church made upon their generation.

What made the difference? Fifty days after the death of Jesus, He proved both to His few followers and to the world that He was alive, by filling them with the Holy Spirit. Jesus filled those who believed in Him with the same Spirit through Whom He had lived a life of power, love, and spotless purity. The outpouring of the Spirit made the disciples of Jesus as zealous as He had been. This despised sect demonstrating breathtaking miracles and reaping such a harvest of souls had to succeed. They could not fail. For they were motivated by the Power of the Spirit.

Missionary-statesman Oswald J. Smith has declared that the most urgent work of the Church is the evangelization of the world. Today, as never before, the Great Commission of our Lord to "preach the Gospel to every creature" (Mark 16:15) stands to challenge us anew to the work He has commanded us to do. This is not only for pastors, evangelists, mission workers and missionaries. The command to be a witness for Christ is for *all believers*. Today there are many more people in India alone, waiting to be told the Good News of Salvation through Christ, than were alive in the **whole world** on the Day of Pentecost! In terms of magnitude, our task is greater than theirs.

The Church Reaping

There are forces arrayed against the Church to-day, that the early apostles knew nothing of. Yet despite the fact they had been with Jesus for more than three years, cast out devils by His power, and seen the Risen Lord, the apostles were commanded not to go forth with the Evangel "**until** *ye be endued with Power from on high*" (Luke 24:49). Their efforts would be futile unless they were filled with the Holy Spirit.

But today, our task is even greater. It is not enough that we experience our own personal Pentecost and be filled with the Spirit. We dare not stop at Sinai. If we are to be reaping in this great harvest, we must go on to Zion, and experience personally the Restoration of the Tabernacle of David. For the fullness of the Power of His Presence is found there.

We may try "to do God a service," but we will never serve God effectively in the great harvest, according to the fullness of our ability **in Him**, until we experience in our lives the Restoration of the Tabernacle of David and the revival this Restoration brings.

Praise God, He has promised us the three-fold outpouring of His Spirit, and the resultant **three-fold harvest** of precious souls in this Last Day revival. He promises to minister to all, supernatural Power and energy to "put ... in the sickle, for the harvest is ripe" (Joel 3:13). God's restored Church shall receive the reviving showers of the Early and the Latter Rain to reap the great harvest;

"Be patient therefore, brethren, unto the coming of the Lord. Behold, the husbandman waiteth for the precious fruit of the earth, and hath long patience for it, until he receive the early and latter rain" (James 5:7).

Then shall the Lord Jesus Christ return:

"Be ye also patient; stablish your hearts: for the coming of the Lord draweth nigh" (James 5:8).

Bring Up The Ark

God is restoring the Tabernacle of David. Hear the voice of rejoicing and praise. The Ark of the Covenant is on its way. Unity. Freedom. Fellowship with God. Restoration. Revival and renewal. Reaping the great harvest.

Will you, like David's wife, stay inside your own house, and miss this Last Day move of God's Spirit? Is the sacrifice too great? Is the reproach too unbearable?

Or will you join with David? Will you obey God's commandment to bring again the Ark of our God to us, and enjoy the fullness of the Power of His Presence?

The choice is up to you.

About the Author

Graham Truscott came to Christ as a youth in a Methodist church in Christown, New Zealand. During his college years, he was baptized in the Holy spirit and began itinerant ministry. He eventually traveled to over thirty nations preaching the Gospel. In 1960, Graham and his wife Pamela moved to India as full-time missionaries. The Truscott's Gospel campaigns gathered crowds as large as 25,000, with dozens of churches being planted in west India. After moving to the United States, they began Restoration Temple (now the Life Church—Mission Bay) in San Diego, California, where they pastored until 1991.

PRESENCE PIONEERS MEDIA

CHECK OUT THESE OTHER TITLES FROM PRESENCE PIONEERS MEDIA

DAVID'S TABERNACLE
How God's Presence Changes Everything
Matthew Lilley

ENJOYING PRAYER
Knowing God and Transforming the World
Matthew Lilley

10 DAYS
The Unlikely Story of a Global Movement Mourning for the Return of Jesus
Jonathan Friz

JESUS GETS WHAT HE PRAYS FOR
Jonathan Friz

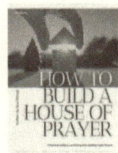

HOW TO BUILD A HOUSE OF PRAYER
A Practical Guide to Launching and Leading Prayer Rooms
Brad Stroup

Available wherever you buy books, or at
https://presencepioneers.org/product-category/books/

To receive updates and discounts on future book releases, visit media.presencepioneers.org or scan this QR code.

www.ingramcontent.com/pod-product-compliance
Lightning Source LLC
Chambersburg PA
CBHW030112240426
43673CB00002B/54